Projecting History

Social History, Popular Culture, and Politics in Germany
Geoff Eley, Series Editor

Ethnic Drag: Performing Race, Nation, Sexuality in West Germany, Katrin Sieg

Projecting History: German Nonfiction Cinema, 1967–2000, Nora M. Alter

Cities, Sin, and Social Reform in Imperial Germany, Andrew Lees

The Challenge of Modernity: German Social and Cultural Studies, 1890–1960, Adelheid von Saldern

Exclusionary Violence: Antisemitic Riots in Modern German History, Christhard Hoffmann, Werner Bergmann, and Helmut Walser Smith, editors

Languages of Labor and Gender: Female Factory Work in Germany, 1850–1914, Kathleen Canning

That Was the Wild East: Film Culture, Unification and the "New" Germany, Leonie Naughton

Anna Seghers: The Mythic Dimension, Helen Fehervary

Staging Philanthropy: Patriotic Women and the National Imagination in Dynastic Germany, 1813–1916, Jean H. Quataert

Truth to Tell: German Women's Autobiographies and Turn-of-the-Century Culture, Katharina Gerstenberger

The "Goldhagen Effect": History, Memory, Nazism—Facing the German Past, Geoff Eley, editor

Shifting Memories: The Nazi Past in the New Germany, Klaus Neumann

Saxony in German History: Culture, Society, and Politics, 1830–1933, James Retallack, editor

Little Tools of Knowledge: Historical Essays on Academic and Bureaucratic Practices, Peter Becker and William Clark, editors

Public Spheres, Public Mores, and Democracy: Hamburg and Stockholm, 1870–1914, Madeleine Hurd

Making Security Social: Disability, Insurance, and the Birth of the Social Entitlement State in Germany, Greg Eghigian

The German Problem Transformed: Institutions, Politics, and Foreign Policy, 1945–1995, Thomas Banchoff

Building the East German Myth: Historical Mythology and Youth Propaganda in the German Democratic Republic, 1945–1989, Alan L. Nothnagle

Mobility and Modernity: Migration in Germany, 1820–1989, Steve Hochstadt

Triumph of the Fatherland: German Unification and the Marginalization of Women, Brigitte Young

Framed Visions: Popular Culture, Americanization, and the Contemporary German and Austrian Imagination, Gerd Gemünden

The Imperialist Imagination: German Colonialism and Its Legacy, Sara Friedrichsmeyer, Sara Lennox, and Susanne Zantop, editors

(continued on last page)

Projecting History

German Nonfiction Cinema, 1967–2000

NORA M. ALTER

Ann Arbor

THE UNIVERSITY OF MICHIGAN PRESS

Published in the United States of America by
The University of Michigan Press
Manufactured in the United States of America
⊗ Printed on acid-free paper

2005 2004 2003 2002 4 3 2 1

A CIP catalog record for this book is available from the British Library.

Library of Congress Cataloging-in-Publication Data

Alter, Nora M., 1962–
Projecting history : German nonfiction cinema, 1967–2000 / Nora M. Alter.
p. cm. — (Social history, popular culture, and politics in Germany)
Includes index.
ISBN 0-472-09812-8 (alk. paper) — ISBN 0-472-06812-1 (pbk. : alk. paper)
1. Documentary films—Germany—History and criticism.
I. Title. II. Series.
PN1995.9.D6 A39 2002
070.1'8—dc21 2002002091

For My Two As

Acknowledgments

I am especially grateful to Geoff Eley for his initial interest in my project, to Elizabeth Suhay of the University of Michigan for sponsoring this book, and to Mary Erwin and Kevin Rennells for seeing it through to completion. The successful completion of *Projecting History* would not have been possible without fellowship support from the National Endowment for the Humanities and the Howard Foundation. Additional summer research funding was provided through the University of Florida Summer Research Scholarship. I am grateful to the Bundesarchiv/Filmarchiv, Berlin (West) and to the Deutsches Rundfunkarchiv, Berlin (East) for giving me access to the films discussed in chapter 1 and to Serge Canto, head of documentation of *L'Humanité,* for providing me with crucial documentation used in chapter 4. My participation at the German Film Institute both at University of Chicago and Dartmouth College provided me with an invaluable knowledge on how to research and write about German film.

Thanks also to the Department of Germanic and Slavic Studies and the Film and Media Studies Program and to the dean's office of the College of Liberal Arts and Sciences at the University of Florida, which generously provided me with the leave time necessary to research and write this book. In particular, I would like to thank the following colleagues, who supported my work both intellectually and administratively: Keith Bullivant, William Calin, Franz Futterknecht, Helga Kraft, Robert Ray, Maureen Turim, and Gregory Ulmer.

I have also greatly benefited over the years from stimulating intellectual exchange from and support of colleagues at other universities: David Bathrick, Russell Berman, Barton Byg, Tom Conley, Tim Corrigan, Thomas Elsaesser, Gerd Gemünden, Sander Gilman, Anton Kaes, Marcia Klotz, Lutz Koepnick, David Levin, John McCarthy, Gerald Prince, Eric Rentschler, Azade Seyhan, Frank Trommler, and Geoff Waite.

I am grateful to Caroline Constant for her generous help as a critical reader of the manuscript. In addition, I am indebted to Margit Grieb for the preparation of the manuscript, including images and index. Thanks to the anonymous readers for University of Michigan Press, whose insightful comments helped sharpen and strengthen the text. Finally, I thank Ellen Goldlust-Gingrich for her meticulous and thoughtful copyediting.

In addition, I thank those individuals who helped make my life a little easier by providing me with the space to complete this project: Jean V. Alter, Maria P. Alter, Michelle Caroly, Ana Lizon, and Jordan McDuff. And for relief, humor, and the proper perspective, I thank Arielle. And finally for patience, support, and understanding in more ways than can be acknowledged, I thank Alex Alberro.

Portions of this book have appeared previously. They have all been substantially revised for inclusion in this book.

Chapter 1 appeared as "Excessive Pre/Requisites: Vietnam through the East German Lens," *Cultural Critique* 35 (winter 1997): 39–79, published by the University of Minnesota Press.

Chapter 3 appeared as "The Political In/visible in the Essay Film: Farocki's *Images of the World and Inscriptions of War,*" *New German Critique* 68 (spring/summer 1996): 165–92.

Part of chapter 4 appeared as "Documentary as Simulacrum: *Tokyo-Ga,*" in *The Cinema of Wim Wenders: Image, Narrative, and the Postmodern Condition,* ed. Roger Cook and Gerd Gemünden (Detroit and London: Wayne State University Press, 1996): 136–62.

Part of chapter 5 appeared as "Ottingers' Benjamin: *Countdown*'s Alternative Take on Reunification," *Germanic Review* 73, no. 1 (winter 1998): 50–69; and "Marcel Ophüls' *November Days:* German Reunification as Musical Comedy," *Film Quarterly* 51, no. 2 (winter 1998): 32–43 (by permission of the University of California Press, © 1998 by the Regents of the University of California).

I would also like to thank Harun Farocki for generously allowing me to use an image from *Images of the World and the Inscription of War* as an illustration for the cover of this book.

Contents

Introduction

> The documentary idea after all demands no more than that the affairs of our time shall be brought to the screen in any fashion which strikes the imagination.
>
> —Noël Burch, *Theory of Film Practice*

> Nonnarrative is but another part of cinema, perhaps all the more devious for claiming to be above the deceptive means with which it makes its point.
>
> —Bill Nichols, *Representing Reality*

The term *nonfiction* in the title of this book, *Projecting History: German Nonfiction Cinema, 1967–2000,* deliberately breaks from the prevailing dual system of traditionally opposed terms: fiction and documentary. This divergence is intended to suggest the raison d'être—and justification—for addressing a subject matter that has apparently been thoroughly explored: postwar films in Germany. Indeed, the genre of "nonfiction" film, rarely taken into account by critics, underpins the architecture of this study. This broad category, generally understood to refer to films that do not deal with fictional topics, accommodates scientific reports, travel narratives, newsreels, documentaries, family mementoes, nonnarrative and experimental films, and hybrid works known as essay films. But I am using the term *nonfiction* specifically to refer to films in which the fictional element colors the documentary material. While borrowing many features of documentaries and actuality films, including the appearance of filming "reality," the nonfiction films studied here do not claim to offer an objective—hence, true—vision of that reality. They do not disguise—indeed, they prefer to display—their artificiality, their artful and often biased manipulation of the "factual" images, celebrating these qualities. In sum, they are not content with merely recording events. Rather they put a spin on these events and use them to convey a message, an idea, a point of view. Since nonfiction films, composed through the selection, timing, and montage of documentary images, do not fit into either of the two traditional categories of cinema—fictional features (or narrative films) and documentaries (or nonfictional and nonnarrative films)—such works are generally overlooked and neglected by scholars and critics alike. I seek to redress that imbalance not by rewriting any part of the available extensive criticism of postwar German cinema but rather by adding to it and thereby presenting a revised and reshaped picture of a discrete "nonfiction" unit that is close to, but not entirely part of, dominant feature film production.

Since the 1980s a concerted effort has taken place to study what is heralded as the first German avant-garde since Expressionism: "New German Cinema." Several significant scholarly studies have been published (in English) that put postwar German film on the international film-studies map. These include (in chronological order) Timothy Corrigan's *New German Film* (1983, reissued in 1994), Eric Rentschler's *West German Film in the Course of Time* (1984), Anton Kaes's *From Hitler to Heimat* (1989), and Thomas Elsaesser's *New German Cinema* (1989).[1] Several volumes focusing on women and gender in German films followed in the 1990s, including Julia Knight's *Women and the New German Cinema* and the two-volume *Gender and German Cinema,* edited by Sandra Frieden and others.[2] A number of recent studies have also examined various aspects of German film from a variety of theoretical perspectives: postcolonialism, autobiography, feminism and fascism, cultural studies, gender studies, music, and now former East German film.[3] Monographs

1. Timothy Corrigan, *New German Film: The Displaced Image* (1983; Bloomington: Indiana University Press, 1994); Eric Rentschler, *West German Film in the Course of Time: Reflections on the Twenty Years since Oberhausen* (Bedford Hills, N.Y.: Redgrave, 1984); Anton Kaes, *From Hitler to Heimat: The Return of History as Film* (Cambridge: Harvard University Press, 1989); Thomas Elsaesser, *New German Cinema: A History* (New Brunswick, N.J.: Rutgers University Press, 1989). See also Rentschler's two edited anthologies, *German Film and Literature: Adaptations and Transformations* (London: Methuen, 1986), and *West German Filmmakers on Film: Visions and Voices* (New York: Holmes and Meier, 1988).

2. Julia Knight, *Women and the New German Cinema* (New York: Verso, 1992); Sandra Frieden, Richard W. McCormick, Vibeke R. Petersen, and Laurie Melissa Vogelsang, *Gender and German Cinema: Feminist Interventions,* 2 vols. (Oxford: Berg, 1993).

3. For postcolonialism, see John E. Davidson, *Deterritorializing the New German Cinema* (Minneapolis: University of Minnesota Press, 1999); for autobiography, see Barbara Kosta, *Recasting Autobiography: Women's Counterfictions in Contemporary German Literature and Film* (Ithaca: Cornell University Press, 1994); for feminism and fascism, see Susan E. Linville, *Feminism, Film, Fascism: Women's Auto/biographical Film in Postwar Germany* (Austin: University of Texas Press, 1998); for cultural studies, see Gerd Gemünden, *Framed Visions: Popular Culture, Americanization, and the Contemporary German and Austrian Imagination* (Ann Arbor: University of Michigan Press, 1998); for gender studies, see Alice A.

have focused on individual directors such as Rainer Werner Fassbinder, Werner Herzog, Alexander Kluge, and Wim Wenders.[4] Several anthologies have been devoted to German film, including *Perspectives on German Cinema* (1996) and *Triangulated Visions: Women in Recent German Cinema* (1998).[5] These English-language volumes are highly informative and offer exceptional examples of scholarship and interpretation in the fields of German studies and film studies, outshining much of what has been published in Germany.

Yet the picture of German postwar film produced by these studies is surprisingly homogenous: they focus almost exclusively on narrative feature films that privilege the so-called New German Cinema. This priority is in part indicative of the extraordinary flowering of talent in the context of New German Cinema. Directors such as Herzog, Kluge, Fassbinder, Ulrike Ottinger, Helke Sanders, Helma Sanders-Brahms, Volker Schlöndorff, Wenders, Hans Jürgen Syberberg, and Margarethe von Trotta have made some of the most memorable fictional films of their era. Although these filmmakers are known primarily for their narrative work, most have also made significant contributions in the area of nonfiction. However, due in no small part to their popularity and accessibility—both in terms of reception and availability—feature films attract more scholarly and critical attention. Furthermore, most film theory has generally converged on narrative feature films, which has only increased the allure of this genre for scholars.

The reevaluation of film that has taken place in the past decade has recognized that this bias ignores a large body of films. As a result, there

---

Kuzniar, *The Queer German Cinema* (Stanford: Stanford University Press, 2000); for music, see Caryl Flinn, *The New German Soundtrack* (Berkeley: University of California Press, forthcoming, 2003); for East Germany, see Sean Allan and John Sanford, eds., *DEFA: East German Cinema, 1946–1992* (New York: Berghahn Books, 1999).

4. Thomas Elsaesser, *Fassbinder's Germany: History, Identity, Subject* (Amsterdam: Amsterdam University Press, 1996); Wallace Steadman Watson, *Understanding Rainer Werner Fassbinder: Film as Private and Public Art* (Columbia: University of South Carolina Press, 1996); Timothy Corrigan, ed., *The Films of Werner Herzog: Between Mirage and History* (New York: Methuen, 1986); Peter C. Lutze, *Alexander Kluge: The Last Modernist* (Detroit: Wayne State University Press, 1998); Roger Bromley, *From Alice to Buena Vista: The Films of Wim Wenders* (London: Praeger, 2001); Roger F. Cook and Gerd Gemünden, eds., *The Cinema of Wim Wenders: Image, Narrative, and the Postmodern Condition* (Detroit: Wayne State University Press, 1997).

5. Terri Ginsberg and Kirsten Moana Thompson, eds., *Perspectives on German Cinema* (New York: G. K. Hall, 1996); Ingeborg Majer O'Sickey and Ingeborg von Zadow, eds., *Triangulated Visions: Women in Recent German Cinema* (Albany: State University of New York Press, 1998); see also Randall Halle and Maggie McCarthy, eds., *German Popular Film* (Detroit: Wayne State University Press, forthcoming).

has been an explosion of studies on nonfiction and documentary film.[6] At the same time, the latter are gaining popular acceptance and slowly entering into mainstream theaters. Ironically, this shift is taking place at the same time that new possibilities of digital manipulation have discredited even further whatever truth claims the documentary image was still thought to make. I do not think that this is a coincidence. Rather, the popularity of the genre of documentary film has increased in direct proportion to the decrease in this genre's indexical link to actuality. Since documentary films' truth claims are more tenuous than ever, viewers can take in such films the same way they do fully fictional feature films. In addition, major technological advances following from the development of the video recorder camera (or portapak) and digital editing systems have made it much easier to produce nonfiction films. The relatively inexpensive, widely available technology enables virtually anyone with a minimum of expertise to make actuality films (especially videotapes). Identification with the process of production in this way has surely also contributed to the increased interest in nonfiction cinema in the theaters.

What, then, might explain the neglect of this genre by German film studies? Emerging in the 1960s as a revolt of the postwar generation against Hollywood and "daddy's cinema," the New German Cinema immediately thrived. Its reputation only grew as it embraced (and was embraced by) successive waves of fashionable avant-gardes: radical or moderate feminism, new historicism, gender studies, postmodernism, and the like. New German Cinema's avant-garde, experimental style

---

6. Ian Aitken, ed., *The Documentary Film Movement: An Anthology* (Edinburgh: Edinburgh University Press, 1998); Erik Barnouw, *Documentary: A History of the Non-Fiction* (Oxford: Oxford University Press, 1993); Richard M. Barsam, *Nonfiction Film: A Critical History,* rev. and exp. ed. (Bloomington: Indiana University Press, 1992); John Corner, *The Art of Record: A Critical Introduction to Documentary* (Manchester: Manchester University Press, 1996); John Corner, ed., *Documentary and the Mass Media* (London: Edward Arnold, 1986); Jane Gaines and Michael Renov, eds., *Collecting Visible Evidence* (Minneapolis: University of Minnesota Press, 1999); Barry Keith Grant and Jeannette Sloniowski, eds., *Documenting the Documentary: Close Readings of Documentary Film and Video* (Detroit: Wayne State University Press, 1998); William Guynn, *A Cinema of Nonfiction* (London: Associated University Presses, 1990); Kevin MacDonald and Mark Cousins, eds., *Imagining Reality: The Faber Book of Documentary* (London: Faber and Faber, 1998); Bill Nichols, *Blurred Boundaries: Questions of Meaning in Contemporary Culture* (Bloomington: Indiana University Press, 1994); Michael Renov, *Theorizing Documentary* (New York: Routledge, 1993); Alan Rosenthal, ed., *New Challenges for Documentary* (Berkeley: University of California Press, 1988); William Roth, *Documentary Film Classics* (Cambridge: Cambridge University Press, 1997); Dai Vaughan, *For Documentary* (Berkeley: University of California Press, 1999); Diane Waldman and Janet Walker, eds., *Feminism and Documentary* (Minneapolis: University of Minnesota Press, 1999); Charles Warren, ed., *Beyond Document: Essays on the Nonfiction Film* (Hanover, N.H.: University Press of New England, 1996); Brian Winston, *Claiming the Real: The Documentary Film Revisited* (London: British Film Institute, 1995).

was particularly appealing to intellectuals and critics. Yet it self-consciously remained on the periphery of dominant film production (that is, Hollywood and its clones), which may explain why an even more marginal and ambitious filmic practice was ignored. Already on the periphery, why should a critic or scholar go beyond to the outermost circles of that map?

But there is another reason for the neglect of nonfiction German film, inherently intertwined with historical circumstances. Here it is revealing to note that this genre frequently summoned predecessors such as Hans Richter's experimental films of the 1920s, Walter Ruttman's *Berlin, Symphony of a Great City* (1927), and Robert Siodmak's and Fred Zinnemann's *People on Sunday* (1929). Significantly, all of these films were made before 1930—before, that is, the formidable entry of documentary filmmaker Leni Riefenstahl. Her almost instant domination of the field (she claimed her films were not documentary newsreels)—the way in which her practice formed the ground rules for how nonfiction films should be produced, received and critiqued—extended well beyond the Third Reich. If the New German Cinema directors had a father to kill, nonfiction filmmakers were confronted with a devouring mother. And it is Riefenstahl's triumph that her films continue to fascinate and command a great deal of attention and criticism.[7] Understandably, Riefenstahl's dominance in this genre has colored the field and led to a critical silence about other nonfiction productions.[8] This study seeks to give them voice by taking up the interrupted dialogue of the 1920s and early 1930s concerning the possibilities and potentiality of nonfictional production.

The Nazi past played a special role in the postwar German imaginary, as many struggled to deal not only with this period's unprecedented crimes against humanity but also with the physical and psychological pain felt by the nation. In contrast to the nearly silent generation of the immediate postwar years, those crippled by what Alexander and Margarete Mitscherlich referred to as an "inability to mourn," politically active artists and intellectuals in the 1960s took up the challenge to master and work through their problematic recent history.[9] New German Cinema

7. See, for example, Barnouw, *Documentary;* Barsam, *Nonfiction Film;* Grant and Sloniowski, *Documenting the Documentary.*

8. Individual films such as *Germany in Autumn* have been widely discussed and debated. But with a few exceptions, there has been no extensive study of nonfiction cinema. An anomaly is Barton Byg's tour de force, *Landscapes of Resistance: The German Films of Danièle Huillet and Jean-Marie Straub* (Berkeley: University of California Press, 1995).

9. Alexander and Margarete Mitscherlich, *Die Unfähigkeit zu trauern* (Munich: Piper, 1967); on films and recent German history, see Eric L. Santner, *Stranded Objects: Mourning, Memory, and Film in Postwar Germany* (Ithaca: Cornell University Press, 1990); Kaes, *From Hitler to Heimat.*

addressed the past with an aggressive platform that called for radically different films about a new vision of history. The systematic preference for (narrative) feature films implied, among other things, that history should be depicted in terms of fictional though typical individual lives by means of personal guilt or redemption. With some exceptions, this fictionalized "history as film" reduced complex historical and political events to highly individualized and personal stories.

Most of the nonfiction films I have chosen to discuss do not depict individual protagonists. Rather, they focus on political-economic forces and structures. The films address basic problems of German history, including its overall "peculiarity" within the European context, and, in particular, the specific ways in which the National Socialist legacy continues to haunt Germans. The process of mastering or working through the troubled German past that I scrutinize in these nonfiction films is subject to a double perspective: as a national cinema in centripetal relation to internal German problems (including terrorism, the divided state, and reunification) but also as a transnational cinema in centrifugal relation to external problems such as the ways that, under postindustrial conditions, global images of totality (and hence imaginary structures of communities larger than a nation) proliferate and remain politically viable. Within this national-transnational structure, I examine not only how the nonfiction genre develops within Germany but also how the films are in dialogue with nonfiction films produced elsewhere and thereby contribute to a transnational genre that stands fundamentally opposed to Hollywood feature film production.

My account provides an alternative to Corrigan's claim in *New German Film: The Displaced Image* that the New German filmmakers have not lived up to the radicalism of their initial project of social criticism: "Like the old order they once engaged, these filmmakers, inadvertently in most cases, have arrested audience expectations at the borders of their own films and have in many ways closed the channels of an ongoing dialogue with pertinent social issues."[10] While Corrigan's assertion may be true of much traditional narrative film production in Germany, it is less true of German nonfiction cinema, including that produced by otherwise traditional filmmakers. The reasons for this are ultimately linked to issues of production and funding. First, new technology has made it easier for established filmmakers to shoot low-budget nonfiction films without having to apply to film-funding boards. This increased freedom from financial ties and obligations has also enabled a significant amount of artistic experimentation and play. Hence, it is important to emphasize that most of the films

10. Corrigan, *New German Film,* 187.

under consideration, with the exception of those made in the former East Germany, did not have expectations for a large public or even box office release.

Methodologically, I have found Bill Nichols's analysis of nonfiction films in *Representing Reality* (1991) to be productive. Nichols shows that although nonfiction films and films with a fictional narrative are structurally and ideologically similar, the "differences—if not distinctions," between the two genres are more significant.[11] More specifically, I shall show that despite their sometimes easy accessibility and seeming straightforwardness, nonfiction films contain crucial encoded moments that are simultaneously visible and audible to some viewers and invisible and inaudible to others. Nonfiction filmmakers often cleverly use this mechanism of im/perceptibility in canny attempts to control their films' reception. Intentions are a complex matter, however, and the dialectical collision of the visual and the audible often prevents political critiques or simple messages from being received. Political meanings tend to come together indirectly and often in surreptitious ways in films, fiction and nonfiction alike. Thus, not only thematic but also formal and technological elements of production must be examined to comprehend the various meanings of any nonfiction film. Meaning is just as much the product of subject matter as it is of film craft and techniques, including the use of camera, editing, and voice-over for the purpose of constructing and manipulating the point of view and viewer's identity (whether positively by identification or negatively by abjection). To present German cultural politics or individual films from an exclusively thematic or, for that matter, purely formal or technological perspectives is to deny their complexity.

One type of film within the nonfiction genre, the essay film, deserves particular mention here since several of the productions under consideration in this book are of this sort.[12] The essay film was first formally articulated by avant-garde filmmaker Hans Richter just prior to his 1940 departure from Europe. In "Der Filmessay: Eine neue Form des Dokumentarfilms" (The Film Essay: A New Form of Documentary Film), Richter proposes a new genre of film that would enable the filmmaker to make the "invisible" world of thoughts and ideas visible on the screen.[13] Unlike the documentary film, which presents facts and information, the essay film produces complex thought that at times is not grounded in real-

11. Nichols, *Representing Reality,* xi.

12. To date there is no book-length English study on the essay film. In German, see Christa Blümlinger and Constantin Wulff, eds., *Schreiben Bilder Sprechen: Texte zum essayistischen Film* (Vienna: Sonderzahl, 1992).

13. Hans Richter, "Der Filmessay: Eine neue Form des Dokumentarfilms" [1940], in *Schreiben Bilder Sprechen,* ed. Blümlinger and Wulff, 195–98.

ity but can be contradictory, irrational, and fantastic. This new type of film, according to Richter, no longer binds the filmmaker to the rules and parameters of the traditional documentary practice, such as chronological sequencing or the depiction of external phenomena. Rather, it gives free reign to the imagination, with all its artistic potentiality.[14] The term *essay* is used because it signifies a composition that is in between categories and as such is transgressive, digressive, playful, contradictory, and political.[15] Richter cites his own production, *Inflation* (1928), as an early example of what an essay film might look like. The genre was further formulated in the late 1940s and 1950s in France by Alexandre Astruc, whose influential essay, "La caméra-stylo" (1948), promoted a type of filmic "writing just as flexible and subtle as written language."[16] Developments in Germany in the 1980s, with *Filmkritik* commentary, as well as in France in the 1970s, with the self-reflexive cinema verité and the work of "essayists" Jean-Luc Godard and Chris Marker, continued to delineate the main features of the essay film as a genre—or, rather, as a nongenre, since, like Adorno's literary "heresy," it strives to transgress structurally and conceptually traditional boundaries.[17] To a certain extent, contemporary German filmmakers

14. "In diesem Bemühen, die unsichtbare Welt der Vorstellungen, Gedanken un Ideen sichtbar zu machen, kann der essayistische Film aus einem unvergleilich größeren Reservoir von Ausdrucksmitteln schöpfen, als die reine Dokumentarfilm. Denn da man in Filmessay an die Wiedergabe der äußeren Erscheinungen oder an eine chronologische Folge nicht gebunden ist, sondern im Gegenteil das Anschauungsmaterial überall herbeiziehen muß, so kann man frei in Raum und Zeit springen: von der objektiven Wiedergabe beispielweise zur phantastische Allegorie, von dieser zur Spielszene; man kann tote wie ebendge, künstliche wie natürliche Dinge abbilden, alles verwenden, was es gibt und was sich erfinden läßt—wenn es nur als Argument für die Sichtbarmachung des Grundgedankens dienen kann" (Richter, "Der Filmessay," 198).

15. For a theorization of the essay as form, see Theodor W. Adorno, "Der Essay als Form," in *Noten zur Literatur I* (Frankfurt am Main: Suhrkamp, 1981); Georg Lukács, "On the Nature and Form of the Essay," in *Soul and Form* (Cambridge: MIT Press, 1980).

16. See Alexandre Astruc, "The Birth of a New Avant-Garde: La Caméra Stylo" [1948], in *The New Wave: Critical Landmarks,* ed. Peter Graham (Garden City, N.Y.: Doubleday, 1968), 17–23. Also see his *Du stylo à la caméra et de la caméra au stylo* (Paris: L'Archipel, 1990). Astruc argued that the fate of the avant-garde hung in the balance. The essay film was a historical necessity because "the cinema is now moving toward a form which is making it such a precise language that it will soon be possible to write ideas directly onto film" ("Birth," 19). Astruc's notion of literal inscription of texts on the celluloid was to be enriched by other ways of inscribing ideas on films.

17. Filmmaker Harun Farocki was involved as a coeditor of *Filmkritik,* notably during the influential 1983–84 period. But as early as 1979, German filmmakers' Hamburg declaration acknowledged the need for a synthesis between the "feature film" and "documentary . . . films that reflect on the medium," anticipating two major traits of the essay film, self-reflexivity and the (equivocal) use of objective images to tell a subjective message ("The Hamburg Declaration" [1979], in *West German Filmmakers on Film,* ed. Rentschler, 4). Such a program challenged Siegfried Kracauer's influential separation of cinema into realistic and

who work in the genre of the essay film—and generally within the category of nonfiction film—are genealogically linked to the violently interrupted project of the historical avant-garde.

The period covered in this book, 1967–2000, starts at the height of student protest and activism in West Germany. Film production also underwent significant transformations in the mid-1960s, including the birth of New German Cinema. The endpoint of my project corresponds not only to the end of the century but also to the end of a number of practices of audiovisual production and distribution current in the twentieth century. Everything has changed with recent developments in the field of computer technology, as digitally generated images proliferate. National cinemas are also becoming obsolete as new forms of transnationalism come to dominate production, distribution, and consumption.

Yet I do not seek to give a comprehensive overview of nonfiction film production in Germany in the second half of the twentieth century. Rather, I have selected only a handful of filmmakers, all of whom have achieved a considerable degree of success or mastery in their filmmaking careers: Walter Heynowski and Gerhard Scheumann and Winfried and Barbara Junge (the leading East German documentarists); Fassbinder, Schlöndorff, and Wenders (the leading German feature filmmakers); Ottinger (a maker of feminist films that problematize gender constructions); Ophüls (an international documentary filmmaker); and Farocki and Kluge (the top essay filmmakers). Their works all explore the potentiality of this genre in between fact and fiction, and I argue that these explorations are encouraged, even mandated, by the political unconscious of their topics—whether terrorism or reunification. The films produced are highly demanding of spectators, requiring that they actively work to coproduce meaning.

---

formalistic films, with documentary falling more toward the former than the latter. See Kracauer, *Theory of Film: The Redemption of Physical Reality* (New York: Oxford University Press, 1960), 33–37. For French cinema verité, see Birgit Kämper, "*Sans soleil*—ein Film erinnert sich selbst," in *Schreiben Bilder Sprechen,* ed. Blümlinger and Wulff, 33–59. From its inception, essay film theorists and practitioners have followed the example of the written essay (dating back at least to Montaigne and Bacon and extending to De Sade, Leopardi, Nietzsche, Lukács, Adorno, Benjamin, and Barthes), which entails resisting the temptation to situate the essay in stable generic terms. The essay has also been described as not merely "between" other genres but as their repressed *Urform.* See Réda Bensmaïa, *The Barthes Effect: The Essay as Reflective Text,* trans. Pat Fedkiew (1986; Minneapolis: University of Minnesota Press, 1987). Because it is a genre that resists closure, tends to be nonlinear in argumentation, and is often openly personal, it has been perceived as particularly well adapted to feminism. See Ruth-Ellen Boetscher Joeres and Elizabeth Mittman, eds., *The Politics of the Essay: Feminist Perspectives* (Bloomington: Indiana University Press, 1993). See also the special issue "Versuch über den Essayfilm," *Augenblick* 10 (1991).

The first chapter, "Excessive Requisites: Vietnam through the East German Lens," explores the little-known nonfiction Vietnam films produced between 1968 and 1978 by the East German film collective Heynowski and Scheumann. The contrast between these films and coeval Western documentaries demonstrates how communist ideology and politics generated a concrete documentary aesthetic that differed from the Western standard of the 1960s and 1970s. In light of the then official dictate that anti-imperialist filmmakers had to "practice solidarity with their weapon: camera," I question the relationship between war and documentary filmmaking. What happens when the war becomes a form of documentary and the documentary a form of war? As a case in point, what happens when the human body is graphically represented in the context of war, as for example, when U.S. pilots were interviewed by Heynowski and Scheumann in a prisoner of war camp outside of Hanoi? This leads me to the problematic of identity and identification as it emerges from the representation of one body and culture by another: in this case, North Americans and Vietnamese viewed through the East German lens.

The next chapter, "Framing Terrorism: Beyond the Borders," examines the 1978 omnibus production *Germany in Autumn,* made by nine West German filmmakers in direct response to incidents of terrorism in West Germany in the 1970s and their distorted representation in the mass media. I use this film as a transitional work between the East German perspective of Heynowski and Scheumann (including their notion that the war in Vietnam builds on the legacy of National Socialism) and more recent concerns about right-wing trends in the West. From that angle, I draw attention to the role the hybrid nature of the film—part archival footage, part fictional re-creation—plays in conveying the complexity of terrorism. Another notable feature of the film is the way it employs the representation of women defying the state in its analysis of political violence. Throughout the chapter, I pay particular attention to moments of slippage between fiction and nonfiction and to the blurring of canonical boundaries between factual reports and imaginary scenes. The destruction of these (and other) traditional forms, in the context of this film, metaphorically functions as a quasi-terrorist assault on formal cinema.

Chapter 3, "The Political Im/perceptible," focuses on film essayist Harun Farocki's *Images of the World and the Inscription of War* (1988–89). As it articulates formalistic aesthetics with politico-economic history, especially in the context of the Cold War, Farocki's complex and quasi-philosophical film creates a dialectic between a not-so-distant past, scarred by the Holocaust and the Algerian War, and a present-day Germany wedged between the Cold War superpowers. After discussing Farocki's work as an example of the contemporary essay film, I present the film as a modernist investigation of the nature of vision, visuality, and visibility in relation to new technologies of image production and reception. Picking up on the political thread of the previous chapters, I analyze the film as a direct confrontation with the fascist past. Farocki's text becomes an inscription of war, advocating the recourse to radical solutions through the logic of the political im/perceptible.

Chapter 4, "Global Politics, Cinematographic Space: Wenders's *Tokyo-Ga* and *Notebooks on Cities and Clothes,*" considers Wenders's two essay or "diary" films as symptomatic of his theory of film. Geographically, these films point to the nexus among Germany, France, and Japan, with the United States as an absent signifier. Both films testify to a fascination with Japan. This is especially strong with regard to Tokyo and the way a highly developed form of technoculture has been overlaid on a ritualized traditional culture in this megacity. Wenders is particularly interested in probing the tension in Japan between the modernist ideal of originality and the postmodern sway of simulation and simulacra.

Chapter 5, "Reunification in a Decentered Lens: Ottinger and Ophüls," examines two relatively marginal films that feature unorthodox representations of a major political event: the reunification of Germany. In a radical departure from her usual style of filmmaking, Ulrike Ottinger's *Countdown* is haunted by the specter of Weimar and the Third Reich as it counts down the ten days before monetary reunification. Marcel Ophüls's *November Days* interweaves phenomena of the Third Reich and current neo-Nazism in a musical comedy that satirizes a prodigal son's return to his father's Germany, which now seeks a place within the larger European context. The film indirectly raises the still nebulous question of what will happen to East German artists now that their world has fundamentally changed?

The epilogue, "History in the Making: The Children of Golzow Project," begins to answer Ophüls's question. It follows a remarkable film project that two former East German filmmakers, Winfred and Barbara Junge, have been carrying out since 1961, documenting the lives of the people of Golzow. The Junges' forty years of filmmaking offer a record of a small town's history along with glimpses into Germany's progress toward reunification. While chronicling the life of a group of children as they mature into adults, the films also provide glimpses of the profound impact postwar modernization and the demographic move to Western cities has had on (former) East Germans. The Golzow Project is particularly important in this context because it shows the changes that took place in documentary filmmaking practices from the early 1960s to the late 1990s and thereby sums up the thematic and formal evolution of nonfiction German film.

CHAPTER 1

Excessive Requisites: Vietnam through the East German Lens

> Until the day I emigrated to North Vietnam I didn't let the film camera out of my hand. It was my weapon, just as once the rifle had been.
>
> —To Cuong, "Baut die Strassen zum vorwärts schreiten"

> The body is a battle site of contending values and their representation. Images of the stable, fixed, and secure serve as a kind of talisman, warding off the mutable, vulnerable and malleable qualities of the body. A vast repertoire of popular myths and heroes complements the stereotypes and biases . . . to form a cultural diorama in the social imaginary.
>
> —Bill Nichols, *Representing Reality*

> A reciprocal play of different points of view and one's own, creative intent and communicative result.
>
> —Walter Heynowski and Gerhard Scheumann, *Dokument und Kunst*

I. Historical Background

The Vietnam War provoked an international response among leftist cultural workers throughout the world, including Europe. A dominant target of national and international student protests, the war was the direct focus of playwrights writing in West Germany, such as Peter Weiss, Rolf Hochhuth, and Günther Grass. Like their colleagues in Great Britain, France, and Italy (and to a remarkably greater extent than those in the United States), these German writers used their stage not only as a political call to arms in solidarity with the North Vietnamese but also as a more or less disguised forum to speak of their own nation's problems, past and present, including the Third Reich and its legacy.[1] This aspect of Vietnam protest literature took many forms. Austrian Marxist poet Erich Fried, living in exile in England and broadcasting for the BBC to East Germany, devoted a collection of verse, *und Vietnam und* (1966),[2] to the antiwar movement, arguing that there are in fact "many Vietnams" in history and around the world. There were direct and indirect allusions to Vietnam in numerous films and novels of the period. And of course, as chapter 2 will demonstrate, protest against the war initially served to coalesce student activists who later became members of the Red Army Faction. What is far less well known, however, is the impact of the Vietnam War on the former East bloc, including film production in the German Democratic Republic.

Fidel Castro proclaimed 1967 as the global Year of Vietnam. The Vietnam War was a main theme of that year's Leipzig Documentary Film Festival and remained a topic of interest into the 1970s.[3] In 1967 two groups of European filmmakers petitioned to travel to North Vietnam. Hanoi denied the first request, by Swiss French avant-garde director Jean-Luc Godard; this refusal resulted in his contribution to *Loin du Vietnam* (Far from Vietnam, 1967), a celebrated collaborative film conceived and organized by Chris Marker. Its title alludes to the fact that the Western filmmakers (with the exception of Dutch documentarist Joris Ivens) were unable to visit the Democratic Republic of Vietnam (DRV), so they filmed various forms of reaction to the war from afar. They used documentary footage of U.S. warships off the coast of Vietnam as well as demonstrations and interviews in the United States and France. Godard also employed self-consciously fictive re-creations to bring the war home or, as he put it, "to create Vietnam in ourselves."[4]

Hanoi did grant visas, however, to a second European film team (Ivens had filmed alone), the first foreign one to be allowed into the DRV: the leading East German production collective, Walter Heynowski and Gerhard Scheumann, commonly known as H&S. A year earlier, they had made *400 cm³* (1966), a short film about GDR blood donations for the North Vietnamese. The acclaim it received from the DRV delegation at

---

1. For a comprehensive analysis of the international theatrical response to the Vietnam War, see my *Vietnam Protest Theatre: The Television War on Stage* (Bloomington: Indiana University Press, 1996).

2. Erich Fried, *und Vietnam und* (1966). *Gesammelte Werke,* vol. 1, ed. Volker Kaukoreit and Klaus Wagenbach (Berlin: Klaus Wagenbach, 1973), 361–400.

3. Hans-Dieter Tok, "Chile, Vietnam, und unser Zeitgenosse: Überlegungen nach der XVI. Internationalen Leipziger Dokumentar und Kurzfilmwoche für Kino und Fernsehen 1973," *Film und Fernsehen* 2 (1974): 5.

4. As cited from Godard's sequence, "Camera-oeil," in *Loin du Vietnam* (S.L.O.N., 1967), 35 mm, 115 minutes.

Leipzig emboldened H&S to make their petition.[5] The result was a series of documentaries about Vietnam that were shot, edited, and shown from 1967 to 1978—that is, until after the war, when H&S returned for a second visit. In total, H&S produced fourteen films related to the Vietnam War and its legacy. Filmed to a large extent on location, this series of documentaries employed a variety of techniques more or less conventional to the genre: interviews, found archival footage interspliced with fictional recreations, and so on.[6] These 35mm films varied in length from four to ninety minutes: many were in black and white, some were in both black and white and color, and a few were in color only. Some are available in several language versions, including English.[7] At the time of their release on East German television, in movie houses (preceding feature films), and at international film festivals around the world where they were uncensored, these films received considerable national and international recognition, especially in the socialist bloc but also in countries not directly involved in the conflict in Southeast Asia or with officially "neutral" positions (particularly Scandinavia).[8]

The H&S films can be divided into three (not quite chronological) categories. The first is films made during the war but not on location in Vietnam. These works are openly agitative, calling on the viewers to commit themselves to the cause of the war in whatever way possible. These films include *400 cm³* (1966), *100* (100 Pushups, 1971), and *Remington Cal. 12* (1972). The second group consists of interview or single-person films, including *Der Zeuge* (The Witness, 1967), a studio conversation in Leipzig with Vu Nam, filmmaker of the South Vietnamese National Liberation Front; and the four-part, on-location series *Piloten im Pyjama* (Pilots in Pyjamas, 1968); *Yes, Sir; Hilton Hanoi; The Job;* and *Die Donnergötter* (The Thunder Gods), a psychological portrait and investigation of the lives, backgrounds, and psychological and ideological makeup of downed U.S. pilots in prison in Hanoi. The third category includes on-location films made in the immediate aftermath of the war, alluding to the rebuilding process of postwar Vietnam on all levels—cultural, intellectual, political, and economic. The films in this group are *Die Teufelsinsel* (Devil's

5. "Werkstattgespräch Studio H&S," in *Dokument und Kunst,* 94.

6. For a complete filmography of H&S's work up to 1978 (in German, English, French, and Spanish), see Robert Michel, ed., *Die Filme Heynowski & Scheumann, Peter Hellmich, 1965–1978* (East Berlin: Nationales Druckhaus, [c. 1979]).

7. On the problem of translating H&S films into other languages, including the German translation of the U.S. pilots' English, see Wolfgang von Polentz, "Wie dolmetschen? Sprachliche Übertragungen für Dokumentarfilme von Heynowski & Scheumann," in *Dokument und Kunst,* 63–67.

8. See Morgens Rukov, "Respekt vor der Autorität der Tatsachen: Zur Rezeption der H&S Filme in Westeuropa," in *Dokument und Kunst,* 37–40.

Island, 1976); *Eintritt kostenlos* (Free Admission, 1976); *Der erste Reis danach* (The First Rice Thereafter, 1977); *"Ich bereue aufrichtig"* ("I'm Truly Sorry," 1977); *Die eiserne Festung* (The Iron Fortress, 1977); and *Am Wassergraben* (At the Water Trench/Grave, 1978).

To appreciate fairly H&S's work, it is helpful to juxtapose three quotations that together produce a matrix of problems, each condensing one focal point of the films. To Cuong articulates in the 1970s what architect and cultural theoretician Paul Virilio codified as theory in the 1980s: the ancient notion of "the eye's function being the function of a weapon" has developed into a situation in which "a war of pictures and sounds is replacing the war of objects (projectiles and missiles)."[9] In 1976 an East German journal of media studies, *Film und Fernsehen* (Film and Television), cited To Cuong as recalling, "Until the day I emigrated to North Vietnam I didn't let the film camera out of my hand. It was my weapon, just as once the rifle had been."[10] More generally, anti-imperialist filmmakers were asked to "practice solidarity with their weapon: camera."[11] Both To Cuong and Virilio thus make an equation at least as old as the American Civil War between the shooting of weapons and the shooting of pictures. What remains is a reciprocal relationship between war and the peculiar part fiction, part fact type of filmmaking known as documentary. The boundaries between the two types of shooting is further blurred when war becomes documentary and documentary becomes war.[12]

The second epigraph problematizes the physical appearance of the human body in the documentary film. In *Representing Reality* (1993), Nichols argues, "The body is a battle site of contending values and their representation. Images of the stable, fixed, and secure serve as a kind of talisman, warding off the mutable, vulnerable and malleable qualities of the body. A vast repertoire of popular myths and heroes complements the stereotypes and biases . . . to form a cultural diorama in the social imaginary."[13] This thesis is part of a widespread concern in cultural studies with the "body" that has developed out the work of historical materialists as

9. Paul Virilio, *War and Cinema: The Logistics of Perception,* trans. Patrick Camiller (1984; London: Verso, 1989), 3, 4.

10. To Cuong, "Baut die Strassen zum Vorwärts schreiten . . . : Aus dem Tagebuch eines vietnamesischen Dokumentaristen," *Film und Fernsehen* 8 (1976): 11.

11. Tok, "Chile, Vietnam, und unser Zeitgenosse," 5.

12. As Polish director Andrzej Brzozowski said about antiwar filmmaking: "I don't believe that this kind of film is not also militant [*kämpferisch*]. It would be a huge letdown for me if I were to learn that my Vietnam films were not militant films" ("Das Publikum kann auch harte Nüsse knacken" [interview], *Film und Fernsehen* 2 [1974]: 14). For essays on the history of the relationship between war and cinema, see *Historical Journal of Film, Radio, and Television,* special issue, "War, Film, and History" 14:4 (1994).

13. Bill Nichols, *Representing Reality: Issues and Concepts in Documentary* (Bloomington: Indiana University Press, 1996), 239.

well as of Friedrich Nietzsche, Martin Heidegger, Michel Foucault, Gilles Deleuze, Felix Guattari, and Judith Butler, among others.[14] At stake for Nichols is what he calls "raising political consciousness" through a "historical dialectic." He goes on to propose that in the documentary film, the body of the subject represents a surplus of meanings (supplemental "magnitude") in excess of those immediately intended by the referential film frame.[15] In other words, the phenomenological effect of the human body on the viewer will generate a series of unpredictable and uncontrollable chains of references never anticipated during the making of a film. Nichols argues that the confrontation with the re/presented human body on film raises "political consciousness" by addressing "the contradiction between individual consciousness and a historical dialectic. It attends to those magnitudes that implant themselves in the person, the body, and its consciousness, and yet exceed it."[16] Some of these magnitudes arise due to the race, class, gender, and cultural or national composition of the filmed subject. But just as this physical excess is not necessarily intentional on the part of the filmmaker, so also I would suggest that the viewer is not necessarily able to convert it into meaning or raise it to consciousness—political or other—at least not in the immediate act of direct viewing. But this excess or magnitude of meaning exists nonetheless and will be fundamental to my analysis of H&S's Vietnam films.

I will focus on the "excessive" and specifically politicized bodies in H&S's films, particularly as these bodies bear on the question of precisely whose consciousness is raised when it cannot, by the definition of *excess,* be that of the filmmakers themselves. Moreover, the bodies here in dispute are not only human—that is, U.S. "air pirates," Vietnamese on both sides

---

14. See Jonathan Crary and Sanford Kwinter, eds., *Incorporations* (New York: Zone, 1992); Michel Feher, ed., with Ramona Naddaff and Nadia Tazi, *Fragments for a History of the Human Body* (New York: Zone, 1989). On the importance of the body and materialism in the Heideggerian tradition, based on Nietzsche, among others, see Theodore Kisiel, *The Genesis of Heidegger's "Being and Time"* (Berkeley: University of California Press, 1993), esp. 26, 33–38, 40–47.

15. See Bill Nichols, "Questions of Magnitude," in *Documentary and the Mass Media,* ed. John Corner (London: Edward Arnold, 1986), 107–22; Nichols, *Representing Reality,* 229–66 ("Representing the Body: Questions of Meaning and Magnitude"); Bill Nichols, "'Getting to Know You. . . .' Knowledge, Power and the Body," in *Theorizing Documentary,* ed. Michael Renov (New York: Routledge, 1993), 174–91; "The Trials and Tribulations of Rodney King," in Bill Nichols, *Blurred Boundaries* (Bloomington: Indiana University Press, 1992). The Rodney King incident has become something of a test case for these issues, including the meaning of video verité. See, e.g., Paula Rabinowitz, *They Must Be Represented: The Politics of Documentary* (London: Verso, 1994), 205–15 ("Video *Vérité:* Rodney King in the City of Angels of History"); Avital Ronell, *Finitudes Score: Essays for the End of the Millenium* (Lincoln: University of Nebraska Press, 1994), 305–27 ("Trauma TV: Twelve Steps beyond the Pleasure Principle").

16. Nichols, *Representing Reality,* 243.

of the war, and H&S themselves—but also material objects. In other words, I want to extend Nichols's "historical dialectical" thesis about the excessive and disruptive presence of bodies in documentary to include what might be called H&S's dialectical materialist way of filming humans alongside inanimate objects—what they call *Requisiten.* This emphasis on the material object recalls the German theatrical tradition best exemplified by Bertolt Brecht and Erwin Piscator, where *Requisiten* means "requisites" or "indispensable objects" but also "stage devices" or "properties."[17] In contrast to this strategy of consigning to objects an active role in the production of meaning, I suggest that Nichols's almost exclusive focus on human bodies to illustrate his theory of magnitude may unintentionally reinforce certain tendencies of what used to be called bourgeois humanism—or, in cinematic terms, the tendency to reduce complex historical events to specific human bodies whereby film becomes a "machine for the production of the couple"[18] and abandons efforts to represent larger collectives and structures (in the manner, say, of Eisenstein in *October* or *Battleship Potemkin*).

The third quotation is H&S's definition of their documentary work: "A reciprocal play of different points of view and one's own, creative intent and communicative result."[19] It leads to the problematic of self-identity that emerges—not necessarily as intended—in the representation of bodies and cultures by another: in this case, North Americans and Vietnamese viewed through the East German lens. It remains to be seen how this reciprocity works itself out in terms of filming and revisioning "Vietnam" as a complex allegory—not necessarily conscious and necessarily incomplete—for the history and problems of postwar East German society in particular and capitalist society in general. Thus, at this level of complexity, documentary film brings "foreign" wars and other "foreign" events uncannily close to home.

II. Vietnam in/as Film

A renewed look at "foreign" representations of the Vietnam War—including those of H&S[20]—is warranted because, in its multiple representations

17. For an extensive and acute discussion of the East German theory of requisites as applied in H&S's films, see Günter Agde, "Von der Sprache der Dinge: Gedanken zum Einsatz von Requisiten in den Vietnamfilmen von H&S," in *Dokument und Kunst,* 40–46.

18. Slavoj Žižek, "'In His Bold Gaze My Ruin Is Writ Large,'" in *Everything You Always Wanted to Know about Lacan (But Were Afraid to Ask Hitchcock),* ed. Žižek (London: Verso, 1992), 241.

19. *Dokument und Kunst,* 3

20. H&S were by no means the only filmmakers to focus on the Vietnam War. The war produced an international response by documentary filmmakers both in the East and the

and subsequent critical appraisals, the Vietnam War is still too often viewed as an exclusively American affair. Most treatments of the war in Southeast Asia begin and end with American occupation—from the presence of "advisers" in the 1950s to the final troop withdrawal and notorious airlift out of Saigon in April 1975. With the exception of the tenacious POW/MIA lobby, life in 'Nam ceased for the American public on that day. Reunified Vietnam sank back into obscurity, leaving a legacy of more or less repressed and suppressed materials to be played and replayed, worked through and acted out, over the next decades. It is as if Vietnam had no history from a Western perspective before the American occupation and none thereafter. In the words of Vietnamese-born, French-educated, American-based filmmaker and theoretician Trinh T. Minh-ha, "For general Western spectatorship, Vietnam does not exist outside the war. And she no longer exists since the war has ended, except as a name, an exemplary model of revolution, or a nostalgic cult object for those who, while admiring unconditionally the revolution, do not seem to take any genuine, sustained interest in the troubled reality of Vietnam in her social and cultural autonomy."[21] Nonetheless—as demonstrated by the heated reaction to Robert S. McNamara's apologia for the war[22]—while Vietnam, like any other event, is coopted by the postmodern society of the

---

West, including, of course, the United States. In addition to the omnibus film *Loin du Vietnam* (1967), there is Godard's *Letter to Jane* (1972); the British Peter Brook's *Tell Me Lies* (1968) and James Cameron's *Eyewitness—North Vietnam* (1966); the Dutch Joris Ivens's *The Seventeenth Parallel* (1968); the West German Michael Verhoeven's *O.K.* (1970) and Harun Farocki's *Before Your Eyes: Vietnam* (1981–82); the East German Gitta Nickel's *Vietnam 73* (1973); the Polish Andrzej Brzozowski's *The First Ten Days of Peace* (1973); the Cuban Santiago Alvarez's *Hanoi, Tuesday the 13th* (1968), *Laos: The Forgotten War* (1968), and *The Seventy-nine Springtimes of Ho Chi Minh* (1969); the Canadian Michael Rubbo's *The Sad Song of Yellow Skin* (1970); and the Japanese Kentaro Musada and Takashi Koizumi's *Vietnam* (1970). Among the most well known Vietnamese films are the collective productions *A Day of Plane Hunting* (1968) and *U.S. Techniques and Genocide in Vietnam* (1968) and Nguyen Chi Phuc's *Women of Telecommunications Station #6* (1969) and *Young Puppeteers of Vietnam* (1968).

21. Trinh T. Minh-ha, *When the Moon Waxes Red: Representation, Gender, and Cultural Politics* (New York: Routledge, 1991), 100. Trinh's major film about Vietnam is *Surname Viet Given Name Nam* (1989), in which she interviews Vietnamese women about their experiences in Vietnam after the communist victory. The viewer is intentionally misled to assume that these women are relating their own life histories, but they are acting out roles from a scripted text. The controversy surrounding this "interview" technique has tended to overshadow other aspects of the film, which seeks to re/present the continuing history of Vietnam from the points of view of women. See further Trinh, *Framer Framed* (New York: Routledge, 1992), 42–91.

22. Robert S. McNamara with Brian Van DeMark, *In Retrospect: The Tragedy and Lessons of Vietnam* (New York: Random House, 1995).

spectacle, it still retains some power to exceed absolute commodification for some Americans, retaining at least some of its unresolved mystique.

Though far removed geographically and culturally from the Western world, Vietnam was at the time of the war thrust into the center of global attention, becoming a triggering sign with multiple meanings in virtually all political and cultural discourses. Yet the overall concern of North American and Hollywood cultural production concerning Vietnam has been the impact of the war on American society in general and the body of Vietnam veterans in particular. Cultural works or scholarly studies from the United States rarely focus on more broadly defined non-American representations of the war, let alone Vietnamese representations,[23] even when Vietnam held the keen interest of nations throughout the world and was in the forefront of political debates. The American avoidance of non-U.S. material manifests itself not only on the level of cultural production but also on the level of intellectual analysis. Most English-language articles on documentary films about the Vietnam War focus exclusively on American documentaries.[24] If such foreign films as Pierre Schoendorffer's *The Anderson Platoon* (1966) are mentioned, it is only in passing and without regard to their unique perspective: in the case of Schoendorffer, the viewpoint is that of a French infantryman who was stationed in Vietnam during Dien Bien Phu.[25] "I went back to discover the Vietnam I had left thirteen years ago with the French Army," Schoendorffer's voice-over intones, "but except for a few poignant scenes, I discovered above all

23. I find it not surprising that the 1993 Pulitzer Prize for fiction was awarded to Robert Olen Butler's novel, *The Alleys of Eden* (New York: Henry Holt, 1981), in which all the old Caucasian masculinist, middle-class biases about Vietnam are alive and well.

24. See, for example, Michael Renov, "Imaging the Other: Representations of Vietnam in Sixties Political Documentary"; David Grosser, "We Aren't on the Wrong Side, We Are the Wrong Side"; Peter Davis, "Targets (American) Hearts and Minds"; Barry Dornfield, "Dear America: Transparency, Authority, and Interpretation in a Vietnam War Documentary," all in *From Hanoi to Hollywood: The Vietnam War in American Film,* ed. Linda Dittmar and Gene Michaud (New Brunswick, N.J.: Rutgers University Press, 1990). David E. James is an exception when discussing *Loin du Vietnam* in "Documenting the Vietnam War" in the same volume. See further Claudia Springer, "Military Propaganda: Defense Department Films from World War II and Vietnam"; Rick Berg, "Losing Vietnam: Covering the War in an Age of Technology"; John Carlos Rowe, "Eyewitness: Documentary Styles in the American Representations of Vietnam," all in *The Vietnam War and American Culture,* ed. John Carlos Rowe and Rick Berg (New York: Columbia University Press, 1991). And see the essays collected in the special issue of *Cultural Critique* 3 (spring 1986), "American Representations of Vietnam," ed. Rick Berg and John Carlos Rowe. Finally, on feminist counterdocumentaries and on Vietnam War reporting by women, see Rabinowitz, *They Must Be Represented,* esp. 107–29, 199–204.

25. James mentions *The Anderson Platoon* only to the extent that it is "representative of such documentaries that propose the G.I. as the site of exemplary understanding" ("Documenting the Vietnam War," 242).

America." Foreign documentaries about the war are commonly delegated to endnotes or are dismissed as propaganda, even while it is recognized that all documentary images are to some extent propagandistic or can be read that way.[26]

In "Eyewitness: Documentary Styles in the American Representations of Vietnam," John Carlos Rowe remarks that Emilio de Antonio's *In the Year of the Pig* (1969) is exceptional when compared to more mythic American documentaries, such as Eugene Jones's early *A Face of War* (1968) or Peter Davis's later *Hearts and Minds* (1974–75), in managing "to overcome the tendency of viewers to transform the documentary's politics into such mythic propaganda."[27] But, as Michael Renov has noted in "Imaging the Other," even *In the Year of the Pig* remains "more about the United States than about Vietnam," with the latter depicted only to be rendered "domesticated, made familiar." Renov continues,

> The nativist character of *In the Year of the Pig* results in part from its attention to American diplomats, journalists, and military men whose testimony slowly, meticulously builds a mosaic and in so doing charts one nation's collision course with a fateful intervention. The film is conspicuously American in another way as well: it is one part the rationalist discourse of a philosopher trained in the American, analytical tradition (de Antonio did indeed teach philosophy), one part the creative tapestry of a New York–based artist influenced by his contemporaries, the Abstract Expressionists. In this instance, the Other is a topos defined less by Vietnamese geography or custom (though these concerns are addressed in numerous interviews) than by the outer limits of the American imperial mind projected abroad with fateful consequence."[28]

It is important, therefore, to turn to documentary filmmakers trained in a radically different philosophical tradition (historical and dialectical materialism), with a more explicit political commitment (East German communism), and an aesthetics derived not from modernism but from (socialist) realism, to yield an alternative—anti-imperialist but no less "fateful"—way of defining the Vietnamese Other. In his discussion of *In the Year of the Pig,* Rowe mentions in passing that de Antonio "relies on U.S. censorship of news footage taken by the North Vietnamese (or in some cases the East Germans), and this footage edited into his documen-

26. For a relevant history of the concept and practice of propaganda, see Peter A. Foulkes, *Literature and Propaganda* (London: Methuen, 1983).

27. Rowe, "Eyewitness," 156.

28. Renov, "Imaging the Other," 262–63.

tary thus appears as utterly new to his American audience." According to Rowe,

> It is a documentary that tries to make the American audience "see" with the eyes of the North Vietnamese, and it is thus far more effective in terms of questioning not only our myths about ourselves but also many of our Orientalist myths about the Vietnamese. The risk of such documentary filmmaking is obvious. Before *In the Year of the Pig* was screened in one Texas theater during the war, the screen was splashed with red paint, and demonstrators at many other theaters protested such "communist propaganda."[29]

It is imperative to rescue Rowe's nameless East German producers and their potentially disruptive images from parenthetical obscurity. To do so properly requires problematizing, if not rejecting outright, the explanatory power of the overused term *propaganda*—which is part of the "prison house of language" (Fredric Jameson via Nietzsche) and almost always conceals more than it reveals. At the same time, documentary should not be valorized as necessarily more "true" than feature films or any other genre, precisely because, in Nichols's terms, documentary is "a fiction (un)like any other."[30]

III. A Call to Arms

H&S's first "Vietnam" film—*400 cm³* (1966)—is barely five minutes long, yet it is one of their most effective. It was shown as a short before feature films throughout the GDR, and was intended as a direct appeal to East Germans to donate blood to the North Vietnamese. The title of this tersely edited film alludes to the cubic measurement of blood piped from the human vein to container for shipment to its destination. *400 cm³* crosscuts between found footage from Vietnam of starving, wounded, and napalmed people in hospitals to East Germans giving blood. The synchronized music and image track crescendo builds to the penultimate shot of a clenched East German fist pumping blood from its veins to the raised triumphant fist of a North Vietnamese soldier. The bridge between the two distant lands is forged musically and visually, as real and symbolic blood flows between two races and cultures in a gesture of international comradeship. The rhythmic beat of Paul Dessau's musical score echoes the

29. Rowe, "Eyewitness," 156.
30. Nichols, *Representing Reality,* 105–98.

blood life pulsing against the war.[31] *400 cm³* opens with a quotation from Friedrich Hölderlin's hymn "Der Tod fürs Vaterland" (Death for the Fatherland): "Oh nehmt mich, nehmt mich in die Reihen auf!" (Oh, enlist me, enlist me in the ranks!). In an interview, H&S say that this allusion makes evident at the outset that their film "is not the reporting of an event, but an interpretation and an evaluation."[32] H&S call their work a "film-hymn."[33] *400 cm³* ends with the image of Vietcong shooting down an American bomber. Just as Hölderlin had enlisted his verse in the opposition against the French foreign aggressor under Napoleon, so do H&S appeal to the East Germans to aid the North Vietnamese materially, bodily, against imperialists in Indochina—the United States, inheritors of the French legacy there. In short, the documentary goes to war across time and space; its referents are music and blood, both linked in a mesmerizing somatic rhythm.

Two later films in this category address the body in both possible senses: human and material. The first—*100* (1971)—is six minutes long and consists of a medium close-up of a male body doing pushups while a superimposed mechanical counter, at the bottom right of the screen, counts down from one hundred to zero with the sound of a metronome relentlessly ticking off camera. Also superimposed in double exposure are Vietnamese faces of various types. A diegetic voice in English screams repeatedly three words: "Dog, Pig, Monkey!" At the count of forty-three, the male body shows signs of exhaustion, breaking down completely at eight, at which point the counter is instantly reset to one hundred. Then, as penultimate image, the following text appears on frame: "Mark Lane in his book *Conversations with Americans* (New York, 1970): 'Soldiers in U.S. Marine units are ordered to do 100 pushups if they refer to a Vietnamese as Vietnamese and not as a dog, pig, or monkey.'" The final image is found footage: a U.S. training film of marine infantrymen screaming during bayonet practice.

In *Remington Cal. 12* (1972), H&S trace the historical evolution of the Remington 12-gauge shotgun and demonstrate its current uses. The tech-

31. For the East German take on H&S's use of music in their films and on its function in documentary film generally, see Wolfgang Thiel, "Bausteine zu einer Ästhetik der Dokumentarfilmmusik," in *Dokument und Kunst,* 52–57.

32. H&S further explain their choice of the Hölderlin citation by saying that "we named distant events with our own literary and artistic traditions to make clear that the cause that is being fought over there is also our most fundamental cause [*ureigenste Sache*]" ("Werkstattgespräch Studio H&S," 95). Nearly every imaginable political cause in Germany has cited this poem at one time or another, from the far Right and the Nazis to the far Left and the Red Army Faction and every place in between.

33. "Werkstattgespräch Studio H&S," 100.

nique in this fifteen-minute expository film is one of dialectical montage (H&S are particularly influenced by Eisenstein and Vertov),[34] in which contradictory images and sounds are juxtaposed to draw the spectator to certain conclusions. The appeal is less to gut emotion (as in *400 cm³* or *100*) than to common sense and reason. The primary focus of *Remington Cal. 12* is on the "requisite" eponymous shotgun. Here the Remington shotgun is systematically taken apart to demystify the audience about the way it works, so that the lethal shell becomes a "dead object," as H&S put it.[35] And they film this object close-up with almost loving irony, as if it were a classical still life. Using American and West German Remington advertisements, H&S show the discrepancy between one particular 12-gauge shotgun, marketed for the hunter, and the owner's manual, which recommends not using it on animals because it completely destroys the flesh, making it worthless for hunting. The next sequence of images derives from John Wayne's fictional feature film *Green Berets* (1968), with its good-natured and benevolent GIs, immediately followed by documentary footage of their less fictional compatriots in mortal combat in Vietnam, using Remington shotguns. By means of this montage, the audience is made to compare images presented to an American public by Hollywood and the advertising industry with another, equally mediatized reality: instructions and attitudes of U.S. combat troops who have modified their Remington shells (in conscious violation of the Geneva and earlier conventions and in contradiction to official U.S. government press releases) to shoot tiny, flesh-tearing aluminum missiles that cannot be detected by X rays. Wounding is a more productive way of waging war than is killing because it uses more people and resources. As laconically put by one interviewed grunt, the Remington is "a very fine weapon." The final sequence in *Remington Cal. 12* shows pumpkins, filled with a liquid that looks like blood, being shot—by weapon and camera—over and over again. Ostensibly horrifying us by showing what happens to the human body when it is shot, the end of the film assaults the viewer much like the Remington assaults its victims. But this violent use of blood, in contrast to its role in *400 cm³*, raised questions about the film's effectiveness, even at the time. One East German who saw the film when it was first released recalled in conversation with me that "most of us [East Germans] were convinced that the war was wrong and we didn't need such exaggerated theatrical techniques to persuade us." The film does indeed leave the spectator with little room to draw any conclusions other than the obvious, thus running

34. On the sources and uses of visual and aural montage in the films of H&S, see Erwin Reiss, "Den Feind im Visier, den Feind vor Augen: Visuell-verbale Montage des historischen Materialismus in Filmen von H&S," in *Dokument und Kunst,* 20–30.

35. "Werkstattgespräch Studio H&S," 133.

the risk of backfiring, so to speak, in terms of raising political consciousness. Interesting in this regard, however, is that H&S intended the style and structure of *Remington Cal. 12* to be a satirical mimicry of advertising, calling it a "Werbefilm."[36]

Throughout their films, interviews, and "studio conversations" (*Werkstattgespräche*), H&S attempt to deconstruct the status of Vietnam as a "television war": that is, the hegemonic control of television over the production and consumption of images representing both the war and the protests against it and the general inflation of images in the society of the spectacle. As H&S note, the primary source of images of Vietnam came (and still are coming) from American TV.[37] For them, the advertisements for their films that ran on East German television were part of the definition of cinema tout court. In this expansive definition, H&S's cinema includes their team of film critics and theorists—the entire cinematic apparatus. The corollary of H&S's recognition of the role of television is to use their films to train viewers to be critical of that more powerful and popular mass medium. Documentary is not only a matter of filmmaking but of instructing the viewers, à la Brecht, in "the art of viewing."[38] The same strategy is at play in the "Children of Golzow" series filmed by former East German filmmakers Winfried and Barbara Junge (see chapter 6).

No doubt by design, the spectator in *Remington Cal. 12* is rather heavy-handedly positioned as passive in constructing meaning. The documentary style in these prelocation films is confrontational, overtly political, and in that sense subjective and manipulative—all in direct contrast to the dominant trend in American and European documentary at the time. Both direct cinema and cinema verité outwardly strove toward as much objectivity and neutrality as possible, thus concealing their own irreducibly subjective, tacit, ideological perspective.[39] In contrast, H&S reject that kind of objectivity, tending toward a comparably more subjective style that was part of a general type of documentary filmmaking in East bloc countries. When speaking about the 1973 Leipzig documentary film festival and exploiting the double meaning of German *Objectiv,* Karl Eduard von Schnitzler comments, "The lens [*Objectiv*] of our camera is not 'objective' [*objectiv*] but rather highly partisan. That is to say, the cam-

36. "Werkstattgespräch Studio H&S," 121. On the use of satire in H&S documentary, see Peter Schöning, "Das Satirische bei H&S," in *Dokument und Kunst,* 46–51.

37. "Werkstattgespräch Studio H&S," 98–101.

38. "Werkstattgespräch Studio H&S," 110–11. A similar strategy was practiced in international Vietnam protest theatre.

39. For a detailed account of American direct cinema and cinema vérité in this context, see Brian Winston, "The Documentary Film as Scientific Inscription," in *Theorizing Documentary,* ed. Renov, 37–57.

era and film represent more than ever a weapon in the global conflict of systems in an ever more polarized and direct ideological class war."[40] In response to the direct question of whether their films were documentary or propaganda, H&S responded on Swedish television that "even the totally unpolitical film is in the last analysis enormously political, for it attempts to depoliticize social (hence: political) life."[41] This response—precise or evasive—leaves the question of the distinction open, if not moot.

IV. The Body Politic

H&S's second group of Vietnam films, *Pilots in Pyjamas* (there is an English and a dubbed German version) is shot entirely on location in Vietnam. It comprises four segments ranging between sixty and ninety minutes in length: *Yes, Sir; Hilton Hanoi; The Job;* and *The Thunder Gods.* In the GDR, the release of the film series in 1968 (it was first shown in its entirety in North Vietnam in 1976 and in the South a year later) was immediately preceded by publication of the film book *Pilots in Pyjamas* (1968), which contains translated transcripts of the interviews with the pilots arranged sequentially (the interviews in the book are somewhat less extensive and do not crosscut among the pilots, as the interviews in the film do) as well as documents relating to the making of the films and some of the controversy surrounding them. H&S also reprinted and discussed the U.S. military code of conduct, pilots' affidavits that they were being interviewed without coercion, reproductions of their letters home, statistics relating to the pilots' military lives, and an interview with H&S from the West German magazine *Stern.* The front cover of the book depicts all the high-tech equipment taken from a downed U.S. pilot; the graphically matched back cover shows the simple prison uniform, the "pyjamas" worn by much of the Vietnamese population and now the American "air pirates" as well. The book sold 80,000 copies in the GDR immediately after publication.[42] This success may be attributable not merely to a fascination with (U.S.) pilots but also, at a deeper level of consciousness, with all mechanisms of "just following orders."

---

40. Cited in Tok, "Chile, Vietnam, und unser Zeitgenosse," 4.

41. Mogens Rukov, "Respekt for der Autorität der Tatsachen: Zur Rezeption der H&S Filme in Westeuropa," in *Dokument und Kunst,* 38.

42. "Werkstattgespräch Studio H&S," 117. The film book *Piloten im Pyjama* was first published in East Germany (East Berlin: Verlag der Nation, 1968) and subsequently appeared in West Germany, Austria, and Switzerland (Munich: Kindler-Verlag, n.d.). The book was also translated into Russian (Moscow: Iskusstwo Moskow, 1971). All citations are to the East German edition.

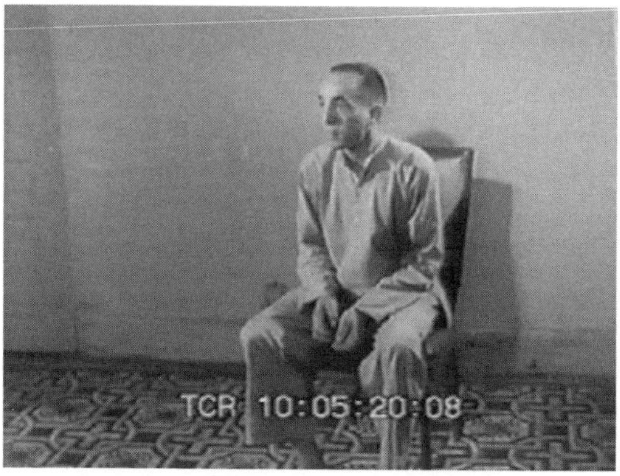

Risner in *Pilots in Pyjamas* (1968)

The four films in *Pilots in Pyjamas* consist mainly of interviews that H&S carried out with ten U.S. jet pilots in a prisoner-of-war camp in North Vietnam dubbed the Hanoi Hilton by the Americans. H&S make clear both in the films and in written remarks that two pilots refused to be interviewed. The others were "permitted" and/or coerced to "speak for themselves" to expose their more or less unconscious and ideological contradictions, motivations, and legitimations. The film owed its relatively high profile less to its aesthetic, cinematographic, or even ideological aspects than to its raw evidential status as testimony to the existence of pilots otherwise presumed missing or dead, including Colonel Robinson Risner, a former *Time* magazine cover subject.[43] H&S were relatively suc-

43. Risner had appeared on the cover of the Atlantic edition of *Time*, April 23, 1965, under the heading "Who's Fighting in Vietnam: A Gallery of American Combatants." Ironically enough, thirty years later, almost to the day, another U.S. pilot occupied a comparable position in the public eye: Scott O'Grady bailed out over Bosnia and was rescued by U.S. forces (see "A Pilot's Story," *Time*, June 19, 1995). One of many U.S. pilots who were not "heroically rescued" in an analogous situation during the Vietnam War was Navy pilot Joseph Dunn, who was shot down over Chinese territorial waters in February 1968. Robert S. McNamara, then secretary of defense, in a recently released classified document, ordered, "No rescue attempt should be made. It's not worth it." Dunn's widow, Maureen, recalled this incident during a confrontation with McNamara at the Kennedy School of Government, April 25, 1995 (see *Harpers*, July 1995, 14–15). After his release from prison, Colonel Risner returned to the United States and wrote *The Passing of the Night: My Seven Years as a Prisoner of the North Vietnamese* (New York: Random House, 1974). His account of his interview with H&S differs radically from that of Heynowski and Scheumann: Risner claims, among other things, that he was threatened by the North Vietnamese. In my opinion, H&S effectively counter these charges, including the one that the question-and-answer sessions

cessful, both filmically and in their writings, in combating the accusation of coercion that was commonly made against them by the U.S. and West European press at the time.[44] However, H&S freely admitted that, here as always, the ultimate decision was in the viewer's court.[45] The key *factum brutum* of the pilot's bodies on camera—so very much alive and loquacious—overshadows questions of coercion or propaganda or of the many other aesthetic and ideological reservations that might remain even three decades later. The films are of interest, in part, because of their status as evidence that appeals to what Nichols refers to as "epistophelia." H&S describe the unintended effect of all their films in slightly different terms: "what we didn't calculate is the fact that for the viewer—or rather many viewers—the information that the film provides puts itself into the foreground, and that possibly in the discussion of this information the value of the film as a gestalt is hardly recognized insofar as one is so intensively engaged by the matter at hand that one likely ignores much that is visible and audible."[46] In any case, any deeper information about or poetics of H&S's documentaries—conscious or unconscious—was effectively buried in the West under the visual and auditory weight of these remarkably talkative U.S. pilots, once in uniform and now in pyjamas.[47]

---

were scripted, and Risner's account contradicts itself internally in important details (compare "Ein Pilot im Pyjama," *Dokument und Kunst: Vietnam bei H&S* [Berlin (GDR): Akademie der Künste der Deutschen Demokratin Republik, 1977], Arbeitsheft 27, 167–69; and "Werkstattgespräch Studio H&S," esp. 114–16, to Risner, *Passing,* esp. 161–75). Part of H&S's point, however, is that this controversy is up to each viewer and reader or ideological constituency to adjudicate in his, her, or its own way.

44. The existence of *Pilots in Pyjamas*—and hence also the first incontrovertible photodocumentation of the existence of U.S. pilots in the North—was widely reported by both the socialist and capitalist international press in the fall of 1967, including *Algerie-Actualité* (Algiers); *Stuttgarter Zeitung; Land og Folk* (Copenhagen); *Zie* (Antwerp); *Vorwärts* (Basel); *Sunday News* (New York); *Paris Match;* and *Life* (cover story of the Asia edition), October 30, 1967, under the heading "U.S. Prisoners in North Vietnam." NBC also showed the stills from the H&S films on the Nightly News. The West German weekly *Stern,* vol. 43, 1967, ran an interview in which H&S explained the circumstances of their film. *Stern* had been denied permission by Hanoi to travel to North Vietnam to interview the pilots and retaliated against H&S by refusing to publish their accompanying text to the still photographs. The interview was *Stern*'s gesture of compromise. *Stern* also ran an editorial that began, "It is well-known that not all liars are communists, and, alternatively, it can not be ruled out that a communist can tell the truth," ostensibly allowing readers to determine the truth content of H&S's images. See further "Werkstattgespräch Studio H&S," 114–15; and *Piloten im Pyjama,* 408–15.

45. "Werkstattgespräch Studio H&S," 116.

46. "Werkstattgespräch Studio H&S," 102.

47. For a discussion of the poetics of documentary, see Michael Renov, "Toward a Poetics of Documentary," in *Theorizing Documentary,* ed. Renov, 12–36.

Pilots in Pyjamas consists mainly of a string of interviews conducted in the prison near Hanoi, with occasional crosscutting to other footage collected from the war, including in the South.[48] H&S chose to focus on the pilots because they wanted to discover to what extent one can portray or represent an individual life as part of a historical process and structure.[49] An additional fascination with pilots presumably results from something that has been noted by combatants and noncombatants alike from the inception of aerial warfare onward: the startling, wrenching juxtaposition experienced by people on the ground when they suddenly see the faces of low-flying airmen in their cockpits. At this moment the so-called cult of the young pilot that began in World War I is exploded.[50] The lethal impersonality of warfare is suddenly brought uncannily close to home and earth. In World War I and the Spanish Civil War, or even sometimes in World War II and Korea, this was an experience that could be shared—in principle at least—by both those on the ground and the pilots themselves, as the latter momentarily came face to face with their "soft targets" (as current U.S. military jargon has it). With the nuclear holocaust in Japan and the high-level saturation bombings of World War II in Europe and Vietnam, however, the world arrived at an almost totally impersonal modern and postmodern technowarfare in which visual or physical contact between pilot and ground troops or civilians was almost wholly eliminated—except, as *Pilots in Pyjamas* shows, when fighter or bomber pilots are captured.

Part 1 of the pilot cycle opens with loud dramatic music and footage of bombing raids viewed from the ground—that is, from the point of view of the victims rather than the aggressors—with a voice-over asking, "We have seen murderers in the sky—what do the insides of their heads look like?" The film tries to uncover the individual and collective psyche of the pilots and the possible motivations behind these "crimes against humanity." But H&S proceed not, as one might automatically expect, by means of a psychoanalytic theory—individual or collective—but rather by a complex filmic application of historical and dialectical materialism. H&S

48. The South Vietnam film footage used in many of H&S's films was made by one of their cameramen, Peter Hellmich, who traveled into the South in 1967 while Heynowski and Scheumann were interviewing the pilots in the North ("Werkstattgespräch Studio H&S," 97).

49. Rolf Richter, "Die Geschichte als Prozess oder Über einige Vorzüge der Dokumentarfilme von Heynowski und Scheuman," in *Dokument und Kunst,* 7.

50. Bernd Hüppauf, "Modernism and the Photographic Representation of War and Destruction," in *Fields of Vision: Essays in Film Studies, Visual Anthropology, and Photography,* ed. Leslie Devereaux and Roger Hillman (Berkeley: University of California Press, 1995), 109.

attempt to show that all individual agents of history—themselves no less than the U.S. pilots—are caught up in a dialectic with larger structures within which responsibility and culpability are shared. Similarly, in their theory, any documentary film is also caught up in another, intersecting dialectic between being limited to its immediate occasion—and hence to ephemerality and temporality—and being part of the long march of history. As such, documentary outlives its occasional status to gain relative transhistoricality. Admittedly, this view is itself ideological and teleological: class struggle is the ultimate motor of history, and H&S fight with their camera on the side of what they assume is the side of the victors, albeit with no absolute guarantee of success.[51] It remains to see how this ideological problematic is translated into specifically cinematic terms, wherein active editing interventions such as montage play a key role.

H&S are guided by what they see as the fundamental "difference between live news reportage of current events and the documentary film, which sums up events by means of montage, and thus sublates [*aufhebt*] factual events into permanence."[52] This overall dialectic shuttles between the individual and the universal, between the mortal and immortal bodies of films as well as individuals. The more specific but related dialectic relegates the more or less fetishistic fascination with the bodies and testimonies of captured pilots on screen to the genre of documentary. For according to Nichols, documentaries more than fiction activate "conventions that prepare us to expect a privileged status for the indexical link between sign and referent." He continues, "Our apprehension of this link anchors the image in the specificity of a given moment. Such moments are understood as subject, at the moment of filming, to the vicissitudes of history rather than the coherence of narrative. Some quality of the moment persists outside the grip of textual organization."[53] In other words, part of

51. Robert Michel, "Die beargewöhnte Alliance: Dokfilm und Kunst," in *Dokument und Kunst,* 80, 88.

52. "Werkstattgespräch Studio H&S," 118. Formally speaking, this problematic is not reducible to any one ideology—Left, Right, or Center. Thirty years prior to H&S, Leni Riefenstahl encountered and resolved it in her determination not to make "newsreels" of the Nuremberg rallies or Olympic Games but rather simply "films" defined as "art"—including a very active, interventionist use of camera, editing, and montage. The difference, however, is that while Riefenstahl subsequently denied her own adherence to National Socialism—indeed, to any politics at all—H&S openly affirm their commitment to both national and international communism. Ironically, with the alleged "death of communism," H&S's films, theories, and practices are sinking into oblivion, whereas Riefenstahl—censored by the Allies after World War II—still lives on to fight another day in the public imagination.

53. Nichols, *Representing Reality,* 231.

the fascinating quality of the films is in the feeling that a "real" piece of history is in the making before our eyes.

Politically speaking, Castro's "One, Two, Three Vietnams!"—cited by Godard in *Loin du Vietnam*—becomes the historical backdrop for H&S montage technique. As they put it in their "Studio Conversations," "Imperialism always has the same face, whether in Chile or South Vietnam or elsewhere."[54] They self-consciously position their oeuvre in the broad sweep of history from the October Revolution to the "thirty years war" in Southeast Asia and into the future.[55] Cinematographically speaking, H&S address the perennial question of whether a documentary film is "directed" (and the concomitant question, Are the U.S. pilots in any sense reading a script?) by arguing that, dialectically viewed, the irreducibly partisan and subjective manner in which camera and editing "intervene in reality" does not necessarily entail the latter's "violation [*Vergewaltigung*], but rather its re/organization for the purposes of the camera."[56] In short, H&S distinguish between *arranging* and *directing,* freely admitting the former and denying the latter.[57] At the same time, however, H&S concede that viewers will dispute the degree to which the filmmakers succeed in this endeavor, determined by contingencies that are both individual and collective. This phenomenon is determined by the way in which the bodies in their excessive magnitudes, scripted or not, relate to the viewers experience of the filmic text.

H&S repeatedly remind the interviewed pilots that neither the filmmakers nor their North Vietnamese comrades in arms hold the Americans responsible for what they have done, since they are tools or puppets of an imperialist, capitalist system: "The bosses never go to war, only their intermediaries," H&S tell the pilots, echoing the thesis of Brecht's *Mother Courage.* The pilots reduce this negotiating back and forth between the problem of individual and structural accountability—that is, the pilots' denial of the former and refusal to engage in the latter—to "I was just following orders." This has been of course a searing question for Germans, as H&S remind the pilots, from Nuremberg on, and it has reappeared in the more recent defense mounted by former GDR border guards. Though

54. "Werkstattgespräch Studio H&S," 119.

55. "Werkstattgespräch Studio H&S," 93. This perspective lives on in the work of certain critics, including Aijaz Ahmad, who writes, "The whole of this contradiction—revolutionary anti-colonialism; the most advanced socialist political practice in the most backward peasant economy; the direct, historic, prolonged combat between socialism and imperialism; the utterly unequal balance of forces—was condensed in the Vietnam War" (*In Theory: Classes, Nations, Literatures* [London: Verso, 1992], 28).

56. "Werkstattgespräch Studio H&S," 108.

57. "Werkstattgespräch Studio H&S," 108.

U.S. involvement in an undeclared war, as H&S also remind each pilot, is obviously the primary focus of these films, another excessive theme begins to emerge between the lines: a diachronic and synchronic reference to the German past—Nuremberg, but also, more than likely, the Allied fire-bombing of Dresden. According to Nichols, in documentaries, "affective ties must be forged, obliquely, between viewer and representation but in relation to the historical referent."[58] But in 1967, American viewers would obviously have seen the film rather differently than East German viewers, whose memory of Dresden would be triggered as the Americans' would not.[59] Further association would then be triggered by more or less involuntary allusions to the East German present. According not only to Nichols's theory but also to their own, H&S are only partly in control of all these referents.

H&S pointedly ask each pilot if he has ever been in the Federal Republic of Germany or visited the GDR. Several have been stationed on airbases in the FRG, and a few have even taken bus tours of the East Berlin that they had been trained to bomb if so ordered. H&S want to tease out of these pilots the analogy between a divided Germany and a divided Vietnam—each with half under capitalist domination, the other socialist by choice. Asked by *Stern* in 1967 why they were permitted to travel to North Vietnam when "even European communists are not," H&S surmised that it was because of the direct parallel between the two divided countries.[60] In *Pilots in Pyjamas,* the U.S. pilots are led, apparently for the first time, to see the parallel, a realization that also entails admitting that they are fighting for the political economy of capitalism as much as for the United States as a nation. Nevertheless, most of the pilots retain their ideological conviction that both capitalism and Americanism are preferable to communism, at least as they have been brought up to understand it.[61] H&S harbor no illusions about their ability to convert the pilots, which is expressly not the filmmakers' intent. Indeed, even before the release of the films, H&S stated that at most one or two of the pilots might have been changed in any way by the interview process.[62] These films are less a pedagogical lesson in enlightenment than an example of audiovisual class struggle between rival ideologies, one of which is aware that it is an ideology, the other of which denies it.

58. Nichols, *Representing Reality,* 234.

59. See, for example, Rolf Hochhuth's play *The Soldiers,* which dealt explicitly with the Allies' firebombing of Dresden.

60. *Piloten im Pyjama,* 408.

61. This point is made particularly clear in the interview with Major David Henry Duart. Also see *Piloten im Pyjama,* 212.

62. *Piloten im Pyjama,* 386.

H&S also ask the pilots whether they believe that every nation or group has the right to self-determination, reminding them that the constitution of North Vietnam is modeled (at least de jure) on that of the United States and its Bill of Rights. Just at the point when the pilots express surprise at this fact and agreement with the right of self-determination, they revert to the position that they are, after all, professional military men, "just following orders"—echoing the Nuremberg trials. H&S and the pilots reach an almost palpable physical blockage or aporia, since each camp is positioned as class enemies without the possibility of mediation; only combat remains. For the pilots, the constitutive contradictions include the classical ones between individualism and nationalism, between free market and monopoly, between the democratic claims of civil society and the restraints of political economy. For H&S, the constitutive contradiction is between the science of history and an ideology of political struggle in which H&S, too, are "just following orders," although in another sense and for another cause. The parallel that H&S wish to draw between Vietnam and Germany will be made more obvious in the second sequence of films, made after Vietnam has achieved independence under hegemony of the decimated North and when the South is being reconstructed, but this parallel remains no less problematic; indeed, it is arguably more so. This aporia partly accounts for H&S's mode of interviewing, which is at once aggressive and passive and thus relatively distinct from the Western documentary poetic. The filmmakers sometimes berate the pilots with Marxist-Leninist technical terms (expressing particular frustration because the pilots are ignorant of politics and history), but at other times H&S exchange little jokes.

In *Yes, Sir,* H&S remind the pilots that the U.S. military code of conduct states that a captured soldier may give only his name, rank, serial number, and date of birth to his captors. By being interviewed and re/captured on film, these U.S. pilots are blatantly violating that code. In fact, H&S's film book *Piloten im Pyjama* begins with an in-depth reconstruction and analysis of the history of the code from its inception, inspired by Dwight David Eisenhower, in 1955. The concern during the Korean conflict was that fully one-third of American POWs might have been brainwashed to no longer believe that they were fighting yet another good fight. This brainwashing would have occurred not necessarily as a result of physical or overt psychological torture but for reasons that were and remain unclear.[63] In the film *Pilots in Pyjamas* virtually all the pilots violate—more or less willingly and without explanation—the six articles of

63. *Piloten im Pyjama,* 19. For the classic Hollywood treatment of this theme and its personal and social implications, see John Frankenheimer's *The Manchurian Candidate* (1962)

the code of conduct. But the implications of this violation are far in excess of the particular Vietnam situation, since it could occur in virtually any political struggle, involving Hitler, Stalin, Pol Pot, Sendero Luminoso, and so on. To quote one pilot (First Lieutenant Edward Lee Hubbard), strict adherence to articles 2 and 3, which demand that soldiers resist capture "by every means possible," would have been tantamount to suicide.[64] Most of the pilots declare themselves to be religious, an admission that broaches a further subtext of contradictions with their jobs. Equally violated are articles 4 and 5, which absolutely limit communication with captors to the aforementioned bare facts. This, too, is a contradiction the pilots cannot resolve, though not far from their minds must have been the possibility that their physical survival would be made more likely by virtue of their filmic re/capture.

In the ensuing filmed dialogues, H&S are particularly eager to elicit the social, familial, educational, religious, and class backgrounds from which each pilot comes. But more interesting is how all four films in the cycle shift from this discussion of relatively straightforward facts—that is, from living human bodies—to inanimate requisites or props. In each interview, H&S eventually place four objects into the hands of the pilots: a now empty service revolver (which makes some of them bolt), a charred clump of rice, a bomb fragment, and a heavy straw hat. This sequence is carefully plotted (though the responses are not): from the useless and unused hand-held weapon whose use was defined in the equally neglected code of conduct to the incinerated staple food of a large region of the globe, to a high-tech, impersonal airborne weapon of destruction directed against this staple as well as against people, and finally to the pathetic premodern attempt to defend oneself against such bombing from the sky. Thus, H&S try to overcome the abstract distance and removal that these pilots felt when they dropped their bombs and to elicit the feeling of alienation—in the strong Marxist sense—of men "just doing their job."

First Lieutenant Herbert Benjamin Ringsdorf, holding his old weapon, is asked why he did not resist capture, as he was trained and required to do, by firing his Smith and Wesson six times. Ringsdorf expresses his astonishment that women and children had captured him, a circumstance none of the pilots can get over. Then, as his German ancestry comes up, Ringsdorf indignantly interjects, "I am not a killer!" Here H&S aggressively point out that this is a remarkable statement in light of the fact that he had successfully completed fifty-six bombing runs before capture. Ringsdorf is silent. According to H&S's film theory, such a contradiction can be shown to us but not to the interviewees, and it is the role

64. See also *Piloten im Pyjama,* 59.

of the "requisite" to make this transfer into (class) consciousness. H&S raise the question of responsibility for war from yet another angle. In an interview conducted in an earlier film, H&S elicit from a West German mercenary—the so-called Congo Müller—the cheerful admission that, yes, he is a killer, and what of it?[65] This forces H&S to distinguish structural and existential guilt and accountability. Whereas, on a personal level, they obviously prefer the U.S. pilots to Müller, on a structural level H&S consider them to be more dangerous, for American pilots represent not merely exceptional individual killing machines but an entire system of potential mass destruction motored by capitalist and imperialist greed. The everyday life of petty bourgeois American society can at any moment produce and legitimate mass murder.[66] As a professional soldier of fortune, Müller is not in principle (ideologically) opposed to H&S, whereas the U.S. pilots and H&S are mortal enemies in class war. In any case, when Ringsdorf remains silent in *Pilots in Pyjamas,* this overdetermined moment seems to define major limits of the documentary medium.

According to the theory developed by the H&S collective and best formulated by H&S film theorist Günter Agde, the proper effect of requisites is to give the viewers more insight into their historical function than is available to the interviewed subject who holds the requisites in his hand.[67] Thus, for example, in the sequence when the charred piece of rice is placed in the pilots' hands, H&S crosscut to scenes of Vietnamese cultivating rice fields, harvesting and storing the food staple, and eventually preparing meals. This "excessive" insight, for H&S, must be collective rather than individual, as reflected not only in H&S's collaborative way of producing films but also in their insistence that what they mean by *documentary* includes the reception of their films, group discussions of them, and so forth. This is where historical materialism differs from what is imagined to be—and often is—a bourgeois theory and practice in which the individual body first and last supposedly carries the day from production to consumption. Where a specifically dialectical-materialist elaboration comes into focus is made evident in Agde's remark that a "double confrontation" is at work in H&S: "The requisites are confronted *among themselves,* that is, independently of any viewing subject." In other words, we deal with a dialectic of nature. Taking the example of the aerial bomb and the straw hat, according to Agde, "the maximum thinkable contradiction: terrible

65. Congo Müller's admission is made in H&S's film about the man also known as Ko-Mü—*Der lachende Mann* (The Laughing Man, 1966)—and is included again as montage in their post–Vietnam War film *Die eiserne Festung* (The Iron Fortress, 1977).

66. *Piloten im Pyjama,* 360.

67. Günter Agde, "Von der Sprache der Dinge: Gedanken zum Einsatz von Requisiten in den Vietnamfilmen von H&S," in *Dokument und Kunst,* 42.

destruction/simple protection."[68] On the one hand, this formulation seems insolubly caught up in another contradiction, due to the hermeneutic requirement that each viewing subject or formation interprets objects differently.[69] On the other hand, this formulation extends Nichols's thesis about magnitude. H&S demonstrate that not only human bodies carry out the most basic and complex work in documentary film; inanimate objects such as rice or a straw hat have the capacity to take on equally active roles.

Part 1 of the Vietnam cycle, *Yes, Sir,* is especially intriguing because it gives unusual spin to the thesis that documentary filmmaking is an act of war. The sequence begins by showing on camera H&S and their film crew and equipment. Following the celebration of "foregrounding the device" (from the Russian formalists and Brecht to *Cahiers du Cinema* in the 1960s and 1970s), we have learned that there is nothing necessarily or automatically "progressive" (in the sense of producing not merely an active, as opposed to passive, viewer but one aligned with one's own political beliefs) in the self-reflexive act of exposing the filmic as filmic. Nonetheless, such moments in the documentary can have the advantage of making visible—exposing—the still common widespread Hollywood effect of verisimilitude. What is specifically fascinating in *Yes, Sir,* however, is that this moment of self-reflexivity is eventually followed—immediately after the segment with the pilots being reunited with their old revolvers, crosscut with scenes from a Hollywood Western shootout—by footage of the capture of a pilot by Vietnamese peasants. Like several similar scenes viewed earlier, it looks like a documentary. But this particular footage is in fact taken from a short DRV feature film in which First Lieutenant Robert Peel had starred, helping to re-create his own capture after having flown a single combat mission over North Vietnam. This moment does seem to exceed all permissible deviations from any military code of conduct. The warrior becomes actor for the enemy, war becomes documentary of collaboration. This extraordinary segment in *Hilton Hanoi* is neither recorded nor alluded to in the film book *Piloten im Pyjama,* except perhaps as a picture of a pilot "Pete" Peterson—which, appropriately enough, may be a still from the movie rather than a record of his first capture. But, no matter how it is read, this overdetermined moment calls into question the status of H&S's own film as documentary rather than feature—is the film authentic, unrehearsed truth or an artificially (and artfully) constructed narrative fiction. So extreme, so excessive, is this moment that it cannot be sublated theoretically or practically. Nor can it be apodictically worked through; it can only be ignored or reenacted by other means. This includes displacing the

68. Agde, "Von der Sprache der Dinge," 42.
69. "Werkstattgespräch Studio H&S," 111.

entire problematic onto objects—that is, requisites. Yet this scene must be read in a more complex manner, for it simultaneously highlights the fact that in a certain sense, everything on the screen may be staged in the theater of war as well as in the movie theater. Alternatively, nothing is staged: everything is equally "real." The distinction between reality and fiction seems irrevocably shattered. This is a moment, in Nichols's terms, of true magnitude, true excess. In addition, this sequence raises the question of coercion—to what extent were the pilots willing players in front of H&S's cameras? Not only is the body of one pilot in question but also an entire body of filmic production and consumption.

Following this segment, H&S return to crosscut among pilots, who are now shown a U.S. military film they had seen during their training. This found footage stages what will happen to them if they are captured. In retrospect this film's visual and rhetorical hyperbole is risible even to the pilots themselves. More profoundly, this example of military indoctrination or propaganda, when viewed in the context of the immediately preceding segment of the North Vietnamese feature film, continues the process of exposing all film (whether feature, pseudodocumentary, documentary, or *Hilton Hanoi*) as a potentially manipulative medium. Yet paradoxically, nonfiction film retains to some extent a certain rudimentary, irreducible truth index, epistemology, and logic: "I see and hear it, ergo it is true." This may lead to the question of whether H&S are any more believable than the pilots. In their "Studio Conversations," H&S admit that they censored at least one scene from *Pilots in Pyjamas:* a U.S. pilot receiving medical attention and given a transfusion of blood from GDR donors, perhaps inspired by *400 cm³*. H&S made this cut on the grounds that East Germans would have been outraged to see where their blood was going. Throughout their work, H&S argue that the distinction—"the threshold," as they call it—between feature film (fiction) and documentary (fact) always exists as a problem; nevertheless, they insist that it is not absolutely automatic or necessary to assume that a "subjective element" informs all documentary, just as it does all features.[70] The real, in Lacanian terms, may be what resists symbolization absolutely, but it does not therefore cease to exist and it still make its appearance in oblique and fleeting images. For H&S, the struggle over how much reality can be manipulated and how much artifice is allowable is no less significant than the class struggle itself and is indeed intimately related to it.[71]

The prelocation and location films made by H&S prior to the capitulation of South Vietnam all display a combination of passive-aggressive

70. "Werkstattgespräch Studio H&S," 103.

71. "Werkstattgespräch Studio H&S," 102, 103.

interviewing techniques and the active participation of the filmmakers as visible warriors: they appeal directly to the audience to get involved in the struggle on the side of communist North Vietnam. In other words, documentary and war commingle. Yet at the same time, a certain excessive element is also articulated that is not quite in the control of either H&S or the documentary format but seems to have the power to deconstruct any and all monolithic or "pure" political intent. What happens, then, after the war is over and H&S's side appears to have won?

V. Aftermath

H&S made their third and final group of Vietnam films between 1976 and 1978, when Vietnam was rebuilding an ecologically and humanly devastated country. Unlike in many capitalist representations, East Germans were not interested in Vietnam only while it was at war with the United States.[72] The first postwar H&S film, *Devil's Island* (1976), focuses on the South Vietnam prison Co Son. It is devoted almost entirely to an interview with Le Quang Vinh, who had been held prisoner there for political reasons during much of the war. Against his voice-over describing his experiences, H&S film the now empty cages and cells, looking for possible inscriptions or signs left by prisoners. Historical photos show the U.S. commandants of the camp as well as the South Vietnamese thugs who enforced the Americans' orders. Approximately halfway through the film, the interviewer starts to replace the term *Devil's Island* with *Insel KZ* (concentration camp island), as the film crosscuts to show a plaque with the names of French military personnel who had been in charge until 1953. A double link is thus forged both to Vietnam's colonial status and, via the French, to Europe and its own camps. The filmic style, tone, shots, and voice-over bear an uncanny similarity to Alain Resnais's *Night and Fog* (1955). (*Night and Fog*'s initial release was delayed in France until the documentary footage of French officers helping Germans was removed.) The beginning of the fourth reel of *Devil's Island* makes the bridge to Europe even stronger, with images from Buchenwald and Bergen-Belsen, with the accompanying voice-over remarking, "No one thought it would exist but it still does: 1940–41." Then a montage sequence follows, cutting to a U.S. corporal saying, "Co Son is not a Death Island but a vacation spot for Boy Scouts"—words reminiscent to a German audience of the famous Nazi propaganda movie *The Fuhrer Gives Jews a City,* in which the extermination camp Theresienstadt is portrayed as a spa for the Jewish people.

72. For H&S's account of their postwar trip to Vietnam, see Walter Heynowski and Gerhard Scheumann, *Filmen in Vietnam: Tagebuch* (East Berlin: Henschelverlag, 1976).

(Unbelievably, Co Son is currently being transformed into a $298 million tourist resort in a project involving PMC Jinwon of South Korea and Ba Ria-Vung Tau Province.) In *Devil's Island* the conceptual link is forged between Germany and Vietnam—both trying to come to terms with a past and epoch indelibly inscribed by death camps. One may also recall the proximity of Weimar to the Buchenwald concentration camp, which also served as a political prison in the GDR. What H&S hammer home is the German trauma and guilt, which does not necessarily exclude—official propaganda to the contrary—citizens of the GDR.

Free Admission (1976) is an eleven-minute short depicting a tour through a war museum in Hanoi, showing U.S. bomb fragments, uniforms, weapons, and so on. Admission is free, a plaque explains, because "it cost the American people 56,369 dead and $146 billion." Once again, the camera lingers over requisites: in this case, objects that were once lethal and now are themselves dead. Speaking for H&S, Scheumann states bluntly, "I see no direct contradiction between sometimes letting people speak and, alternatively, showing objects. I believe that things also speak, in their own way. I have to say that I like to photograph 'dead objects' because they always express something about people—not only about the people who produced them but also about those with whom they later come into contact."[73] This fascination with "excessive requisites"—as they are filmed, edited, and received—informs not only *Free Admission* but all of H&S's post–Vietnam War works and, indeed, their films generally. Nor are they unique in this regard.[74]

In the third film in the postwar series, *The First Rice Thereafter* (1977), H&S track down the former chief West German military adviser to the United States in Saigon, a General Holtorff. He had been a Nazi officer and even in 1977 continues to wear his Iron Cross from World War II. He is heard on tape from the Vietnam War advising the Americans to find a "final solution" to the Vietnam "problem," even to annihilate the entire Vietnamese population. The next sequence of montaged images depicts a current Vietnamese political leader relating his imprisonment in Co Son. This is followed first by reference to GDR leader and former resistance fighter Erich Honecker and his incarceration by the Gestapo and then by two leaders—East German and North Vietnamese—embracing at a meeting. The implication is clear: fascism and capitalist imperialism are

73. "Werkstattgespräch Studio H&S," 133.

74. The precedents for the notion that documentary films help objects speak include most notably Chris Marker and Alain Resnais's 1953 *Les statues meurent aussi* (Statues Also Die), in which a critical political and economic history of colonialism (in the Belgian Congo) is produced from masks, statues, and other objets d'art that are preserved in the First World only for their "cultural value." The film was banned for ten years in Europe.

alive and well but so also is resistance to both. Next, H&S trace the activities of German chemical firms continuing to fabricate poisons in the Third World, including a subsidiary of what was once IG Farben: Hoechst Chile and Hoechst Vietnam. As the publication of secret correspondence with its home office in Frankfurt am Main demonstrated, Hoechst Chile was directly responsible for collaborating with the CIA in the 1973 overthrow of what H&S call the "fraternal" socialist regime that had been elected in Chile.[75] The direct line is thus drawn from the economics of death to current economic "miracles" and disasters. And, in this last instance at least, East Germany cannot be accused of playing a role; if it is not able to control past history, it can control certain present engagements and entanglements.

The fourth film in this cycle (H&S themselves sometimes refer to it as closing the *Pilots in Pyjamas* series) is *"I'm Truly Sorry"* (1977). It concerns the reeducating of former enemies (hence the link to U.S. pilots) but also asks what to do with enemies generally, including South Vietnamese "traitors." In the GDR this film was by far the most controversial produced by H&S, precisely because many East Germans saw the direct and indirect parallels with the question of what to do with former Nazis and their collaborators in post–World War II Germany. Some viewers thought these criminals should simply be "put to the wall and shot," while others, including H&S, argued with equal force for the possibility and necessity of reeducation.[76] In their "Studio Conversations," H&S remark that they put quotation marks around the title of their film to indicate that the matter of sincerity is very much left open to debate. The East Germans clearly had an unbearable problem in mastering the past in a country that officially proclaimed that its break with Nazism was complete and that only the West German capitalists were still complicitous. The reference to "putting enemies to the wall" is particularly telling, though H&S symptomatically do not draw the connection themselves and in a sense do not need to, given the theory of documentary excess. What H&S say in 1977, however, is that one of their greatest failures as filmmakers was that "to date we have not made a film that makes clear to the world public why we needed August 13, 1961," the date of the erection of the Berlin Wall, where people were shot.[77] The shift in the meaning of the pronoun shifter *we* is overdetermined: from "we filmmakers" to "we East German Communists."

"I'm Truly Sorry" follows the life of a former South Vietnamese commander, Lam Van Phat, who served first with the French and then with the American puppet regime. He has been spared execution so he can con-

75. "Werkstattgespräch Studio H&S," 108.

76. *Dokument und Kunst,* 157–64.

77. "Werkstattgespräch Studio H&S," 125.

front the atrocities he committed and experience the "generosity of communism." He served, in effect, as a test case, the implication being that if he could be reeducated, anyone could. H&S discovered that he had a sister who was active on the other side: the highly decorated North Vietnamese war hero Captain Lam Thi Phan. *"I'm Truly Sorry"* crosscuts between brother and sister, reinforcing the thesis that before the massive U.S. intervention, the Vietnam War was a "thirty years civil war" between two rival but fraternal economic systems. H&S detail the problems not only of individual reeducation but also, allegorically, of transforming a once capitalist and colonialist society into a potentially communist one. Here the paradoxical parallels to the GDR are both clear and unstated. H&S say that neither the U.S. airmen in *Pilots in Pyjamas* nor the collaborators in *"I'm Truly Sorry"* "make things easy for the viewer." They explain: "Viewers find themselves in a decision-making situation, in which they have to ask themselves: 'How would I, if I were a judge, pass judgment in this case?' "[78] Left in/visible and in/audible is the "excessive" corollary question: "How would I, if I were the accused, defend myself?"

The title of the next film in the postwar series, *The Iron Fort* (1977), refers to Ho Chi Minh's name for the Mekong Delta, the strongest area of resistance to the French and the Americans. Images taken from the life of U.S. ground troops show their total ineffectiveness and helplessness and are followed by a return to the villages of Son My and My Lai, a decade after the massacre of virtually the entire civilian population. Through a series of interviews with the few survivors as well as the wartime photographs of Ron Haeberle, H&S re-create the massacre. Censured is not only the U.S. military but also the American society that rewarded Haeberle for taking the pictures while inadequately addressing his own culpability—his own inaction—in the "crime against humanity." The film censures the government that pardoned Lieutenant William Calley but even more the capitalist system that allows him to receive two thousand dollars per lecture and a cut every time the "Ballad of Lieutenant Calley" is played. Finally, the entire capitalistic commercial enterprise of South Vietnam is laid bare: bars, drugs, whorehouses, and so on. Only then does the film focus on the alternative, underground infrastructure of resistance that existed throughout Vietnam and the collective will that led the people to victory. Toward the end of the film, a "bureaucrat of death" is asked if he ever heard people in the nearby prison being tortured, and the answer is predictably, "No." The official reasons for the prisoners' deaths were heart attacks, strokes, and so forth—in short, the same fictitious causes of death the Nazis attributed to victims of the Holocaust, used by revisionist histo-

78. "Werkstattgespräch Studio H&S," 116.

rians to this day. Yet the film's overall message also comes dangerously close to an apology for what happened in Nazi Germany. Can individuals be held accountable when larger economic systems are to blame in the notorious "last instance"? As Louis Althusser noted, "From the first moment to the last, the lonely hour of the 'last instance' never comes."[79] The knife of structural analysis cuts several ways: Even as it points the finger at the South Vietnamese puppets and their U.S. masters and at the Nazis and their West German progeny, it cannot be stopped. When audiences emerged from East German movie theaters in the 1970s, they could look around themselves.

It is not entirely fortuitous in this context that the key requisite in the last film of H&S's Vietnam cycle, *At the Water Trench/Grave* (1978), is once again plant life, as had been the case for rice in both *Pilots in Pyjamas* and *The First Rice Thereafter.*[80] Among the charred stubble and dead earth of Son My and My Lai, where Haeberle had once recorded human death, H&S's camera finally locates a tiny spot of new vegetation and water flowing back to produce rice in what had recently been trenches and graves. This requisite is presumably to be seen as a dialectical synthesis between animate human bodies and inanimate material objects. The significance of this requisite for documentary film theory and practice, for grasping a magnitude that is always slightly in excess of fixed meaning, is likely to remain open and impure. H&S's Vietnam cycle thus begins in 1966 with a focus on human blood and ends twelve years later focusing on a spring of water. The first film starts physically in the former GDR; the last ends there metonymically. The basic problematic both directly and indirectly addressed by H&S (that is, the legacy of the Vietnam War and of German fascism) is taken up with a vengeance in both its formal filmic and thematic aspects, by West German filmmakers in 1978, the same year that H&S made their last film about Vietnam. This time the focus is on left-wing terrorism carried out in part in solidarity with the North Vietnamese. And this time the explosion is deep in the heart of Europe, in West Germany.

79. Louis Althusser, *For Marx,* trans. Ben Brewster (1965; New York: Vintage Books, 1970), 113.

80. See also "Werkstattgespräch Studio H&S," 109.

CHAPTER 2

Framing Terrorism: Beyond the Borders

Heime

Heim für Schwererziehbare
Altersheim
Fürsorgeheim

Niflheim
Stadelheim
Stammheim

Unheimlich
was alles
Heim heißt

—Erich Fried

Gudrun Ensslin

Das Kissen weiß, der Kopf in seiner Mitte
Die Haare kurz und etwas ungekämmt
und das Gesicht ein wenig schief, sehr tot
nicht ganz genau mehr auf den Kopf gefügt
vom Obduzenten oder seinen Helfern

Zwischen den schönen Zähnen noch viel Gips
nicht mehr entfernt. Es kommt nicht darauf an
Der Mund halb offen. Ein blutige Stelle
am Kinn. Der Pullikragen hochgeschoben
daß man den Hals nicht sieht und seine Wunde

Die Augen nicht ganz zu, als sähen sie
noch immer—was? . . . Und dieser rote Fleck
—kein Totenfleck—groß an der Nasenwurzel
wie eine Druckwunde von einer Maske
wenn ein Patient betäubt wird, der sich wehrt

Der Sarg aus hellem Holz—fast tröstlich. Aber
Trost kann nicht sein. Kein Trost und kein Vergessen.

—Erich Fried

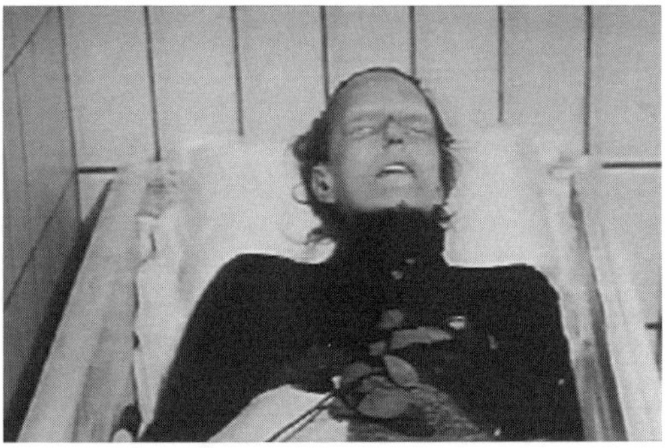

Gudrun Eusslin, from *Germany in Autumn* (1978)

In his introduction to *New German Film: The Displaced Image,* Timothy Corrigan insightfully posits two "symbolic poles" from which to structure his study: the Oberhausen Manifesto (1962), and the omnibus film *Germany in Autumn* (1977–78).[1] The former, an iconoclastic declaration penned by Alexander Kluge but underwritten and signed by other avant-garde West German filmmakers, proclaimed that "old film is dead" and called for a radical restructuring of the West German film industry.[2] *Germany in Autumn,* a collaborative film production that Kluge edited, was made in direct response to the "terrorism" of the 1970s, its distorted representation in the mass media, and the subsequent "media blackout." Corrigan locates the significance of these two declarations in their collective status, in their heroic attempt to create a new cinematic dialogic discourse, in their novel presentation of the complex relationship between artistic freedom and the reality of filmic production and distribution, and, finally, in their own interface: "as the Oberhausen manifesto presents a sketchy theoretical position, *Germany in Autumn* represents an implementation and actualization developing out of that stance."[3] Following Miriam Hansen, Corrigan further argues that *Germany in Autumn* created a new

1. Timothy Corrigan, *New German Film: The Displaced Image* (1983; Bloomington: Indiana University Press, 1994), xv; *Deutschland im Herbst* (Germany in Autumn), 35 mm, 126 min., prod. Filmverlag der Autoren, dir. Alf Brustellin, Bernhard Sinkel, Rainer Werner Fassbinder, Alexander Kluge, Maximiliane Mainka, Edgar Reitz, Katja Rupe, Hans Peter Cloos, and Volker Schlöndorff, 1978.

2. For a full text of the manifesto, see Eric Rentschler, ed., *West German Filmmakers on Film: Visions and Voices* (New York: Holmes and Meier, 1988), 2.

3. Corrigan, *New German Film,* xvi.

type of spectator, one who is active rather than passive in determining meaning.[4] And one of the primary techniques by which the film constructs this new form of spectatorship is the systematic employment of *Gegeninformation* (alternative or combative information), to appropriate Kluge's term, that Corrigan understands as the manner in which "the film scrambles fact and fiction in an intentionally uneven pastiche."[5]

While Corrigan's theses are illuminating, they do not sufficiently address *Germany in Autumn*'s radical departure, both thematically and formally, from earlier West German nonfiction film production; thus, they fail to bring out the full sociopolitical significance of this historically important film. By focusing almost exclusively on its purely cinematic features and downplaying the harsh public events informing and indeed motivating its production, Corrigan presents only half of the picture. In what follows, I supplement his eye-opening work with a close reading of *Germany in Autumn* that shows how the film's hybrid mixture of fact and fiction reveals and projects an intimate and inextricable relationship to terrorism.

I. Historical Background

For many German intellectuals on the Left, the events of October 1977, the background to the German Autumn, were comparable to those of May 1968 for the French—that is, they were taken to manifest a serious crisis resulting from disillusionment with the democratic state but also, more profoundly, with the Left's own ideas and achievements. As Geoff Eley noted, the German autumn "was immediately recognized as a political watershed. In retrospect, it became the moment of the *Wende*—the turning of the public climate to the right after the progressive opening of the Brandt government of 1969–1974—anticipating the return of the Christian Democratic Union (CDU) to government in 1982–1983."[6] In fact, as Eley is quick to point out, this turn to the right began much earlier, and October 1977 merely represented its bloody completion. A full understanding must then include the recollection of key developments leading

4. This emphasis on the role of the spectator and on the creation of an oppositional public sphere is the focus of Miriam Hansen's essay, "Cooperative Auteur Cinema and Oppositional Public Sphere: Alexander Kluge's Contribution to *Germany in Autumn*," *New German Critique* 24–25 (fall–winter 1981–82): 36–56. However, Hansen attributes this strategy primarily to Kluge rather than seeing it as something that concerned all the filmmakers involved.

5. Corrigan, *New German Film*, 12.

6. Geoff Eley, "Deutschland im Herbst," *American Historical Review* 96 (October 1991): 1130–32.

up to the events of the German Autumn and the violent outcome of what started as peaceful left-wing student protests.[7]

As noted in the previous chapter, the Vietnam War triggered critical responses throughout Germany, both East and West. Under the communist regime, that outrage in the East took the form of a vocal, concerted, state-supported, and generally unproblematic solidarity with the North Vietnamese. In West Germany, because of its ties to the United States, the situation was more delicate: supporting the North Vietnamese implied accusing both the United States and West German governments and much of what they both stood for. Protests against the war took place throughout Europe, for the most part peacefully as a part of a larger student unrest that, with the possible exception of France, was more explosive in words and political realignments than in radical deeds. Two tragic incidents that occurred at that time, one perpetuated by the state and one by a left-wing organization, seem to have ignited a spark of violence in West Germany and shifted the rules of conduct on both sides: the June 2, 1967, slaying of student Benno Ohnesorg by the West German police during a protest against the visit of the Shah of Iran and his wife; and the far Left's May 22, 1967, bombing of L'Innovation, a Brussels department store, resulting in the death of three hundred people.[8] The impetus behind the bombing of L'Innovation was presented in a statement broadly distributed throughout West German campuses announcing that these bombs "brought Vietnam home to Brussels." Shortly thereafter, on May 24, 1967, a leaflet handed out at the Freie Universität Berlin raised the omi-

7. For an in-depth study and analysis of the history of the West German counterculture movement from the perspective of the student movements, see Sabine von Dirke, *"All Power to the Imagination!" The West German Counterculture from the Student Movement to the Greens* (Lincoln: University of Nebraska Press, 1997), esp. chap. 3, "Post-1968 Blues: Spontis, Violence, and New Subjectivity." Also useful is Rick McCormick's *Politics of the Self: Feminism and the Postmodern in West German Literature and Film* (Princeton: Princeton University Press, 1991), esp. chap. 1, "'All Power to the Imagination!' From the 1960s to the 1970s," 58–68.

8. The Ohnesorg slaying spawned the armed resistance group June 2. For an "insider's history" of the events leading up to and following 1967, see Stefan Aust's *Der Baader Meinhof Komplex: Erweiterte und aktualisierte Ausgabe* (Hamburg: Hoffmann und Campe, 1997). Aust was closely associated with members of the RAF, and his recollections of the events, as well as the attempt to give an accurate and objective record of what happened, have resulted in an extremely rich 668-page volume. *Der Baader Meinhof Komplex* was originally published in 1985; however, since the fall of the Wall, Aust has added new information gathered from East German secret police files, resulting in the current edition, published on the twenty-year anniversary of the deaths of Ensslin, Baader, and Raspe. Aust's study, in my opinion, is much more fruitful than the predictably conservative English-language account by Jillian Becker, *Hitler's Children: The Story of the Baader-Meinhof Terrorist Gang* (1978; London: Pickwick Books, 1989).

nous question, "When will Berlin stores burn?"[9] What followed was the gradual organization of a radical extreme left West German group that called itself the Red Army Faction (Rote Armee Fraktion, RAF), after the militant radical Japanese Red Army (Rengo Sekigum).

The exact number of RAF members is not known, but a brief recall of the key RAF players and a short timeline of their actions will suffice to rekindle the memory or to re-create the special atmosphere of the times. Andreas Baader (1943–77) and Gudrun Ensslin (1940–77) both died in the Stammheim maximum security prison, as did Jan-Carl Raspe (1945–77), allegedly by suicide. Ensslin had previously been married to Bernward Vesper, with whom she had one son. Vesper, who committed suicide on May 14, 1971, was the son of a prominent Nazi poet and represented part of the generation that rebelled against their fathers' crimes.[10] Ulrike Meinhof (1934–76), an editor of a left-wing publication, *Konkret,* also died in Stammheim. Horst Mahler (1936–) was a lawyer, and Holger Meins (1941–74) was a film student. On the night of April 2, 1968, Baader, Ensslin, Thorwald Proll, and Horst Söhnlein set fire to two Frankfurt department stores, Kaufhaus Schneider and Kaufhof, as a protest against the Vietnam War.[11] There were no casualties. Brought to trial in October 1968, the four young radicals were sentenced to several years in prison but were released in June 1969 to await the outcome of an appeal. Their lawyer at the time was Mahler, who was becoming increasingly involved in RAF politics.

A basic shift occurred sometime around 1970. The topical protest against the imperialist war in Vietnam grew into a general attack on capitalist consumerism in a West German society (at the height of its economic miracle) that Ensslin declared to be governed by "consumption terrorism" (*Konsumterror*). The continued presence of former Nazi officials both in government and industry was increasingly exposed. At the same time, members of the RAF aligned themselves with Middle East radical organizations such as the Popular Front for the Liberation of Palestine, and several (including Mahler) traveled to Beirut and Jordan to train in guerrilla warfare. Armed resistance was becoming internationalized. Protests throughout West Germany increased in violence—the 1972 bombing of

9. The flyer reads as follows: "Ein brennendes Kaufhaus mit brennenden Menschen vermittelt zum erstenmal in einer europäischen Großstadt jenes knisterne Vietnamgefühl (dabeizusein und mitzubrennen), das wir in Berlin bislang noch missen mußten. . . . Wann brennen die Berliner Kaufhäuser?" (cited in Aust, *Der Baader Meinhof Komplex,* 49).

10. Shortly before his death, Vesper wrote *Die Reise* (1977; Reinbek: Rowohlt, 1995), a semiautobiographical account of his relationship to the legacy of the Nazi past and to the present radical movements.

11. "Wir taten es aus Protest gegen die Gleichgültigkeit, mit der die Menschen dem Völkermord in Vietnam zusehen" (cited in Aust, *Der Baader Meinhof Komplex,* 75).

the U.S. military bases at Frankfurt and Heidelberg killed four U.S. military personnel and injured eighteen. Some years later, trying to make sense out of what had happened, Rainer Werner Fassbinder grouped the German terrorists into three generations: the first, in the 1960s, included Baader, Ensslin, Mahler, and Meinhof and was motivated by idealism; the second, increasingly violent and antiestablishment, identified with the 1977 autumn; and the third lacked idealism or ideology and was moved only by sensationalism.[12] French cultural theorist Jean Baudrillard later referred to such sensationalism provoked by terrorism as "pure spectacle."[13] Fassbinder described his film, *The Third Generation* (1978–79), as "a comedy, because the terrorists behave like politicians. They actually work for the system in order to confirm the existing order and make it final."[14]

On May 14, 1970, Meinhof, who previously had only acknowledged her support and sympathy for the RAF in her journalistic writings, aided in the jailbreak of Baader. This act is significant for two reasons: first, the RAF became known as the Baader-Meinhof Gang (with all the Bonnie and Clyde resonances); and second, a guard was seriously injured during the escape, starting a wave of human casualties. Members of the RAF went underground, moving from safe house to safe house throughout West Germany and traveling across Europe and the Middle East.[15] At the

---

12. See Rainer Werner Fassbinder, "Die Dritte Generation" [1978], in *Deutschland im Herbst: Terrorismus im Film,* ed. Petra Kraus, Natalie Lettenewitsch, Ursula Saekel, Brigitte Bruns, and Matthias Mersch (Munich: Das Filmzentrum, 1997), 82–89. In 1978 this categorization undermined and destabilized any terrorists' potential power for political critique.

13. Jean Baudrillard, "Our Theater of Cruelty," trans. John Johnston, *Semiotext(e): The German Issue* 4, no. 2 (1982): 108–15.

14. Cited and translated by Imke Lode, "Terrorism, Sadomasochism, and Utopia in Fassbinder's *The Third Generation,*" in *Perspectives on German Cinema,* ed. Terri Ginsberg and Kirsten Moana Thompson (New York: G. K. Hall, 1996), 415.

15. For a recent insightful essay on the RAF and *Germany in Autumn,* see Thomas Elsaesser's "Antigone Agonistes: Urban Guerilla or Guerilla Urbanism? The Red Army Faction, *Germany in Autumn,* and *Death Game,*" in *Giving Ground: The Politics of Propinquity,* ed. Joan Copjec and Michael Sorkin (New York: Verso, 1999), 267–302. In particular, Elsaesser links recent changes in urban development to the RAF's guerrilla tactics. He notes that "the RAF's preferred theatres of action—the street, public buildings, department stores, nondescript underpasses—designates a topography of visual signs now omnipresent: the city, the urban scene on the move. One suddenly becomes aware to what extent these 'urban guerillas'—and the police that controlled the crowds—were not only part of the more general transformation of the civic realm and the public sphere, but actually played a leading role in making the changes visible. This public sphere in the making has, as we know, radically recoded the cities of the developed world, producing new kinds of mobility, reflecting changed working conditions and leisure habits, imposing new ways of inhabiting and using the domestic environment, in short, making space itself a political category" (285–86).

same time, despite the fear of prosecution by the state and of being labeled as "sympathizers" or "belittlers" (*Verharmloser*), a large number of West German citizens gave both financial and moral support to the RAF.[16] Indeed, a 1971 poll by the Allensbacher Institute for Public Opinion revealed that 25 percent of all West Germans under age thirty felt sympathy for the RAF. Even more politically destabilizing was the sympathy expressed by leading intellectuals such as Erich Fried and Heinrich Böll, who published his provocative article, "Does Ulrike Want Clemency or a Safe Conduct?" in the December 23, 1971, issue of the prestigious *Der Spiegel.* The fear of a swelling of support for the RAF led the state to pass the notorious 1972 *Berufsverbote* or *Radikalenerlaß* legislation, under which members of radical student organizations (and the Communist Party) could be banned from employment in the public sector, notably schools and universities. Between 1971 and 1977, more than 800,000 West Germans were subject to raids and searches by special police forces.[17] During this escalating conflict, the RAF became increasingly violent in its attacks against the state, while the state became more and more brutal in its response and thus gave more credibility to the RAF's claims about state terrorism. At the same time, of course, the credibility of the state's view of the RAF as a violent, ruthless, and irrational menace to society also grew. As noted by Hans-Joachim Klein, who had links to the RAF, to June 2, and to the Revolutionary Cells, "it's the insane reactions of the State that have made a Hydra out of the armed struggle. Every time the State has arrested somebody, it has given birth to five new guerrillas."[18]

Finally, on June 1, 1972, Baader, Meins, and Raspe were arrested in Frankfurt, with Ensslin captured in Hamburg on June 7 and Meinhof caught in Hannover on June 15. But the state did not relent in its pressure, prompting hysterical media coverage of antiterrorist success. On November 9, 1974, erstwhile film student Holger Meins died in prison as a result

16. For an excellent account of the atmosphere at the time, see Margit Mayer, "The German October of 1977," *New German Critique* 13 (winter 1978): 155–63.

17. Writing in 1977, Jack Zipes observed that "political prisoners have been subjected to harsh solitary confinement and maltreatment. Their lawyers have been deprived of their rights as citizens and have experienced an arbitrary curtailment of their legal activities. . . . In addition to these attacks by the state on political activists, police control at all borders and public transportation facilities has been augmented. Even citizens have been mobilized to act like police and to be on the constant lookout for 'enemies of the state.'" ("The Political Dimensions of *The Lost Honor of Katharina Blum*" [1977], in *Perspectives,* ed. Ginsberg and Thompson, 404.)

18. Hans-Joachim Klein, "Slaughter Politics" (interview with Jean-Marcel Bouguereau), trans. Harold Chester, *Semiotext(e): The German Issue* 4, no. 2 (1982): 97. Klein also observed that the RAF was intent on "sharpening the contradictions in such a way as to make the situation become more and more openly fascist" (93).

of a hunger strike.[19] And in 1975 a new maximum-security prison, Stammheim, was built exclusively to house terrorists. The same year the state appointed five judges, rather than a jury, to preside over the trials of Baader, Ensslin, and Raspe. The tension was mounting. On May 9, 1976, Meinhof was found hanging from the bars of her cell window. On April 28, 1977, Baader, Ensslin, and Raspe were given three life sentences plus fifteen years for four murders, thirty-four attempted murders, and six bombings. Shortly before their sentencing, on April 7, the West German federal prosecutor, Siegfried Buback, and his chauffeur were slain by members of the RAF as an anticipated threat of retaliation. The notorious "Buback Obituary" or "Mescalero Brief," which appeared in the student paper *Göttinger Nachrichten* on April 25, 1977, condemned the violence but professed a "furtive joy" about the death of Buback.[20] There followed an increase in state surveillance of university life and the vilification of professors who sympathized with student activism. Professors were now required to sign a new declaration of loyalty to the state or face dismissal.[21] The atmosphere of paranoia and self-censorship grew dramatically, with the media playing fully into the hands of the government.[22] Then, on July 30, 1977, Jürgen Ponto, chief executive officer of the Dresdner Bank, was killed by three RAF members, one of whom, Susanne

19. Meins was one of the first-year film students at the Deutsche Film- und Fernsehakademie in Berlin (DFFB). Other students from his class included Helke Sanders, Harun Farocki, and Hartmut Bitmosky. Meins made several short films, among them *Herstellung eines Molotow-Cocktails* (1968). Farocki directed a documentary about Meins's life and death, *Es stirbt allerdings ein Jeder* 1975. For an informative essay on the relationship between politics and the practices of the DFFB students, see Tilman Baumgärtel, "Ein Stück Kino, das mit Film nichts zu tun hatte," in *Deutschland im Herbst,* ed. Kraus et al., 36–47.

20. For a helpful analysis of the Buback Obituary and its relationship to new subjectivity, see von Dirke, *"All Power to the Imagination!"* 96–103. For a translation of the letter, see "Buback: In Memoriam," trans. Wynn Gundarson, *Semiotext(e): The German Issue* 4, no. 2 (1982): 124–30.

21. The oath is so remarkable that it warrants being cited in full: "In the context of the government investigation of Lower Saxony into the edition of the documentation 'Buback—a eulogy,' I hereby declare: I disavow under all conditions the use of murder or kidnapping or of any kind of violence in our liberal democratic constitutional state [*Rechtsstaat*]. I am aware that I, as a civil servant, have a particular obligation of loyalty towards the state. This demands more than a merely formally correct but otherwise disinterested, cool, privately distanced attitude towards the state and constitution. It demands from civil servants in particular that they unequivocally distance themselves from groups and tendencies which attack, struggle against and slander this state, its constitutional organs and the valid constitutional order. I will live up to my duty of political loyalty. This must be maintained particularly in times of crisis and serious conflicts when the state is dependent upon its civil servants to intervene partisanly for it," as cited in Mayer, "German October," 157.

22. For a scathing report on the self-censorship, see Mayer, "German October."

Albrecht, was his godchild's sister. The state cast the RAF as beyond the pale of human and ethical behavior.

This was the opening of the German Autumn, which was marked by an accelerated sequence of events. On September 5, 1977, Hanns-Martin Schleyer, former SS officer, current president of West German Federation of Industries, and chairman of Daimler-Benz, was abducted. The kidnappers' demands included the immediate release of imprisoned RAF members. On September 8, in complete accordance with the state but exerting self-censorship, the media imposed a full news blackout. Then, on October 13, a Lufthansa flight with eighty-eight passengers on board was hijacked to Mogadishu, Somalia; all hostages were safely released by GSG-9 troopers five days later. Sometime during the night of October 18, Baader and Raspe were shot in their cells, Ensslin was found hanged, and Irmgard Möller suffered serious knife wounds.[23] The next day, the French newspaper *Liberation* received a communication from Schleyer's kidnappers that stated that he had been executed and provided the location of his corpse. Schleyer's funeral was held in Stuttgart two days later, on October 25, in the same city where Baader, Ensslin, and Raspe were buried in the presence of a large number of family, friends, and sympathizers.[24]

The tragic impact of the German Autumn was not confined to Germany: it evoked a response throughout Europe. As Stanley Corngold has noted, the French in particular viewed the outburst of German terrorism as a lightning flash that illuminated the Germans' hidden or repressed blind violence. The latter, in turn, preferred to view it not as a solely German illumination but as a more general European explosion. Corngold points out, however, that German terrorism could be linked back to France's deeply problematic recent history,[25] which might have moved the leading left-wing French intellectual, Jean-Paul Sartre, to pay a highly publicized visit to the prisoners in Stammheim.

II. Cultural Response

More than twenty years later, the German Autumn remains a site of traumatic obsession for the German intelligentsia. Even though members of

23. Ironically and perhaps not coincidentally, Jews were first systematically deported from Berlin on October 18, 1941.

24. Their funeral by no means marked the end of the RAF activities and fatalities as both sides continued their battle well into the 1990s. As recently as April 20, 1998, the state prosecutor in Karlsruhe received a letter announcing the formal dissolution of the RAF. However, the validity of the letter has been called into question since its date marks the hundredth anniversary of Hitler's birth.

25. Stanley Corngold, *The Fate of the Self: German Writers and French Theory* (1986; Durham, N.C.: Duke University Press, 1996), 182–83.

the RAF continued to operate,[26] a period of relative silence followed the initial shock, but this "latency period" ended in the late 1990s with a renewed interest in the events of 1977 on their twentieth anniversary. In a major *Die Zeit* article, "The Dialectic of the German Autumn," Friedrich Christian Delius observed, "Despite all the articles, books, documentations, and films, the theme of '1977' is still burdened by a taboo."[27] This is a theme on which Delius had earlier elaborated at length in his fiction trilogy, *Ein Held der inneren Sicherheit* (1981), *Mogadischu Fensterplatz* (1987), and *Himmelfahrt eines Staatsfeindes* (1992).[28] The "taboo" label of the German Autumn obviously also affected German film production. Wolfgang Landgräber recently noted that many on the Left still remain traumatized by what happened in 1977, and he called for a new generation of filmmakers who would not be inhibited by the taboo and by fear of state reprisals.[29]

By 1977, in attempts to explain the sympathy that many Germans felt for the RAF, the term *trauma* was already associated with the sense of taboo. Writing during that year, Norbert Elias argued that terrorism "suddenly brought to light the latent fissures that exist in West German society

26. For example, a U.S. military base was bombed in Ramstein in 1981 and one in Frankfurt was bombed in 1985; in 1986 AA-Ministrialdirektor Gerold von Braunmühl was assassinated; in 1991 Treuhand director Detlev Karsten Rohwedder was assassinated. For a complete list of continued activities and crimes perpetuated by the RAF, see Aust, *Der Baader Meinhof Komplex,* 659.

27. "Trotz aller Artikel, Bücher, Dokumentationen und Filme bleibt das Thema '1977' von der Aura eines Tabus belastet" (Friedrich Christian Delius, "Die Dialektik des deutschen Herbstes," *Die Zeit* 31, no. 1 [August 1997]: 3).

28. Friedrich Christian Delius, *Ein Held der inneren Sicherheit* (Reinbek: Rowohlt, 1981); Delius, *Mogadishu Fensterplatz* (Reinbek: Rowohlt, 1987); Delius, *Himmelfahrt eines Staatsfeindes* (Reinbek: Rowohlt, 1992). Also of interest are two recent photographic publications: former RAF member Astrid Proll's *Baader Meinhof: Pictures on the Run 1967–77* (Zurich: Scalo, 1998), which consists of a series of photographs that Proll assembled during her time with the RAF; Hans-Peter Feldmann, *1967–1993: Die Toten* (Düsseldorf: Feldmann Verlag, 1998), which contains no commentary and consists only of a series of black-and-white photographs of all those who died either directly or indirectly because of terrorist activities.

29. "Ein großer Teil der Linken [hat] bis heute in fast traumatischer Angst versagt, zur RAF und ihren Protagonisten eine auch emotional begründete und vor allem selbsbewußte Haltung zu enwickeln, aus Furcht, sie könnte als Zustimmung zu Mord als Mittel des politischen Kampfes oder umgekehrt als Kniefall vor der Staatsmacht mißdeutet werden. Bleibt zu hoffen, daß eine neue Riege von Filmemachern sich mit der nötigen Respektlosigkeit und dennoch ernsthaft an das Thema herantraut und die ihm immer noch anhaftenden Tabus aufbricht" (Wolfgang Landgräber, "Das Thema 'Terrorismus' in deutschen Spielfilmen, 1975–1985," in *Deutschland im Herbst,* ed. Kraus et al., 21).

and made them visible to the whole world."[30] Terrorism was perceived as an inevitable, if excessively violent, outgrowth of the "collective trauma" caused by Germany's "inability to mourn" and to come to terms with the unspeakable of the Third Reich.[31] Indeed, a 1978 survey revealed that 24 percent of West Germans still believed that National Socialism was a good idea, albeit poorly implemented. In this context, antiestablishment youth movements and the ideology of the RAF were interpreted as a direct result of the generational guilt of children ashamed of their parents—especially fathers—because of their role during the Nazi period.[32] The trauma\taboo theory certainly helps to explain much overreaction to RAF terrorism.

This characterization of events as traumatic is actually at odds with their treatment as taboo since, rather than a pathological and painful symptom like trauma, taboo is a conventional acknowledgment that particular issues or subjects must be avoided as a protective measure. Whereas taboo implies conscious control of speech, trauma is an unconscious feeling beyond rational control. A thorough analysis of the response to terrorism ought to examine the interplay between unconscious trauma and conventional taboo, exploring what exactly was protected or concealed. For the trauma underlying the German Autumn may very well have had roots in addition to those in the Nazi past, a more pressing tension that can not be easily reduced to one historical jolt. As Alexander Kluge notes, "The fatal catastrophe succeeded in cutting through the amnesia of many. The events did not have much to do with the war directly but '1945' and 'war' were associated with them. . . . The repressed shock breaks out in terrorism, a point that is actually not suited to genuinely coming to terms with the previously repressed material; it may even produce new distortions."[33] Some questions beg to be asked: what were the new distortions in 1977, and what caused them?

---

30. Cited in Anton Kaes, *From Hitler to Heimat: The Return of History as Film* (Cambridge: Harvard University Press, 1989), 24.

31. Kaes, *From Hitler to Heimat,* 24–25.

32. Elsaesser concisely sums up Peter Schneider's earlier argument ("Fathers and Sons Retrospectively," *New German Critique,* 31 [winter 1984]: 11–12): "In other words, these sons did not identify with the official optimism of the West German economic miracle, they also did not have a genuine stake in any (socialist) alternative. Instead they identified with the latent emotions, the ones that the forced optimism and strident efficiency tried to hide. Seeing the father's cover-up, seeing through it, but being sons by flesh and blood, they also had to deal with their own internalization of the father, whose hidden guilt and shame, according to Schneider, returns in the son as self-destructive melancholy. . . . Schneider sees the RAF's theatrical metaphor as apt. The bombings, hostage takings and terrorist acts were nothing less than 'murderous and suicidal' attempts to 'tear off the mask' of official authority behind which they had reason to suspect the guiltily fretting faces of their own fathers" ("Antigone Agonistes," 279).

33. Cited in Kaes, *From Hitler to Heimat,* 25.

The film *Germany in Autumn* sheds revealing light on some deep-seated traumas that emerged or resurfaced in Germany in the fall of 1977. By emerging to the surface—being forced back to the surface—these traumas threatened to disrupt the social order and the social taboos conventionally set up to keep public pathologies under control and thereby to prevent a radical questioning of, or break with, the symbolic entity known as Germany. *Germany in Autumn* represents the earliest and most immediate reaction to the 1977 events. During a time of self-imposed (and/or state-inspired) media blackout, the film's makers sought to create a document that would, in their collective statement, "hold onto memory in the form of a subjective momentary impression."[34] Trying to re-create what really happened during the German Autumn and to provide images diverging from the official state version, the film effectively contributed to produce what Oskar Negt and Kluge theorize as an "oppositional public sphere"—a subversive source of messages pitted against dominant media, notably television.[35] Mixing interviews, fictional reconstitutions, and archival footage from the Third Reich, *Germany in Autumn* sought to add complexity and understanding to the one-dimensional hysterical picture propagated by the mass media.

In addition, the manner in which *Germany in Autumn* resonates with the 1967 French collaborative production *Far from Vietnam* (Godard, Ivens, Klein, Lelouch, Marker, Resnais, and Varda) endows the later film with a special interest for comparative, historical, and theoretical investigation of German postwar cinema. The parallels between the German film and its French precursor were noted and addressed as early as February 1978 in an interview conducted by Bion Steinborn with Brustellin, Kluge, Reitz, Schlöndorff, and Sinkel.[36] True, various critics have also mentioned the influence of the French work in passing, but they have failed to clearly spell out why *Far from Vietnam,* as a "silent interlocutor" on several levels (both structural and thematic), is crucial for a thorough understanding of

34. Kaes, *From Hitler to Heimat,* 27.

35. For an extremely cogent essay on the relationship between Kluge's social theories and *Germany in Autumn,* see Hansen, "Cooperative Auteur Cinema."

36. "Es ist ein erster 'kollektiver Versuch' der deutschen Autorenfilmer, der auch dann interessant und beachtenswert bleibt, wenn der Film nicht alle Erwartungen erfüllen sollte. Denn es ist für ganz Europa das zweite Mal—1966 waren es Joris Ivens, William Klein, Jean-Luc Godard, Claude Lelouch, Chris Marker, Alain Resnais, Agnès Varda, die gemeinsam einen Film über Vietnam machten (*Loin du Vietnam—Fern von Vietnam*)—daß ein kollektiver Versuch des 'Autorenkinos' stattfindet über ein Ereignis von internationalem Interesse" ("'Deutschland im Herbst' oder 'Modell Deutschland?'" [interview with Alf Brustellin, Alexander Kluge, Edgar Reitz, Volker Schlöndorff, Bernd Sinkel], Munich, February 8, 1978, conducted by Bion Steinborn], *Filmfaust* 7 [March 1978]: 3).

Germany in Autumn.[37] *Far from Vietnam* manifests the ambition of some of the most prominent auteurs of the French New Wave to collectively produce a film that would cut through the sensationalized media reports on Vietnam while simultaneously joining the protest against the war. Indeed, on an immediate thematic level, Vietnam provided a link between the two films, since protest against U.S. imperialism was the impetus behind the initial West German terrorist activity in the late 1960s and early 1970s. Moreover, just as *Germany in Autumn* visually mixes the events of 1977 with spliced-in film footage from the 1920s and with newsreels from the Third Reich, stressing the key part played by National Socialism in the past as well as in the present, so too was a dramatic past invoked in the French film, albeit in a more subtle manner. Parts of the soundtrack in *Far from Vietnam* were initially composed by Hanns Eisler for Alain Resnais's 1954 film about the Holocaust, *Night and Fog* (not shown on West German television until 1978).[38] Eisler's haunting music forged a sound bridge between the two French films and between the European and Vietnam tragedies. Similarly, Kluge's use of Haydn's melody (which became the German national anthem) moves the audience back and forth in time—from a mythical past through the Third Reich to the present day and back again.

Far from Vietnam and *Germany in Autumn* also resonate with each other through their participation in protest movements, yet here a major distinction emerges. *Far from Vietnam* was made during a period of optimism and hope in the student movement—Paris '68 and the Prague Spring were a year away, and anything seemed possible. This heady atmosphere is particularly well captured in Marker's extensive shots of and interviews with antiwar protesters in France and in the United States. By contrast, *Germany in Autumn* is about defeat and "collective mourning"[39] for a lost opportunity for a better future—lost not just in Germany but throughout the Western world, since, in the interim, the U.S. protest movement came to a halt with the Kent State student massacre and the virtual obliteration of the Black Panther Party and the Symbionese Liberation Army.[40] As Volker Schlöndorff sadly comments, these were the roots of the "situation

37. See Corrigan, *New German Film,* 195; Kaes, *From Hitler to Heimat,* 25; Hansen, "Cooperative Auteur Cinema," 46.

38. It is interesting to note that Marker served as cameraman for that earlier film.

39. See Thomas Elsaesser, *New German Cinema: A History* (New Brunswick, N.J.: Rutgers University Press, 1989), 260.

40. Although the 1960s have been mythologized as a time of revolutionary liberation and protest, the political potential of armed resistance labeled as terrorism in the 1970s ought not to be underestimated. An interesting parallel is punk and Greil Marcus's *Lipstick Traces: A Secret History of the Twentieth Century* (Cambridge: Harvard University Press, 1990).

that produced the Baader-Meinhof Group and immediately produced in turn that complementary disproportionate response which has spread throughout Europe, for example the anti-terrorist convention which is an instrument that one will make use of in ten years to eliminate the opposition movements in France or Italy."[41] And this sense of loss and misguided idealism marks Schlöndorff's *The Legend of Rita* (2000), a feature film about a group of terrorists in the 1970s who are hidden in the former GDR.

Finally, the dialogue between *Far from Vietnam* and *Germany in Autumn* must also be appreciated on an institutional level. Starting with the 1962 Oberhausen Manifesto, New German Cinema has situated itself with reference to and has been in the shadow of the more internationally popular French New Wave. In particular, the direct or indirect influence of Jean-Luc Godard cannot be ignored. Just as Godard, then the most prominent active French director, gave a highly personal accent to his segment of *Far from Vietnam,* so did Fassbinder, comparable in prestige, make a very personal statement in his contribution to the 1977 German production. Just as Marker provided the earlier film with the overarching narrative thread that held it together, so Kluge assumed a similar role in *Germany in Autumn.* But the most telling influence affects the basic structure of the two films, which both offer a striking mixture of fictional and documentary scenes—with *Far from Vietnam* weighing more heavily in on the side of fact and *Germany in Autumn* more loaded with obviously fictional vignettes.

In its striking hybridity, weaving an increasingly complex thread of "objective facts" and "subjective realities," *Germany in Autumn* most resists categorization. It stands in stark contrast to other films that take terrorism as their main subject but can be placed clearly within the genre of fiction or of documentary. Entirely fictional are Schlöndorff and von Trotta's *Die verlorene Ehre der Katharina Blum* (The Lost Honor of Katharina Blum, 1975); Rainer Werner Fassbinder's *Mutter Küsters Fahrt zum Himmel* (Mother Küster's Trip to Heaven, 1975); von Trotta's *Das zweite Erwachen der Christa Klages* (The Second Awakening of Christa Klages, 1977); Richard Hauff's *Messer im Kopf* (Knife in the Head, 1978), awarded the 1979 Federal Film Prize; Fassbinder's *Die dritte Generation* (The Third Generation, 1979); and von Trotta's *Die bleierne Zeit* (Marianne and Julianne, 1981). These contrast with films clearly pre-

41. Volker Schlöndorff, "Cinema et consensus social: Un entretien avec Volker Schlöndorff," *Politique Aujourd'hui* 1–2 (1977): 127, cited in and trans. Zipes, "Political Dimensions," 408–9. Similarly, the events of September 11, 2001, have led to a virtually unchecked assault on American civil liberties in the United States.

sented as documentaries, such as Harun Farocki's *Es stirbt allerdings ein Jeder* (Everybody Must Die, 1975), Wolfgang Höpfner's *Vor vier Jahren—Vor zwei Jahren* (Four Years Ago—Two Years Ago, 1977–79), and Hauff's *Stammheim* (1985), recipient of the Grand Prix/Golden Bear at the 1986 Berlin Film Festival.[42] Why *Germany in Autumn* breaks away from the two traditional genres is one of the central questions at hand. There is more behind the hybrid structure of this film than a simple imitation of *Far from Vietnam.*

III. Between Fact and Fiction

While acknowledging the formal mixture of forms in *Germany in Autumn,* few scholars address this hybridity in its specificity and decode it as a meaningful sign. Corrigan observes that "the film scrambles fact and fiction in an intentionally uneven pastiche."[43] Anton Kaes explains that the "mix of forms in *Germany in Autumn* corresponds to the ambiguity of its political agenda."[44] Hansen reaches a similar conclusion, arguing that "the mixing of documentary footage with scenes or images of a varying degree of fictional and representational coding creates a space in which alternative readings of political events become possible."[45] Although these critics seem to be aware of the capital role that hybridity brings to the collective work envisaged in the filmmakers, these commentators still break the film into its separate and autonomous parts, assigning individual responsibility to each director and focusing on individual contributions in the spirit of canonical auteurism, which is at odds with the objectives of the cooperative project. As a result, critical discussion has centered on three episodes viewed independently of each other: the opening sequence filmed by Kluge, dealing with Schleyer's funeral and with Gabi Teichert, the history teacher searching for Germany's buried past; Fassbinder's twenty-six minute personal expository statement (by far the longest); and Schlöndorff's narrative (scripted by Heinrich Böll), about attempts to get a staged performance of

42. For a summary of West German films and their connection to the German Autumn, see *Deutschland im Herbst,* ed. Kraus et al. Marking the twentieth anniversary, is Heinrich Breloer's made-for-television docudrama *Todesspiel* (Death Game, 1997), a popular hit. For an insightful analysis of the problematic nature of Breloer's film, see Elsaesser, "Antigone Agonistes," 2. Most recently, Christian Petzold's award winning 2001 film, *Die innere Sicherheit,* cowritten with Harun Farocki, concerns the delicate balance between national security and everyday life in the wake of derailed utopianism of the 1960s.

43. Corrigan, *New German Film,* 12.

44. Kaes, *From Hitler to Heimat,* 26.

45. Hansen, "Cooperative Auteur Cinema," 50.

Antigone accepted by television censors.[46] These three directors were at the time, and remain today, the best known participants in the collective project, and their privileged place in the scholarly literature exemplifies the same process of scholarly realigning of the film's meaning that resulted in the uneven reception of discrete parts of *Far from Vietnam.* In the case of *Germany in Autumn,* this process was particularly unfair to overarching artists, such as Beate Mainka-Jellinghaus, whose editing of the film remains largely ignored.[47] Minimizing the film's structural scheme not only undercuts the initial intentions of the filmmakers but also blocks new readings and interpretations, for it is precisely "the cooperation which helped to create a new perspective."[48] Extracting a few scenes out of the total puzzle destroys the integrity of the work and encourages fragmentary value judgments, "high" and "low" hierarchy, and dismissal as trivialities some basic points of the film's complex critique. In that sense, to consign certain parts as mere "family melodrama" or "embarrassing sketch[es]" is to throw the collective work out of balance, to sabotage its full meaning.[49]

This same type of hit-and-miss criticism and/or analysis still dominates representation of the RAF. As mentioned earlier, the focus was first centered on individuals that the media named, the Baader-Meinhof Gang, presenting a force in the international armed resistance as an isolated conspiracy of a few misguided delinquents, thereby minimizing the militant organization's subversive potential. That focus on the individual is a long-recognized bourgeois strategy that reduces complicated social-political-economic problematics to personal issues. By the same strategy, much was

46. For Kluge, see Hansen, "Cooperative Auteur Cinema"; Corrigan, *New German Film;* Kaes, *From Hitler to Heimat;* for Fassbinder, see Elsaesser, *New German Cinema;* Elsaesser, *Fassbinder's Germany: History, Identity, Subject* (Amsterdam: Amsterdam University Press, 1996); Hansen, "Cooperative Auteur Cinema"; Kaes, *From Hitler to Heimat;* Rentschler, *West German Filmmakers on Film;* Kaya Silverman, *Male Subjectivity at the Margins* (New York: Routledge, 1992); for Schlöndorff, see Elsaesser, "Antigone Agonistes"; Hansen, "Cooperative Auteur Cinema"; Rentschler, *West German Filmmakers on Film.*

47. According to both Kluge and Brustellin, Mainka-Jellinghaus's work on the film cannot be underestimated. "Für diese Montage zeichnet kein einzelner Filmer, sondern Beate Mainka-Jellinghaus" ("'Deutschland im Herbst' oder 'Modell Deutschland?'" 9). Hansen, "Cooperative Auteur Cinema," for example, gives Kluge full credit for the film's montage sequences.

48. As Kluge observes, "Erst die Kooperation schafft hier eine neue Perspektive. Und hier hat dieser Herbst 1977 bei unseren so verschiedenen Geistern verändernd gewirkt. Für einen Moment war sonst üblche Kleinstaaterei des 'Autorenfilms' vorbei. Vielleicht nur für eine Woche, also gerade nur so viel, um einen Plan zu fassen" ("'Deutschland im Herbst' oder 'Modell Deutschland?'" 6).

49. Elsaesser declares that with the exception of the Schlöndorff and Fassbinder sections, "*Germany in Autumn* became the transcription of political history into a family melodrama" (*New German Cinema,* 261); for Hansen's description of the Cloos/Rupe sequence, see "Cooperative Auteur Cinema," 46.

made of personal relationships, jealousies, and fights among the imprisoned RAF members. A similar humanist or auteurist perspective applied to film downplays or completely misses the careful selection of sequences aimed at suggesting or outlining a basic subtext and theory for the events of fall 1977. Only when the film is viewed as a whole in its manifold collective hybridity do the invisible, repressed, and unrepresentable come to the surface and break through the taboo to reveal the real political agenda.

Thus, according to Brustellin, the decision to mix fiction and documentary capped a sustained investigation of the general nature of political films; finding that no singular form could adequately address the issue, the filmmakers chose to use many different strategies, even at the price of ambiguity.[50] For Bernd Sinkel, for example, the film's original mix of perspectives did not seek merely to relate the diversified experiences of fall 1977 but also to interrogate what the film as film could or could not address—the limits of representation.[51] And Kluge argued that the interplay between fiction and nonfiction corresponded to the "coexistence of fact and desire in the human mind."[52] Most artists involved in producing *Germany in Autumn* were keenly aware of the pitfalls inherent in the representation of history in the powerful audiovisual medium of film. And since the events of 1977 were problematic and unresolved, it became crucial to find a form of expression that maintained both openness and ambivalence. As Brustellin noted, "If you take a character, and it is one dimensional, then it is dead. For history, it is the same thing. Only when there are contradictions does it begin to live."[53] There are of course various ways of resolving such contradictions. One traditional tactic in avant-garde film production at the time was to create a disjuncture between the sound and image tracks, thereby forcing viewers to change their perspectives.[54] Another road to the same goal is to systematically confuse the viewers about whether they are seeing fact or fiction. Western spectators have long

50. According to Brustellin, "Wir haben alle Formen des politischen Films befragt, ja richtig befragt, bis wir zu dem Ergebnis kamen, alle möglichen Filmformen zu verwenden: den Montagefilm wie den Dokumentarfilm, ebenso wie den Spielfilm und den Showfilm" ("'Deutschland im Herbst' oder 'Modell Deutschland?'" 9).

51. "Wir haben deshalb Formen, die der Film erfunden hat, daraufhin überprüft, ob sie geeignet sind, uns Perspektiven zu geben. Wir haben also nicht versucht, die Ereignisse des Herbstes 1977 darzustellen oder Teile daraus, sondern was der Film darüber aussagen kann oder nicht" ("'Deutschland im Herbst' oder 'Modell Deutschland?'" 10).

52. Cited in Hansen, "Cooperative Auteur Cinema," 49.

53. "Wenn man eine Figur nimmt und diese eindeutig ist, ist sie tot. Für Geschichten gilt dasselbe. Erst wenn ich sie mit Widersprüchen ausstatte, fängt sie an zu leben" ("'Deutschland im Herbst' oder 'Modell Deutschland?'" 12).

54. According to Brustellin, "Wenn man also z.B. Bilder und Töne verschiebt, die eine feste Zuordnung zueinander haben, dann entsteht ganz automatisch ein neuer Denkansatz" ("'Deutschland im Herbst' oder 'Modell Deutschland?'" 12).

been trained to receive a film differently if it is coded as a fictional feature versus a documentary.[55] When traditional rules of cinematic categorization and production are violated, seemingly in an arbitrary way, all stable meaning is called into question, and, therefore, reflection and further inquiry are called for. The ensuing process becomes dialectically explosive but also enriching, demonstrating that film is a multifaceted medium that can both provide documentary footage as an image of "truth" and, in the words of Edgar Reitz, explore the world of fantasy and imagination.[56]

Let us briefly return to the Buback Obituary. The reaction the Mescalero letter provoked went far beyond that justified by a contribution to a student newspaper. Sabine von Dirke compares it with Peter Handke's novel, A *Moment of True Feeling,* observing that the "ambiguity of violence" was not an issue in the novel, whereas the letter targeted precisely that ambivalence.[57] Drawing on Peter Brückner's analysis, von Dirke reiterates that the "linguistic structure of the obituary's argument itself has an oppositional content. . . . The Mescalero insists on his subjective perception, immediate impressions and feelings, and on his subjective language, which is the language of the countercultural environment."[58] Here again is the threat posed by the use of a mixed genre, by supposed objectivity contaminated by subjectivity. Outrageous propositions may be accepted in the realm of fiction, but when a nonfiction mode is utilized, the criteria for accepting them become much stricter. The Buback Obituary starts with an evocation of private fantasy: "For awhile (like so many of us) I savored the activities of the armed struggle, . . . Things I would like to do in my daydreams, but which I never really dared to do."[59] Only then does the author segue to concrete political considerations.

This use of fantasy as a point of departure for rational discourse, and vice versa, is one of the main structures underlying *Germany in Autumn.* Sinkel and Brustellin's opening fiction about domestic violence is followed

55. This phenomenon has been observed by Jean-Luc Godard, who notes that a spectator's eventual recognition of film footage as fiction becomes a "moment of communication" ("Introduction à une véritable histoire de cinéma," *Camera Obscura* 8–10 (1980): 75–88). For further elaboration of this point, see my "Triangulating Performances: Looking after Genre, after Feature," in *Triangulated Visions: Women in Recent German Cinema,* ed. Ingeborg Majer O'Sickey (Albany: State University of New York Press, 1998), 11–27.

56. "Andererseits sind wir die einzigen, die mit der lebendigen Phantasie der Leute ein Bündnis eingehen können" ("'Deutschland im Herbst' oder 'Modell Deutschland?'" 13).

57. "Whereas the ambiguity of violence in literary New Subjectivity was not thematized by the critics, the Buback Obituary was reproached with just such an ambivalent stance, and even misinterpreted as a glorification of violence" (von Dirke, *"All Power to the Imagination!"* 96).

58. Von Dirke, *"All Power to the Imagination!"* 100.

59. "Buback in Memoriam," *Semiotext(e): The German Issue* 4, no. 2 (1982): 126.

by a "real" interview with imprisoned former RAF member Horst Mahler. For Brustellin, the great objective reality of history is what goes on inside the head of the average person, even in drunken ramblings.[60] In this instance, a cinematographic link is forged between the fictional world and the nonfictional world through the story of Franziska Busch, who rescues a victim of domestic violence from her husband and then proceeds to watch a screening of a real interview with Mahler to better understand terrorism. In the interview, Mahler tries to explain the difference between a terrorist and a revolutionary on the basis of a similar structure: both violate established norms of behavior, but the terrorist leaves the moral system, whereas the revolutionary reinforces it. He then suggests that popular sympathy for the RAF stems from moral indignation, or outrage, which the average citizen shares with the terrorists. Busch, it turns out, is directing a contemporary feature film that claims to reproduce the form of a revolutionary film of the 1920s. Shots of that film within a film are presented as authentic documents from the past, yet they clearly are constructions or simulations of history. The entire sequence shows how easy it is to manipulate supposedly objective facts and hence cast suspicion on rational cognition in general.

By erasing the traditional boundaries between fact and fiction, history and its simulation, arbitrariness and meaninglessness, *Germany in Autumn* problematizes all "stable," "rational" systems of representation. Its function, like that of an imaginary "story" for former RAF member Fritz Teufel, is to upset the moral and/or intellectual comfort of the establishment, since a "'b-libi' (in contrast to an alibi) is a story that the accused does not prove and that the court cannot refute."[61] Or, as Baudrillard argued about the RAF, "The secret is to oppose to the order of the real an absolutely imaginary realm, absolutely ineffectual at the level of reality, but whose implosive energy absorbs everything real and all the violence of real power which founders there."[62] Is this an echo of the hopeful slogan of the student protests in the 1960s, "All Power to the Imagination"? All these ambiguous references and allusions, all these games with shadows and light, reality and phantasms, insure for *Germany in Autumn* a privileged place in the evolution of the essay film: it is a hybrid genre that, like

60. "Darstellbare Geschichte ist für mich das, was sich in den Köpfen der Menschen abspielt, und das ist z.B. der Mann an der Theke, der besoffen vor sich hin brabbelt. Und indem er sein Leben erzählt, ist das Geschichte und umgekehrt, in dem er, wild durcheinander, Geschichte erzählt, ist das sein Leben" ("'Deutschland im Herbst' oder 'Modell Deutschland?'" 9).

61. Fritz Teufel, "From A-libi to B-libi," trans. Cesar Loaiza, *Semiotext(e): The German Issue* 4, no. 2 (1982): 136.

62. Baudrillard, "Our Theater of Cruelty," 112.

its literary and philosophical counterpart, the written essay, is the form par excellence of leftist oppositional critique.[63] No wonder that it is precisely to this subversive essayistic mode of articulation that Ulrike Meinhof turned when "straight" journalism became too constraining a form for her political discourse.[64]

A similar observation can be drawn from a close look at two supposedly minor "fantasy" scenes in *Germany in Autumn* and their interplay with serious documentary footage. One often overlooked episode is Cloos/Rupe's "embarrassing sketch" about a female pianist who lets into her home a wounded man who could be a terrorist. The lighting, music, and set are all staged to produce the effect of a teledrama. Though it could appear in a different context as somewhat overly melodramatic and hence trifling, this short scene actually fulfills a capital function in relation to other more serious features of the film: clarifying and reinforcing their message. First, this segment supplies a fictional companion piece to an earlier "nonfiction" episode where Fassbinder's lover brings a young man back to the filmmaker's apartment and offers him a place to stay. It is specified that the man is from Hamburg, an allusion to the network of safe houses and apartments that operated throughout West Germany to provide refuge for the RAF. Fassbinder looks at the man (terrorist?) with apprehension and demands that he leave immediately. The man departs, and Fassbinder looks out the window after him in a shot that graphically matches the shot of the woman looking out the window after the man has left in the Cloos/Rupe segment. Fassbinder then flings himself on the floor, sobbing uncontrollably; it is implied, or at least suggested, that he has capitulated to antiterrorist hysteria promoted by the state, that in his mind he has become a fascist. This scene resonates with an earlier moment when Fassbinder's mother confesses her longing for a benevolent dictatorship and condemns Heinrich Böll for his statements in support of Meinhof. In the same segment, Fassbinder films himself having a panic attack at the sound of a police siren. These three incidents, as well as some others, serve to evoke the paranoia created by the state—the searches and terror to which West Germans were subjected. Fassbinder, who knew Horst Söhnlein, Baader, and Meins, stressed that point in subsequent comments on *Germany in Autumn:* "But of course harassment's really something that

63. For a recent examination of the essay as political form in the theories of Georg Lukács and Theodor Adorno, see Peter Hohendahl, "The Scholar, the Intellectual, and the Essay: Weber, Lukács, Adorno, and Postwar Germany," in *German Quarterly* 70, no. 3 (summer 1997): 217–31.

64. Arlene A. Teraoka, "Terrorism and the Essay: The Case of Ulrike Meinhof," in *The Politics of the Essay: Feminist Perspectives,* ed. Ruth-Ellen Boetcher Joeres and Elizabeth Mittman (Bloomington: Indiana University Press, 1993), 209–22.

takes place inside of you, because you're constantly aware that they know you exist. So you become more cautious, more fearful. . . . Now nothing can get to me, after that film; it took care of a lot of my fear."[65] While it may have served to exorcise Fassbinder's personal paranoia, this segment as a whole is nevertheless clearly coded as a documentary, however self-reflexive, and for the most part has been received as a "true" personal exposition. And yet, as Eric Rentschler suggests, it can also be read as a very scripted series of exposés, no more real than the more obviously fictional parts of the film.[66] Fassbinder uses his camera to play with the spectator's perception just as, on the telephone, he shows himself idly playing with himself. A deliberate confusion of genres is again at work, where what is ultimately important is the atmosphere and the emotion conveyed, not whether these qualities are true to objective reality.

News media images of terrorists. (Video caption from *Germany in Autumn*.)

While obviously fictional, the Cloos/Rupe segment projects the same serious message: the average citizen's fear that an act of kindness (helping someone who is wounded) can label one a terrorist, turn one into a terrorist, which is a message of Schlöndorff and von Trotta's earlier *The Lost Honor of Katherina Blum.* In the words of painter Gerhard Richter, "there's something else that puts additional fear into people, namely that

65. Rainer Werner Fassbinder, *The Anarchy of the Imagination: Interviews, Essays, and Notes,* ed. Michael Töteberg and Leo A. Lensing, trans. Krishna Winston (Baltimore: Johns Hopkins University Press, 1992), 136–37.

66. Eric Rentschler observed, "The Fassbinder sequence, in its singular merger of documentary confession and fictional self-stylization, represents West German film's most provocative variation on the theme of the problematic and problematized subject, a preoccupation that in hindsight more and more looks like the central obsession of intellectuals living in the FRG during the seventies" (*West German Film in the Course of Time: Reflections on the Twenty Years since Oberhausen* [Bedford Hills, N.Y.: Redgrave, 1984], 192).

they themselves are terrorists. And that is forbidden. So this terrorism inside all of us, that's what generates the rage and fear, and that's what I don't want, anymore than I want the policeman inside myself—there's never just one side to us. We're always both: the State and the terrorist."[67] And since the message is always the same (trauma is both individual and collective) it makes no difference in what form (fictional or not) it is delivered. Similarly, the fear and/or paranoia is the same whether or not it is caused by an actual terrorist: "it is in the atmosphere and never directly visible."[68] In that sense, the formal essayistic strategies of *Germany in Autumn* mimic the power of terrorism—nonrational and confusing.

The imaginary Cloos/Rupe episode also provides the first documentary image of real terrorists in the film as the camera pans over a table on which rests a newspaper featuring authentic "wanted" photographs of six RAF activists. Up to this point, Fassbinder and Mahler only mention the activist's names; finally they are given faces—albeit as they appear on police documents. There are two shots of the newspaper: the first shows Ingrid Schubert, Günther Sonnenburg, and Irmgard Möller while still alive and at large; the second shows the faces of Ensslin, Raspe, and Baader. Through a flash working on the viewer's unconscious, these images return the spectator to the film's main theme: representation of the terrorists. The viewer will then have to wait till the end of the film, shortly before the funeral of Ensslin, Baader, and Raspe in the Dornholden cemetery, to see their images again, this time as fully enlarged photos that cover the entire screen: the first is of Raspe, the second of Baader and Ensslin together. The latter picture is taken in court, as they are engaged in conversation, Baader's hand resting on Ensslin's shoulder—a seemingly banal image not of terrorists but of two friends. These images, derived from police shots disseminated by the mass media, together with the segment's teledrama filming style and the constant presence of a television set in the living room, combine to project a powerful critique of mass media and television, their representation of the RAF, and the impact of the resulting hysteria on the average citizen in particular. The form is melodramatic, but it is intentionally so.

There may be another explanation for the film's deliberate confusion

67. Gerhard Richter, *The Daily Practice of Painting: Writings and Interviews, 1962–1993,* ed. Hans-Ulrich Obrist, trans. David Britt (Cambridge: MIT Press, 1995), 186. Richter had a fascination with the RAF movement, despite his claims to the contrary: "the political topicality of my October paintings means almost nothing to me" (177). He revisited the theme no less than three times, first in his *Atlas;* then in his famous 1988 *October 18, 1977,* series; and again in his 1995 *Stammheim.*

68. According to Reitz, "Was uns gesellschaftlich droht, bahnt sich atmosphärisch an und ist nie direkt sichtbar" ("'Deutschland im Herbst' oder 'Modell Deutschland?'" 8).

of moods and genres, which may have been intended as a relief from tragic violence. As a daily threat, violence always seems to be always both omnipresent and denied, an obsession and a taboo. In Mayer's words, "Violence, the analysis of which no one seriously demands, but which is in fact conjured up, is held at a distance and declared as taboo."[69] Thus, any taboo plays both on attraction and revulsion, lust and censure. The author of the Mescalero letter unveils this duality, or ambiguity, of violence, leading Thomas Elsaesser to conclude that instead of representing merely a return of the uncanny (*Unheimlichkeit*), terrorism thrives on a collective experience of vicarious pleasure (*Klammheimlichkeit*).[70] This vicarious pleasure and its connection to violence are dangerous. And taboo and violence are both linked to the deaths of the imprisoned RAF members imperfectly concealed and still festering. Even the strictest censorship seems helpless to eradicate the fear. But it tries. In 1975 Jean Marie Straub and Danièle Huillet could not release their film *Moses and Aaron* with the dedication "For Holger Meins, J.M.S. and D.H."—it was felt to be too dangerous.[71] Not only the deeds are threatening but also their representation.

IV. Obscured Politics

The deaths of Meinhof, Baader, Ensslin, and Raspe in Stammheim have become inseparable from their lives. And because these deaths were cloaked in ambiguity and mystery, everyone was trapped, in Baudrillard's terms, "in the hysterical search for truth, which is the best way to abolish the symbolic futility of death."[72] Did they or didn't they commit suicide?[73] The dangerous aspect of "this deliberate ambiguity concerning the facts" is, continues Baudrillard, that "it insured that the truth about this death, and not the death itself, became fascinating."[74] The political implications of this transference clearly play into the state's hands. If one focuses morbidly on the factual death of individuals, one ceases to examine the ideology and politics behind their actions, and the revolutionary impact of the RAF movement becomes nullified. But the deaths as such have their own significance. The filmmakers' hard task is to negotiate a fine line between addressing the reality of the deaths and moving beyond them to a cogent

69. Mayer, "German October," 161.

70. Elsaesser, "Antigone Agonistes," 12.

71. Recollected by Renate Sami in Margaretha Huber's "Also, was ist denn wirklich? Zu dem Film von Renate Sami über Holger Meins 'es stirbt allerdings ein Jeder . . .'" in *Deutschland im Herbst,* ed. Kraus et al., 71.

72. Baudrillard, "Our Theater of Cruelty," 111.

73. The obsessive quest for truth concerning death is discussed at length in von Trotta's *Marianne and Julianne.*

74. Baudrillard, "Our Theater of Cruelty," 113.

analysis of their causes. As Reitz observes, "When we look at the suicides at Stammheim as isolated incidents, we will render the experiences in that night of, for example, Ensslin, Baader, Raspe to be incomprehensible. As filmmakers, (we should be held accountable) [for the fact that] history is not created, but that stories will be told."[75]

How, then, are the deaths represented? Through allusion and suggestion, silently but never in a fixed or frozen manner. In one instance, at the end of the interview with Horst Mahler, the camera pans up to the rear wall of the cell, focusing on a grated window. This image has been interpreted in a positive light as signifying hope for the future,[76] but this shot also evokes other cell windows, the ones from which Meinhof and Ensslin were found hanged. Later in the film, historical footage shows the execution of Rosa Luxemburg, followed by a still photo of a hanged female body. Once again, this still evokes other bodies hanging. It asks the viewer to fill an empty spot with the images of these figures because the actual experience of the deaths of Ensslin and Meinhof cannot be conveyed verbally or visually but can be expressed only through indirection or absence. Christian Metz has theorized this problematic between plenitude and absence in cinema from a semiotic point of view, while Mary Ann Doane, arguing from a feminist psychoanalytical perspective, links it to initial castration anxiety and fetishism.[77] The taboo or unspeakable surfaces in the form of absence or void at the site of the trauma. In the period immediately following the traumatic experiences of 1977, the filmmakers could address the Stammheim deaths only indirectly.

Fassbinder provides another instance of implicit referencing in the scene of *Germany in Autumn* that has generated most discussions, the exhibitionist display of his naked body in front of the camera. Rentschler notes that this episode at once "enacts the collective's worst fears, showing a subject so overwhelmed that he cannot actively respond" and serves "to dramatize the deformation of self and the environment, to portray the melancholic left."[78] He also interprets Fassbinder's body as a commodity,

---

75. "Wenn wir die Selbstmorde von Stammheim als Ereignisse behandeln, werden wir dazu beitragen daß die Erlebnisse von Ensslin, Baader, Raspe z.B. in dieser Nacht für immer unverständlich bleiben. Wir sollten als Filmemacher dafür sorgen, daß Geschichte nie entsteht, aber Geschichten erzählt werden" ("'Deutschland im Herbst' oder 'Modell Deutschland?'" 10).

76. Rentschler, *West German, Film in the Course of Time,* 195.

77. For a concise treatment of absence as a site of production, see Mary Ann Doane, "Film and the Masquerade: Theorizing the Female Spectator" [1982], in *Issues in Feminist Film Criticism,* ed. Patricia Erens (Bloomington: Indiana University Press, 1990), 41–57. Christian Metz, *The Imaginary Signifier: Psychoanalysis and the Cinema* (Bloomington: Indiana University Press, 1995).

78. Rentschler, *West German Film in the Course of Time,* 193.

as a narcissistic surface, and as a corpse that foreshadows the director's own death in 1982. Whether foreshadowing Fassbinder's death or not, the representation of his naked male body evokes an actual corpse or perhaps two corpses—Baader's and Raspe's—a basic image that Schlöndorff picks up in his Antigone episode, where the naked corpse of the dead Polyneices is shown lying akimbo on the stage. The same tragic theme reverberates in footage from the early 1930s where revolutionaries sing a song with the refrain, "There stands a man, man. . . . Perhaps by tomorrow, he too will be a corpse like so many freedom fighters." In this instance, the filmmakers' sympathies clearly lie with the dead "terrorists," which are linked to "freedom fighters."

Many other scenes evoke the death of the subject, overtly or implicitly—not only the deaths of the RAF members but also those of their victims. One difficult problem in shooting *Germany in Autumn* was the treatment of Hanns Martin Schleyer's death. The RAF held Schleyer hostage: as an "innocent victim," he was eventually executed to serve as an example. Conversely, Schleyer's politics and ideology—he was a former SS member and a modern industrialist (chief executive officer of Mercedes-Benz)—were tainted with virtual guilt and hence potentially justified from a radical left-wing perspective. The way out of this dilemma could be shown only indirectly. Thus, during Schleyer's funeral in the opening sequence of the film, the camera lingers on the face of a middle-aged man with a *schmiss* (dueling scar) on his cheek, indicating the authoritarian legacy that placed him in the position of a high-ranking officer. This image is followed by an upward pan of the camera coming to rest on three Esso flags flying against a clear sky. The two successive images function, like Tom Conley's "film hieroglyphs," as a bridge linking Schleyer's Nazi past and his contemporary association with big industry.[79] If the Esso logo suggests the past—at least a past with the SS—it also refers to the global politics of oil and, indirectly, the associated automobile industry. Furthermore, on the level of intertextuality, Esso refers to the symbolic function of the Esso sign in *Far from Vietnam,* where it evokes the Third World exploitation by imperialism and by war crimes in Vietnam. It was, after all, outrage against the Vietnam War that prompted the nascence of the RAF movement.

These suggestions were not sufficient to dispel the ambivalence of Schleyer's tragedy. His Nazi past emerges finally in the reading of his September 9–10 letter, a testament before his death, which concludes with the haunting words, "it is never sweet and agreeable to die for the fatherland."

---

79. Tom Conley, *Film Hieroglyphs: Ruptures in Classical Cinema* (Minneapolis: University of Minnesota Press, 1991).

The viewer is left to fill in the picture suggested by these allusions. The only "real" visual image of Schleyer appears on a television monitor shown during his funeral: it is the official publicized media image. In that sense, the cameras treat Schleyer as neutrally as they do Baader, Ensslin, and Meinhof. He seems to be privileged by the acoustic resonance of his words when Kluge reads Schleyer's letter to his son; however, because Kluge's voice is heard, the words are already removed from Schleyer to a certain degree and appropriated by the filmmaker. Finally, the certitude of death—anyone's death—emerges as the underlying theme of the film. This is not an optimistic message, but, then, on the side of pseudodocumentary content, *Germany in Autumn* narrates a grim true story.

V. Gendering Violence

A more optimistic message is conveyed by two fictional figures, Gabi Teichert and Franziska Busch, who, by virtue of the porosity of the essay genre, are threaded throughout *Germany in Autumn.* Teichert is a schoolteacher who, dissatisfied with the history told in textbooks, sets out on a quest—across snow-covered fields and woods—to discover Germany's "true" history that has been hidden from public knowledge.[80] Busch seeks to make sense of what is happening by questioning images that had been recorded technologically: we see her viewing a filmed interview with Mahler, attending a recording session with Wolf Biermann, and filming her own revolutionary film. Her understanding of history is always mediated. In contrast, Teichert seeks to find answers in contemporary politics and attends public meetings. Both Busch and Teichert are thus interpreters with whom the viewer can identify. They have an interactive experience with history to create an alternative public sphere that competes with that of mass media, thereby providing an alternative model for spectators to follow.

It is not coincidental that both characters are female. Throughout *Germany in Autumn,* opposition to the establishment voice is resolutely gendered. Much has been made of Schlöndorff's contribution, which deals with passing through censors a made-for-television staged production of *Antigone,* one of the great female figures of the mythical past. As Elsaesser notes, "Antigone's name trails with it an entire post-romantic politics of interpretation, connoting rebellion and opposition to the State, as well as an order of refusal and resistance of such categorical negation that it challenges the foundations of any form of government, a subject of evident rel-

80. Kluge subsequently developed this vignette into a full-length film, *The Patriot* (1978).

evance in West Germany, since the Bonn government considered itself the sole representative of the German Reich, an ambiguous mandate given the Nazi legacy, and precisely the one contested by the RAF's violent protest."[81] There is an evident connection both to Meinhof and Ensslin and to Sophie Scholl and Rosa Luxemburg, who (as cited in the film) said that Germany has only two choices: "socialism or barbarism." With *Antigone,* the figures of female "enemies of the state" are reinforced and their public "punishment" is once again condemned. Antigone's story calls to mind how women in the RAF, especially Meinhof and Ensslin, were vilified on the basis of their gender, typified by the mass media as "whores," "unnatural mothers," or even "crazies." Of course, Antigone, and hence her posterity, were heroines up to and including the moment of their death.

A similar theme permeates the song recorded in *Germany in Autumn* by Wolf Biermann, *Mädchen aus Stuttgart* (Girl from Stuttgart):

> I met a girl and that hurt
> Tears were streaming down her face
> She cried, who says, who says
> Who says she killed herself
> In Fibinger's Superjail, that'd be a joke
> Just like Ulrike—who says so
> They always twist it around to suit themselves
> Baader, Ensslin, Raspe
> The alchemist of the revolution
> I think it's both—They did it
> And it was done to them
> Despairing of themselves, despairing of us
> And they took the last dark steps
> As a threesome, all alone
> Yes, if the poor disheartened girl was right
> And if it came clear within a year that their
> Suicide wasn't a suicide
> You, don't fool yourself, too many would like it
> This way, beer would taste better, they'd be
> Happy, like about those splendid fellows at
> The GSG9
> Then it will turn out otherwise—the number of
> People in this lovely country who die by their own
> Hand would increase rapidly

81. Elsaesser, "Antigone Agonistes," 5.

What to do with the tears
What is to become of her, what about the
Girl, specially in this blooming land of crisis?
I'll probably be seeing her picture soon, it'll be in a row with
the others,
In the window of the bakery, and a hand armed with a pen
Will scratch out with a scrawl her human face.

Biermann's song parallels Baudrillard's remarks about the public obsession with the truth (or lie) of the RAF's alleged suicides. Biermann observes how once the label *terrorist* is affixed, all personal identity is effaced—something that the filmmakers of *Germany in Autumn* sought to avoid in their decision neither to use the term nor to directly display media images characterizing them as such. The film's photos Ensslin and Baader show them exchanging smiles in a Paris café, looking like any young people, a choice that fails to explain why the press and the public sphere, including the state, focused so much on these women's gender. What remains unanswered is what made the women seem to be more threatening than men, what taboo they had broken.

Catherine Clément argues that the figure of the bourgeois woman gone awry is particularly threatening to the public sphere.[82] To be sure, at the time of Baader-Meinhof, much was made in the press of Meinhof and Ensslin's middle-class backgrounds, university educations, and (failed) roles as mothers. Percolating beneath the surface is fear—fear of an explosion destroying the clichéd view of women as passive individuals and obedient citizens. On a certain level, the RAF movement could be read as a gendered rebellion directed against the fatherland. The anonymous German tract "Violent Women," written in response to the German Autumn, states, "The State, this super-father, who sends with a deafening roar his glistening penises into the skies, erects his petrified penises so that we can't see our neighbors, not to mention the sky."[83] The RAF movement was certainly perceived as a revolt by the younger generation against their fathers' and Hitler's Germany. But the break of sons with their fathers has been for some time a regular trope in Western civilization, becoming, as it were, domesticated. What has not been domesticated and remains scandalous is the revolt of women. "Violent Women" concludes, "We who are hated, who are betrayed, the new youth: women, sons, children, the elderly, the

82. Catharine B. Clément, "Charlatans and Hysterics," in *The Cabinet of Dr. Caligari: Texts, Contexts, Histories,* ed., Mike Budd (New Brunswick, N.J.: Rutgers University Press, 1990), 191–204.

83. "Violent Women," trans. Wynn Gundarson, *Semiotext(e): The German Issue* 4, no. 2 (1982): 149.

insane, criminals, terrorists, anarchists, gays, radical leftists—in a word, social outcasts. *We,* the partisans of life, the swamp of your dreams, which you have to dredge in vain. *We,* your crazy people. Get out of our way, otherwise fur will fly! Viva Medusa!"[84] One hears the echo of the dream-like fantasy evoked in the Buback Obituary. For the nightmarish visions of the RAF showed how the political views that had been persecuted under Hitler continued to be persecuted by the state in the 1970s. The RAF females in particular seemed to call for an uncanny return of the evil mother—an "uncanny effect," which, according to Freud, is "produced when the distinction between imagination and reality is effaced, as when something that we have hitherto regarded as imaginary appears before us in reality," releasing the secrets buried in a swamp.[85] From a Freudian perspective, the German Autumn brought to the surface an underground explosion of the repressed potential of the Other.

One could continue to explore the murky terrain of the uncanny. Why all the references to hanging? Was there somewhere between conscience and the unconscious, a truly uncanny memory, or trigger, released by another primal scene, another tragic woman who hanged herself in a prison cell? Could it have been the ghost of Ilse Koch of Buchenwald camp, imprisoned after the Nuremberg trials and found dead in 1967? A double-edged sword is pointed at women: on the one hand, they stand as revolutionary victims of the male state; on the other hand, their suppressed violence, failing to be directed toward progressive causes, can be used in the gory service of the state. Is it equally important for new generations to question their mothers as well as their fathers?

VI. The Future

A last double question remains: to whom is the film ultimately addressed? What is it intended to achieve? It opens with Schleyer's funeral and his letter to his son. Following the funeral, Kluge reads another letter aloud, this one written in 1945 by a Frau Wilde, who identifies herself as a mother of five and proclaims, "When cruelty arrives at a certain point, it is no longer important who initiated it; it should only stop." These exact words fill the

84. "Violent Women," 150.

85. Sigmund Freud, "The 'Uncanny'" [1919], in *The Standard Edition of the Complete Psychological Works of Sigmund Freud,* ed. James Strachey (London: Hogarth Press, 1955), 17:244. Freud cites from Gutzkow: "'The Zecks [a family name] are all 'heimlich'. 'Heimlich'? . . . What do you understand by 'heimlich'? "Well, . . . they are like a buried spring or a dried-up pond. One cannot walk over it without always having the feeling that water might come up there again." "Oh, we call it 'unheimlich'; you call it 'heimlich'. Well, what makes you think there is something secret and untrustworthy about this family?" ("The 'Uncanny,'" 223).

screen at the end of the film. Letter from a father, letter from a mother—the entire structure of *Germany in Autumn* is dominated by such historical doubling.[86] It reaches historical irony with the figure of Rommel, then the mayor of Stuttgart, who, without consulting the city council, decided to allow Baader, Ensslin, and Raspe to be buried in a city cemetery. The same Rommel is introduced early on in the film. Following Gabi Teichert's first forays in her attempt to unearth German history, footage from the 1930s is borrowed from a Third Reich newsreel that records the funeral of Feldmarschall Erwin Rommel, the Desert Fox. Nazi Party members are believed to have pressured that Rommel to commit suicide. In a voice-over accompanying the old footage, Kluge identifies the figure of Rommel's son, witnessing the hypocrisy of the pompous state funeral. This son shows a streak of humanity in dealing, with speed and dignity, with the burials of Baader, Ensslin, and Raspe and thus redeems the uncertain memory of his father, perhaps a decent man but certainly a soldier for Hitler—a filial act of contrition. A son, we have seen, is also evoked at Schleyer's funeral, both as recipient of a letter and a target of the camera—he is about the same age as young Rommel during his father's funeral. There is another son. During the burials of Baader, Ensslin, and Raspe, a young boy is filmed watching silently as the metal caskets are placed in the earth; as he leaves the cemetery he is again captured by the camera, shooting through the rear window of a car. The child is always alone, never identified, but it seems pretty clear he is the orphaned son of Ensslin and Vesper. The camera lingers on his face, begging the question of what his future will be. In a seemingly unmotivated slice, right before the funeral scene, a print is inserted of Leonardo da Vinci's image of a child in utero, about to be born. This poignant image suggests an as yet unborn hope that lies in the future generation. It also evokes the words of Rosa Luxemburg that Kluge spoke earlier in the film: "I was, I am, I will be." The penultimate visual image on the screen before the letter of Frau Wilde is that of a long tracking shot following from behind the figures of an anonymous mother and daughter as they leave the funeral trying to catch a ride in the rain; the music on the sound track is a Joan Baez folk song, *Here's to You,* that honors two Italian anarchists, Nicola Sacco and Bartolomeo Vanzetti, who were executed in United States in 1927. The filmmakers of *Germany in Autumn* are clearly forging a link between the manner in which states all over the globe punish antiauthoritarian political idealism regardless of age or gender. Baez's refrain, "The last and final moment is yours, their agony is your triumph," echoes hauntingly over the final images.

86. Elsaesser, "Antigone Agonistes," explores the implications of this doubling structure.

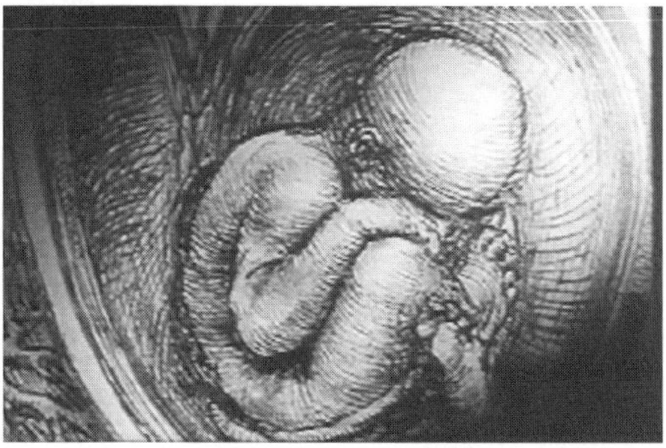

da Vinci print. (Video caption from *Germany in Autumn.*)

Young boy. (Video caption from *Germany in Autumn.*)

The unborn child in its mother's womb, the daughter and mother leaving the funeral—these are figures of a future that seems to have no roots in the filmic present. They are about to break or have broken with a past heavy with guilt and memories and a present that celebrates the public death of those who openly confronted and challenged the status quo.

Within the time set of the film is a more tangible tomorrow, flowing from the past and the present without a real break but as ambiguous as its sources. It is presented in the form of a triple pattern of two generations: three sons—three males, like most previous German leaders—who are set free to shape the new history after the ritual death of their parents, and three sets of parents, identified with fathers in two cases and with the mother in a more hopeful third. First comes the son of Schleyer, the standard-bearer of the terrorist state, ridden with old Nazis: a heavy inheritance indeed, further burdened with the memory of the father's execution. Will that first son's background and understandable resentment, so symptomatic for many youth of the 1960s, direct him to the same right-wing politics as his father? Will he and his peers and their sons in turn freeze the flow of time into an eternal winter, withering the hopes of the German Autumn? Or will the second son, the young Rommel, come to terms, like his father, with the need to compromise ethical values or to close the eyes and the ears of conscience to efficiently protect the state against its political and economic enemies? Will he turn his back on the ambiguous death of his father, forgive or forget the past, and, emulated by the new leaders of the German miracle, exemplify the model of the successful young manager? The film gives no hints about his fate or of the fate of the modern Germany that he might build up. Nor are predictions made about the third child, Ensslin's son. Her death, carried out by the state, and her female gender make her a positive parental figure (like the woman with the daughter); by the film's internal logic, her son could be expected to carry on the good fight, to rally around the memory of victims of the establishment: soldiers killed during the war, poor or unemployed workers, minorities—the best of the youth, ready for sacrifices in the name of idealism. The last, highly symbolic scenes—the reading aloud of a mother's letter and the unidentified mother and daughter walking away from the camera to the strains of Joan Baez's guitar—evoke an image of nurturing motherhood that seeks to replace that of deadly male aggression. Left open is what role the third son will play—will his legacy be that of Antigone's, or will he be inserted in the patriarchal continuum of history? The future is both distant and unpredictable; however, it is interesting to note that not only male children were left behind: Ulrike Meinhof had twin daughters, one of whom, Bettina Röhl, exposed the hypocrisy of German foreign minister Oskar Fischer. (Fischer, like many, sought to hide his earlier affiliation with left-wing organizations. Disgusted by his disavowal, Röhl sent to the press a photograph of Fischer hitting a police officer during a demonstration.)[87]

Without giving clear answers, *Germany in Autumn* poses the questions and encourages thinking about them and formulating ideal answers. In other terms, without saying so, it urges spectators to become committed to a political idea, specifically a left-wing ideology. Nothing is totally clear, all is suggested between the lines, and yet the final message is as persuasive as an essay film can make it—or, rather, as only an essay film could make it. In the form of representation, in the blurring of boundaries between

87. Röhl is finishing a book, *Sag mir, wo Du stehst,* about the history of student protest organizations and the RAF. For further information, see <www.bettinaroehl.de/home.html>.

documents and art, in the heterogeneous fragments telling the same story—in short, in all the cracks in the filmic texture—one is faced with a disturbing evocation of something hidden, half-buried. This mystery subtly reflects the mystery surrounding the RAF and the fate of its leaders. Only the essay film format, with its whispered questions, could refer so effectively, yet inconclusively on the surface, to the fine line between good and bad terrorism, between political and criminal justice, between the Third Reich and the Federal Republic, between the necessity for and censure of violence. The mixed form of *Germany in Autumn* did some violence of its own to the traditional structures and forms of filmmaking in Germany. It was not a coincidence that one year later, in 1979, the groundbreaking Hamburg Declaration by young film directors noted that they would no longer let their work "be divided—the feature film from the documentary film."[88] Following on the steps of the most radical postwar political upheaval in Germany and perhaps responding to the same social and cultural developments, a formal filmic revolution was preparing the ground for an eye-opening new series of committed essay films such as Harun Farocki's *Images of the World and the Inscription of War.*

88. "The Hamburg Declaration" [1979], in *West German Filmmakers on Film,* ed. Rentschler, 4.

CHAPTER 3

The Political Im/perceptible: Farocki's *Images of the World and the Inscription of War*

> The essay's innermost formal law is heresy. Through violations of the orthodoxy of thought, something in the object becomes visible which is orthodoxy's secret and objective aim to keep invisible.
>
> —Theodor W. Adorno, "The Essay as Form"

> Once more, but in a different sense, filmmaking has to go underground, disperse itself, make itself invisible. . . . Only by turning itself into "writing" in the largest possible sense can film preserve itself as [what Harun Farocki calls] "a form of intelligence."
>
> —Thomas Elsaesser, "Working at the Margins"

> Just as weapons and armor developed in unison throughout history, so visibility and invisibility now began to evolve together, eventually producing *invisible weapons that make things visible.*
>
> —Paul Virilio, *War and Cinema*

During the 1970s and 1980s Harun Farocki was not as well known as Fassbinder, Schlöndorff, and Kluge—the group that comprised what came to be known as New German Cinema. Yet Farocki's films constituted more of a departure from or radical alternative to dominant cinematic practice. Farocki was a member of the first year class of the Deutsche Film und Fernsehakademie Berlin (DFFB), and his classmates included Helke Sanders, Hartmut Bitmosky, Wolfgang Peterson, and former protester and activist Holger Meins. Though Farocki was not an active member of the RAF, he, like many of his colleagues, clearly sympathized with RAF politics, and during the late 1960s he produced several collaborative agitational films such as *Nicht löschbares Feuer* (Inextinguishable Fire, 1968); *Anleitung, Polizisten den Helm abzureißen* (Instructions on Taking Away Security/Power from the Police, 1968); and *Drei Schüsse auf Rudi* (Three Shots at Rudi, 1968). In 1975 he paid direct tribute to Meins with an experimental memorial film, *Es stirbt allerdings ein Jeder* (Everybody Must Die), and in 1981 Farocki made *Etwas wird sichtbar* (Before Your Eyes), a meditation on two students who meet each other at an anti–Vietnam War demonstration in Berlin and discuss the possibilities of political resistance and activism within the parameters of acceptable behavior. Farocki has been producing films for the past thirty years, many of the earlier ones in collaboration with filmmakers such as Hartmut Bitomsky.[1] Most of Farocki's films problematize technologies of visual representation and reproduction, generally exposing the views inculcated by mass media and/or contrasting them with more independent coverage of the same events.[2] To some extent, Farocki's films carry on the critique set forth in *Germany in Autumn* and address the differences and similarities between what might be called a visual public sphere and a visual private sphere. His works are clearly informed by Walter Benjamin's critique of "mechanical reproducibility," by Hans Magnus Enzensberger's "consciousness industry," and by contemporary critical theory's exposure of the totalitarian aspect of enlightenment. Thus, for example, Farocki's recent work, *Gefängnisbilder* (I Thought I Was Seeing Prisoners, 2000), examines surveillance tapes from California penitentiaries and exposes the perverse practice of prison employees who arrange and wager bets on (deadly) fights between prisoners.

Although Fassbinder, Schlöndorff, Kluge, and Wenders constructed a filmmaking practice in opposition to "Papas Kino" and Hollywood, they worked within West German funding structures and cinematic institutions. In sharp contrast, since his initial forays into filmmaking as a member of DFFB, Farocki has independently produced—that is, without public sponsorship—almost all of his films. This independence and its

1. For a comprehensive overview of Farocki's career, see Rolf Aurich and Ulrich Kreist, eds., *Der Ärger mit den Bildern: Die Filme von Harun Farocki* (Stuttgart: Europäisches Medienforum, 1998); Tilman Baumgärtel, "Vom Guerillakino zum Essayfilm: Harun Farocki" (Ph.D. diss., Heinrich Heine University, 1997). For a collection of Farock's own writings, see the dual language *Nachdruck/Imprint: Texte/Writings* (New York: Lukas and Steinberg, 2001).

2. For example, his 1981 *Etwas wird Sichtbar* (Before Your Eyes: Vietnam) looks at how the Vietnam War was represented and spectacularized by the mass media, and his 1986 *Wie man sieht* (As You See) stresses that the viewer must always read between the lines of images. More recent are the 1991 *Leben- BRD* (How to Live in the FRG), an ironic critique of self-help groups and the opposition they face, and a year later *Videogramme einer Revolution* (Videogram of a Revolution), in which Farocki compares CNN media coverage of the Romanian revolution to home videos taken by Romanians at the time of the upheaval.

resulting lack of financial resources is an integral component of Farocki's filmic practice, for it informs his politics of image production: formally, stylistically, thematically, and materially. In Farocki's first full-length film, *Zwischen zwei Kriegen* (Between Two Wars, 1977), the filmmaker appears and gives the following statement: "When one doesn't have money for cars, shooting, nice clothes; when one doesn't have money to make images in which film time and film life flow uninterruptedly/independently, then one has to put one's effort into intelligently putting together separate elements: a montage of ideas."[3]

The difficult material circumstances surrounding Farocki's film production have differed significantly from those of Wenders, Ottinger, the former state subsidized H&S, Barbara and Winfried Junge, and other better-known, commercially successful filmmakers who did not work under extreme economic constraints. This economic independence contributed to Farocki's development of his special technique: as an independent avant-garde leftist working on the periphery of the German and European film-subsidy system, he recycled commercial material that he had produced for his paying customers, including German industry and television (though some of his made-for-TV shows were not broadcast).[4] Financing his essay films by making traditional industrial documentaries, he thus participated, however critically, in what is called the *Verbundsystem,* as he stated—not without irony—in a 1975 issue of *Filmkritik:*

> Following the example of the steel industry . . . I try to create a *Verbund* with my work. The basic research for a project I finance with a radio broadcast, some of the books I use I review for the book programmes, and many of the things I notice during this kind of work end up in my television features.[5]

And eventually in his essay films.

In the 1920s Soviet filmmaker Esther Schub perfected the strategy of film production known as compilation film, which relies primarily on using previously shot or existent material. Whereas Schub was working

3. "Wenn man kein Geld für Autos, Schießereien, schöne Kleider, wenn man kein Geld hat für Bilder, die Film-Zeit, das Filmleben von selber verstreichen lassen, dann muß man seine Kraft in die Intelligenz Verbindung der einzelnen Elemente legen: Die Montage der Ideen."

4. See Thomas Elsaesser, *New German Cinema: A History* (New Brunswick, N.J.: Rutgers University Press, 1989), 82–83.

5. Harun Farocki, "Notwendige Abwechselung und Vielfalt," *Filmkritik* 224 (August 1975): 368–69; cited in Elsaesser, *New German Cinema,* 82–83.

with celluloid, Farocki was one of the first German filmmakers to have access to a video camera in the late 1960s. He immediately became aware of the liberating and democratizing potential of the new technology. The video camera enabled him—and others without financial means—to make films on a bare-bones budget, to make something out of nothing. This cinematic practice might adequately be termed a "cinema povera." This economy of means required creative thinking about alternative ways of producing images for his films, since expensive shoots were out of the question. The solution was to shift emphasis onto montage and editing to produce meaning. These choices have important implications, not merely for the material practice of filmmaking (that is, the multiple economic determinations on Farocki as a cultural worker) but also for the im/perceptible political points made—consciously and unconsciously—by his specific films, including his remarkable 1988–89 *Images of the World and the Inscription of War* (Bilder der Welt und Inschrift des Krieges).[6] This film ambitiously brings together crucial aspects of Farocki's filmic theory and production while marking a significant turning point in German history: it was released on the eve of German reunification and the imagined end of the Cold War.

I. Im/perceptibility and Essay Film

Farocki's *Images of the World and the Inscription of War* is an essay film that articulates the formal and aesthetic with the historical and political in the context of modern—and increasingly postmodern—mass media, technoculture, and technowarfare. On the one hand, *Images of the World and the Inscription of War* is a specifically West German leftist response to events of the 1980s; on the other, it raises the perennial problem of the relation between vision and visuality and projects this issue into an uncertain future of technical developments—the digital image synthesis, dubbed "Scitex," and/or the "reconfigured eye"[7]—which render age-old questions about the nature of representation and truth increasingly technologically obsolete yet philosophically relevant. Poised on the shifting boundary between the modern and the postmodern, *Images of the World and the*

6. Harun Farocki, *Images of the World and the Inscription of War,* 16mm, color, 75 min., Harun Farocki Filmproduktion, 1988–89. The English voice-over has been transcribed with slight variations as Harun Farocki, "Commentary from *Images of the World and the Inscription of War,*" *Discourse* 15 (spring 1993): 78–92.

7. See Brian Winston, *Claiming the Real: The Documentary Film Revisited* (London: BFI, 1995), chap. 2, "The Documentary, Scitex and Harry"; William J. Mitchell, *The Reconfigured Eye: Visual Truth in the Post-Photographic Era* (Cambridge: MIT Press, 1993).

Inscription of War addresses aesthetic issues that are transhistorical and transglobal.

Images of the World and the Inscription of War is a technically and ideologically overdetermined work that covers a lot of conceptual and historical ground. Farocki acknowledges that in addition to the financial advantages of working in video, the tapes allow for films that can be seen and reseen, the way one reads a book, thereby allowing for a certain density and unclarity and a crucial shift in the production of meaning onto the spectator. Heavily influenced by Brecht, Farocki stresses that for him, a film is political only to the extent that it has a political effect on the audience, and that effect is mobilized when one can watch it more than once. As implied/applied theory, *Images of the World and the Inscription of War* is an extended investigation into the nature of vision and visuality in relation to modern technologies of image production and into the way of perceiving and interpreting both vision and visuality from a phenomenological point of view. *Vision* here means "sight as a physical operation" (the capacity and action of seeing), and *visuality* means "sight as a social fact" (the understanding and modality of seeing). This duality corresponds roughly to the ancient distinction between nature and culture, reread as what Hal Foster calls "the datum of vision and its discursive determinations." As Foster notes, both sets of distinction are relative: "vision is social and historical too, and visuality involves the body and the psyche."[8] A third key term could also be added here: the Heideggerian category of *Umsicht,* or visibility, which refers to the field of precognitive, prereflective circumspection (expectation of seeing) within which viewers find themselves.[9] Vision could also be converted into Lacanian psychoanalytical terms, in that visibility may also be viewed as seeingness (*voyure*)—an apparently inaccessible category imagined to be anterior to the determining split between "gaze and look," or, as in one of Lacan's succinct for-

8. Hal Foster, *Vision and Visuality* (Seattle: Bay Press, 1988), ix. According to Foster, *vision* and *visuality* are two interrelated but significantly separate terms: "the difference between the terms signals a difference within the visual—between the mechanism of sight and its historical techniques, between the datum of vision and its discursive determinations—a difference, many differences, among how we see, how we are able, allowed, or made to see, and how we see this seeing or unseen therein" (*Vision and Visuality,* ix).

9. See Martin Heidegger, "The Age of the World Picture" [1938], in *The Question Concerning Technology and Other Essays,* trans. William Lovitt (New York: Harper and Row, 1977), 116. For the original, see "Die Zeit des Weltbildes," in his *Holzwege* (Frankfurt am Main: Vittorio Klostermann, 1972). This concept is favored by Thomas Keenan, who has carried out extensive analyses of *Images of the World and the Inscription of War.* For Keenan, Farocki's film is directly related to Heideggerian visibility (see Keenan, "Light Weapons," *Documents* 1–2 [fall–winter 1992]: 147–58).

mulations, "I see only from one point [a look], but in my existence I am looked at from all sides."[10] Like visibility, seeingness is the never quite visible precondition of the radically unsuturable look-gaze split.[11] To grasp *Images of the World and the Inscription of War* adequately, another pair of terms must be subtended to this discussion: the political in/visible and in/audible that moves stealthily beneath, within, and around vision, visuality, and visibility or seeingness.

Visibility, or seeingness, provides *Images of the World and the Inscription of War* with the ontological precondition that anything can be seen or that anything can be revealed or concealed, can be visible or invisible, including any possible "image of the world" or "inscription of war" and its ideological connotations. Farocki addresses that issue, albeit more empirically than theoretically.[12] The film interrogates photographic processes of image making and the surrounding disciplines that use these images: fine arts, engineering, architecture, artisanal and assembly-line production, city planning and urban renewal, military science and practice. In that sense, Farocki's "world" resembles what cultural theorist Fredric Jameson calls the "geopolitical aesthetic" of late capitalism, which is never perceivable as totality.[13] But, at the same time, *Images of the World and the Inscription of War* also focuses on the political in/visible, with additional attention to and manipulation of the political in/audible. In fact, the film's formal and political achievement as well as its limi-

10. Jacques Lacan, *The Four Fundamental Concepts of Psycho-Analysis* [1973], ed. Jacques-Alain Miller, trans. Alan Sheridan (New York: Norton, 1981), 82, 72.

11. This Lacanian framework informs Kaja Silverman's analysis of *Images of the World and the Inscription of War* (see Silverman, "What Is a Camera? or: History in the Field of Vision," *Discourse* 15 [spring 1993]: 3–56; reprinted with minor changes in Silverman, *The Threshold of the Visible World* [New York: Routledge, 1996], chap. 4, "The Gaze").

12. As Silverman notes, Jonathan Crary's work on what he calls "techniques of the observer" helps clarify that aspect of Farocki's *Images of the World and the Inscription of War* as well as Lacanian and Heideggerian approaches to it. Crary problematizes, by historicizing, not only ahistorical theories of the ways viewers and viewing are constructed but also contemporary "attempts to theorize vision and visuality [that] are wedded to models that emphasize a continuous and overarching Western visual tradition." Crary argues that "during the first decades of the nineteenth century a new kind of observer took shape in Europe radically different from the type of observer in the seventeenth and eighteenth centuries," that this paradigm shift had much to do with technologies leading up to and including photography, and that "concepts of subjective vision, of the productivity of the observer, pervaded not only areas of art and literature but were present in philosophical, scientific, and technological discourses." A new viewing subject, an embodied vision, was produced (Crary, *Techniques of the Observer: On Vision and Modernity in the Nineteenth Century* [Cambridge: MIT Press, 1990], 25, 6, 9). Precisely such a viewer is the subject and object of Farocki's film.

13. See Fredric Jameson, *The Geopolitical Aesthetic: Cinema and Space in the World System* (Bloomington: Indiana University Press, 1992).

tations reside precisely in the tension between in/audibility and in/visibility—hence in im/perceptibility.

The "in/visible" is perhaps best captured in a provocative remark by Louis Althusser:

> what classical political economy does not see, is not what it does not see, it is *what it sees;* it is not what it lacks, on the contrary, it is *what it does not lack;* it is not what it misses, on the contrary, it is *what it does not miss.* This oversight, then, is not to see what one sees, the oversight no longer concerns the object, but *the sight* itself.[14]

Althusser specifically means that classical political economy both sees (perceives) and does not see (acknowledge) the determining but not fully representable role of labor and class struggle in history. This perspective is surely applicable to *Images of the World and the Inscription of War* to the extent that the film both reveals and conceals the impact of the political economy on Farocki. Even when *Images of the World and the Inscription of War* draws manifest links between vision and politics, some significant economic determinations may remain im/perceptible, just as, in the dynamics of Theodor Adorno's *Vexierbild,* or picture puzzle of political economy, most workers are increasingly unable to perceive that they are workers.[15] Furthermore, if the political unconscious is indeed *un*conscious and needs investigation "to lead to the unmasking of cultural artefacts as socially symbolic acts,"[16] then one must expect to encounter the political im/perceptible on the un/canny boundaries of the human sensorial grasp of the world. This is also the shifting site of art, since, to quote Adorno, "the *Vexierbild* is a good-natured reprise of the serious vexation perpetrated by every art work. Like art it hides something while at the same time showing it."[17] In his use of preexistent images, Farocki

14. Louis Althusser and Étienne Balibar, *Reading Capital* [1965–68], trans. Ben Brewster (London: NLB, 1970), 21. This remark also figures prominently in Martin Jay's *Downcast Eyes: The Denigration of Vision in Twentieth-Century French Thought* (Berkeley: University of California Press, 1993), in his chapter entitled "Lacan, Althusser, and the Specular Subject of Ideology." But whereas Jay uses Althusser's text to buttress his thesis that "a plurality of scopic regimes" ought to replace his (problematic) claim that recent French thought has "denigrated" vision, my own inclination is to use Althusser's remark more simply as a salutary warning against our assuming that we have seen what we think we have seen. And I argue that this is Farocki's warning as well.

15. Theodor W. Adorno, *Minima Moralia: Reflections from Damaged Life* [1951], trans. E. F. N. Jephcott (London: NLB, 1974), 193–94.

16. Fredric Jameson, *The Political Unconscious: Narrative as a Socially Symbolic Act* (Ithaca: Cornell University Press, 1981), 20.

17. Theodor W. Adorno, *Aesthetic Theory,* ed. Gretel Adorno and Rolf Tiedemann, trans. C. Lenhardt (1970; London: Routledge and Kegan Paul, 1984), 178.

accesses an audiovisual archive, the use of which has been theorized by Alan Sekula as capable of "liberating" the possibility of meaning "from the actual contingencies of use. But this liberation is also a loss," Sekula continues, "an abstraction from the complexity and richness of use, a loss of context. . . . So new meanings come to supplant old ones, with the archive serving as a 'clearing house' of meaning."[18] Farocki finds existent texts to put together an alternative history, and though he removes the documents from their archival context, he attempts to show the other image in the *Vexierbild.* In his words, "One has to encounter an image or thought at least twice to see what happened to it, how it has been transformed by a new context."[19] What is perceptible in some respects remains simultaneously imperceptible in others, but this im/perceptibility is not random: it has specific political causes and consequences for specific instances of production and reception.

Farocki's film illustrates that notion of im/perceptibility in showing that people can look without really seeing. Is this failure conscious or unconscious, natural or cultural, physical or psychological? Farocki offers no answers, nor does he really ask questions. Rather, he manipulates the potential of the essay film to stimulate questions in the viewer's mind. In that sense, he takes up the challenge of Adorno's thesis that in an age of the persistent and irreversible methodological reduction of reason to scientism and instrumentality, "in the realm of thought it is virtually the essay alone that has successfully raised doubts about the absolute privilege of method."[20] Perhaps paradoxically, when showing/concealing the im/perceptible, Farocki expands the realm of thought to a modern audiovisual mass medium—the essay film—that favors techniques of sub-rosa persuasion.[21]

Among the various acknowledged secondary features of the essay film, Farocki's film most manifestly displays techniques requiring reading

---

18. Alan Sekula, "Reading an Archive," in *Blasted Allegories,* ed. Brian Wallis (Cambridge: MIT Press, 1987), 116.

19. "Mindestens zweimal muß ein Bild oder ein Gedanke schon vorkommen, damit man sieht, was aus ihm wurde, wie er sich verändert in einem neuen Zusammenhang" (quoted in Baumgärtel, "Vom Guerillakino zum Essayfilm," 145).

20. Theodor W. Adorno, "The Essay as Form" [1954–58], in *Notes to Literature,* ed. Rolf Tiedemann, trans. Shierry Weber Nicholsen (New York: Columbia University Press, 1991), 9.

21. In addition to Marker and Godard, these essay filmmakers include Derek Jarman, Kidlat Tahimik, Trinh T. Minh-ha, and Orson Welles, as well as, in the German-speaking world, Hartmut Bitomsky, Werner Herzog, Alexander Kluge, Elfi Mikesch, Ulrike Ottinger, Rosa von Praunheim, Helke Sander, and Wim Wenders—to mention but a few. Clearly, this is a not a homogeneous group. And Farocki and his group *Filmkritik* explicitly took their distance, in theory and in practice, from Wenders, Herzog, and Kluge. An in-depth study of the essay film as an international movement remains to be done.

between the lines, or locating the message, as with *Germany in Autumn,* in the splits between documentary versus fiction and truth versus fantasy. It is in the breaks, reiterations, ambiguities, veiled prolapses and anachronisms, misdirections, verbal or visual puns, and other free-play spaces of essay films that *Images of the World and the Inscription of War* conceals and reveals its im/perceptible politics and challenges the attention of viewers (and historians). Conversely, perhaps because of his ideological commitment or theoretical inclination, Farocki avoids the structural tension between narrativity and specularity, the story and the image, that marks many essay films (notably *Germany in Autumn* or Wim Wenders's *Tokyo-Ga* and *Notebooks on Cities and Clothes*) and, more generally, according to Thomas Elsaesser, most of the New German Cinema, including the avant-garde.[22] The same sobriety or single-mindedness accounts for Farocki's ability to elude two perils nurtured by any essay: excessive self-reflection (a Charybdis threatening to become self-indulgence) and documentary illusion (a Scylla threatening to make illicit claims for total objectivity). In all these ways, favoring an intellectual approach, *Images of the World and the Inscription of War* qualifies as a "form of intelligence" (Farocki's preferred term for essay film) and, to yield its full (political) impact, must be actively coproduced by a relatively educated audience.

II. Vision and Its Others

The multiplicity and heterogeneity of the building blocks of *Images of the World and the Inscription of War* enables Farocki to structure it not only visually but also "musically" so that each social practice he depicts can be associated with key images that recur in a more or less rhythmic fashion and thematic variations. For example, at the beginning, in the middle, and near the end of the film appears an identical sequence of a Hannover water-research laboratory. This reiteration, which might seem unmotivated on its own, is integrated in the structure of the film as a whole with some recurring sequences. In fact, *Images of the World and the Inscription of War* has remarkably few really unmotivated sequences—quite an achievement for a film montaged so extensively from commissioned, ready-made, documentary images. And within that network of associations and reverberations, the Hannover sequence turns out to be particularly significant.

When initially filming the Hannover laboratory, Farocki was not pleased with the results; however, members of the film crew brought to his

22. Thomas Elsaesser, "'*It All Started with These Images*'—Some Notes on Political Filmmaking after Brecht in Germany: Helke Sander and Harun Farocki," *Discourse* 7 (1985): 95–120.

attention that the shot he was seeking already existed in a film archive. Why produce new footage of images and sequences if sufficient ones already exist? Why not employ the images of others? Thus, Farocki dispensed with the auteurist practice of producing his own shots. (Interestingly, Wim Wenders faced a similar conundrum when in Tokyo seeking traces of Ozu's Japan, but instead of using Ozu's footage, Wenders reshot many of the same scenes with the same camera and angle, thereby rendering the images his.) Another consequence of this cannibalistic practice—Farocki's use of commercial footage—is his systematic recourse to well-controlled (and controlling) montage to make sense of the accumulated disparate materials. Farocki explains the importance of montage in an interview with Kaja Silverman, underscoring the basic difference between Soviet (that is, ideological) and American (entertaining) cinema:

> Montage for the Soviets meant the juxtaposition of ideas. For the Americans it meant instead the juxtaposition of narrative components. . . . Soviet montage is very out of fashion these days. Only advertisements and political films use it.[23]

As a form of intelligence (or ideas), Farocki's essay films might then be expected, in their intense use of montage, to be inspired not only by an explicit leftist political tradition (notably Eisenstein's "intellectual montage") but also by a powerful medium of consumer capitalism—that is, commercial advertising films that dominate the culture industry so much that "consumers feel compelled to buy and use products even though they see through them."[24] Thus, montage—or the practice of montage or the mastery of tricks that montage can play—links Farocki's two seemingly incompatible filming activities, enabling and encouraging him to feed his (essay) films with previously produced advertising material.

The resulting personal editing technique creates a new global image with fragmented old images, with both ideological and aesthetic results. Most obviously, this new image echoes Farocki's concern with the way that a constructed technological vision relates to a direct natural vision. Do the two compliment or negate one another, or both?[25] Farocki is aware

23. Harun Farocki and Kaja Silverman, "To Love to Work and to Work to Love—A Conversation about *Passion,*" *Discourse* 15 (spring 1993): 63.

24. Theodor Adorno and Max Horkheimer, *Dialectic of Enlightenment* [1944], trans. John Cumming (New York: Continuum, 1972), 167.

25. Thus Hitchcock liked to insist that there is an irreducible difference between the circular field of the human and camera eye on the one hand and the rectangle of the celluloid and screen frame on the other ("I Wish I Didn't Have to Shoot the Picture: An Interview with Alfred Hitchcock" [1966], in *Focus on Hitchcock,* ed. Albert J. LaValley [Englewood Cliffs, N.J.: Prentice-Hall, 1972], 22–27).

that the camera lens often provides information that viewers normally do not see, in spite and/or because of its visibility—recalling Adorno's conceptualization of the *Vexierbild.* One of the most striking examples in *Images of the World and the Inscription of War* involves a 1944 Allied photograph of IG Farben in Auschwitz: the Auschwitz death camp was shown in the photo yet had was not seen by the CIA until 1977.[26] To clarify the other meaning of this image, Farocki takes viewers rhythmically through a complex montage of seemingly unrelated sequences: the work of Alfred Meydenbauer (the inventor of scale measurement by the use of photography); photographs taken by SS officers in Auschwitz; pictures of unveiled Algerian women taken in 1960 by French soldiers; drawings of the Auschwitz camp made by an inmate, Alfred Kantor; a Dior model being made up in Paris; an art school class; and relatively high-tech computer-generated images, robotized industrial production lines, and flight simulators—all in addition to the aforementioned water-research laboratory in Hannover and the aerial photograph of IG Farben/Auschwitz. *Images of the World and the Inscription of War*'s image track thus implies that the historical purpose of photography—whether scientific, military, forensic, or aesthetic—has been not only to record and preserve but also to mislead, deceive, and even destroy: that is, to aid yet obfuscate vision. In other words, to show the in/visible. Of course, this thematic aspect of the film is itself problematic (intentionally or not), since film in general—and, in particular, this film—is subject to the same visual regime as photography and hence must deceive and obfuscate, not only at the level of sight but also at the level of sound.

This dual function of *Images of the World and the Inscription of War* is notably carried out through the interplay of images and Farocki's verbal narrative that in both the German and English version is spoken (ventriloquized) by a tonally objective and neutral female voice-over. Farocki clearly seeks thematic contrasts by superimposing an intentionally fictional and subjective narrative on the documentary and objective photographic facts. But this strategy, while consistent with the theory and practice of the essay film, raises certain questions in its concrete application to *Images of the World and the Inscription of War.* Why is only a woman's voice heard? And why is it accompanied by a minimalist tinkling

26. This photograph—or one from the same series—is on display at the U.S. Holocaust Memorial Museum in Washington, D.C. Although Farocki does not mention it, there were several photographs of IG Farben/Auschwitz: "Allied photorecon aircraft made it to these targets less than two dozen times between 4 April 1944 and 14 January 1945[, and] half of those missions also coincidentally got cover of the death camps—a few frames in each of eighteen roles of film" (Roy Stanley, *World War II Photo Intelligence* [New York: Scribners, 1981], 346; also cited by Keenan, "Light Weapons," 149).

of a piano? In fact, these are questions related to a much more basic interrogation about the instances of Farocki's use of women to make a point in his film. Is he fully in control of his inscription (*Inschrift*) of the re/presentation of women?

In addition to the photo of IG Farben/Auschwitz, three other sequences must be considered here; in each case, the photographed subjects/objects are women. The first sequence has drawn by far the most critical attention in analyses of the film.[27] It can be first examined as a silent image without accompanying female voice-over narration (column 1), then with it we shall add to it the verbal track (column 2).

27. At least it has drawn the detailed attention of Silverman and Keenan—the first, and to date only, extended treatments of *Images of the World and the Inscription of War.* This image, framed by Farocki's hands, also appears as the cover of Michael Renov, ed., *Theorizing Documentary* (New York: Routledge, 1993), though the book mentions neither Farocki nor *Images of the World and the Inscription of War.* Silverman observes, "This text is at first shocking in its imputation to the Jewish woman and her Nazi photographer of viewing relations which we associate with 'normality' and which seem unthinkable within a context like Auschwitz. However, one of the primary functions of this sequence is to stress that although the male subject is at most a privileged 'functionary' of the camera/gaze, the latter is defined as a masculine extension through a whole confluence of institutional, discursive, and representational determinations. At least within the West, the same determinants posit the female subject as the specular object par excellence. Given how overdetermined these relations are, there would seem to be no context—even one as given over to death as Auschwitz—within which they could not somehow be inscribed." Silverman concludes, "to object to the commentary for imputing meaning to these two photographs which was not available to the camera, and which cannot be historically documented, is to overlook another crucial feature of *Images of the World and the Inscription of War*'s interrogation of the visual field—its discourse upon the human look" ("What Is a Camera?" 39–42). It is striking that Keenan, in his article on *Images of the World and the Inscription of War* with the intriguing title "Light Weapons," uses the same citation of the narrative voice-over segment as does Silverman. For Keenan, however the key point is that the image and its commentary are immediately preceded by the click of a shutter, one of the few times in the film where, quite literally, "the light goes out in *Images of the World*"—that is, the screen goes black. This emphasis on "the cut and the darkness that precedes it" is crucial because from a neo-Heideggerian point of view, the cut stands for "the darkness against which an image, a photograph or a film, finds its possibility"—a possibility that is here "brought into the event of the film itself" ("Light Weapons," 151).

Photo from Auschwitz (Reproduced in *Images of the World and the Inscription of War*.)

> The woman has arrived at Auschwitz; the camera captures her in movement. The photographer has his camera installed, and as the woman passes by he clicks the shutter—in the same way he would cast a glance at her in the street, because she is beautiful. The woman understands how to pose her face so as to catch the eye of the photographer, and how to look with a slight sideways glance. On a boulevard she would look in the same way just past a man casting his eye over her at a shop window, and with this sideways glance she seeks to displace herself into a world of boulevards, men and shop windows. (Farocki, "Commentary," 86)

This passage is striking because the description by the female voice-over—if taken at face value—sentimentalizes the soliciting look with too much narrative that, paradoxically, is as problematic as Margaret Bourke-White's famous refusal, when the camps were finally liberated, to inscribe any meaning or consciousness whatsoever to the look of the inmates. She is said, on first arriving at Buchenwald, to have

> set to work immediately. A crowd of men in prison clothes stood silently behind barbed wire. She stood in front of them with a flash to take their picture; not one of them reacted. *The camera, which automatically forces self-consciousness on its subjects, could not do so here; Buchenwald had stripped away self-consciousness and ordinary response.*[28]

28. Vicki Goldberg, *Margaret Bourke-White, A Biography* (Reading, Mass.: Addison-Wesley, 1987), 290. Farocki's SS photo must be contextualized further, however, with regard to another problem of photographing (in) the camps. Thus, the *Picture Post* in 1943, when prison camps in Italy were liberated, captioned a picture of an emaciated female inmate, "Women Want to Be Photographed." In 1945, a *Picture Post* caption of an image of a horrifically thin man claimed that he had demanded to be photographed because "the free peoples of the world should know what a German prison-camp does to a man." See "The Eighth Army Breaks Open a Concentration Camp," *Picture Post,* October 23, 1943, 8; "The Problem That Makes All Europe Wonder," *Picture Post,* May 5, 1945, 11. For these references, I am indebted to an unpublished essay by Barbie Zelizer of Temple University: "The Image, the Word, and the Holocaust: Photojournalism and the Shape of Memory."

What about this image attracts Farocki's camera, and how should this image be read—as text or image? One possible method may be to approach it as a "blur" (the Lacanian *point de capiton*), as the device that according to Slavoj Žižek "denatures" an image, "rendering all its constituents 'suspicious.'"[29] According to Žižek, when viewers are confronted with such a blur, the

> ground of the established, familiar signification opens up; we find ourselves in a realm of total ambiguity, but this very lack propels us to produce ever new "hidden meanings." . . . The oscillation between lack and surplus meaning constitutes the proper dimension of subjectivity. In other words, it is by means of the . . . spot that the observed picture is subjectivized: this paradoxical point undermines our position as "neutral," "objective" observer, pinning us to the observed object itself. This is the point at which the observer is already included, inscribed in the observed scene—in a way, it is the point from which the picture itself looks back at us.[30]

All the photographs filmed by Farocki do indeed "look back at us," implicating us in them in a political way. One of the main reasons for the Allies' failure to see the horror of Auschwitz "in" the comparatively "natural," "familiar," and "idyllic" pictures of IG Farben was precisely an ideological bias. This point—which articulates how the economic base can be occluded by the superstructure—has preoccupied Farocki from the beginning. Thus, for example, in *As One Sees,* he includes a citation from Hannah Arendt: "Work is hidden because working society is ashamed of it." And in *Between Two Wars,* Farocki covers 1917–33 from the perspective of the German working class to show that the military-industrial complex had eliminated the international worker in favor of fascism. For Farocki, ideology may appear in/visible but is revealed in the tensions among vision, visuality, and visibility—and one might add, with Žižek—as "subliminally anamorphic" or, with Adorno, as "puzzled."[31] Indeed, returning to the Allies' failure to see Auschwitz's camp, the practical consequence of that *méconnaissance* was nothing less than horrific for millions and somehow was already inscribed in images.

As for the SS photograph of the Jewish woman, what is at stake is not a more accurate description, or "Truth," but rather the search for alternative and more precise narrative possibilities that could have been occluded from sight. Thomas Keenan insightfully concludes,

29. Slavoj Žižek, *Looking Awry: An Introduction to Jacques Lacan through Popular Culture* (Cambridge: MIT Press, 1991), 91.

30. Žižek, *Looking Awry,* 91.

31. Adorno, *Minima Moralia;* Žižek, *Looking Awry.*

> Farocki seems to understand what it means for the camera to be part of the equipment of destruction, indeed for the destruction to be in a certain sense impossible without the camera. This is what he calls *Aufklärung:* no bombing without reconnaissance, certainly, but also no annihilation without the record of what has been accomplished.[32]

But what about Farocki's film, to which this same function presumably can also be applied? What exactly does it make visible yet simultaneously destroy? What kind of "light weapon" might it be? And what might gender have to do with it? These questions remain without answers.

I now turn to a sequence that occurs early in the film and then is repeated several times. It is a series of photographs of unveiled Algerian women taken in 1960 by a French soldier, Marc Garanger. Farocki films himself leafing through the book in which these images are collected. His face is sometimes directly behind the book, in which, changing point of view, we see the face of one woman in particular, unveiled and reveiled by Farocki's hand. The disembodied female voice-over asks,

> How to face a camera? The horror of being photographed for the first time. The year 1960 in Algeria: women are photographed for the first time. They are to be issued with identity cards. Faces which up till then had worn the veil. (Farocki, "Commentary," 80)

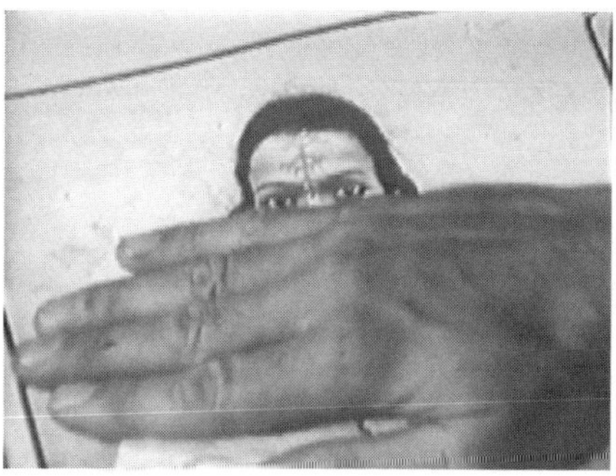

Photo of Algerian woman. (Reproduced in *Images of the World and the Inscription of War*.)

32. Keenan, "Light Weapons," 151. This certainly is not a particularly original observation by either Keenan or Farocki. See, for example, the extensive treatment of this articulation of war and cinema in Virilio's *War and Cinema,* which Keenan cites only in passing and Silverman not at all. Too, there is the infamous case of *Life* photographer Ron Haeberle, who asked that GIs hold their fire for an instant at My Lai so that he could snap his picture of the victims before they were murdered. (He was rewarded with a Pulitzer Prize.) For this and similar incidents, see Susan D. Moeller, *Shooting War: Photography and the American Experience of Combat* (New York: Basic Books, 1989). A similar problematic has been recently addressed from a very different angle in Remy Belvaux's pseudodocumentary *Man Bites Dog* (France, 1992), in which the film crew assigned to "document" the everyday life of a serial killer eventually "participates" in stealing money to finance the film and in raping a victim.

Then there is a third sequence, further toward the end, in which Farocki focuses in on a female prisoner, ostensibly smiling, in a group of inmates that are walking, perhaps to their deaths. The accompanying voice-over says:

Among the shaven heads, a girl who smiles. In Auschwitz apart from death and work, there was a black market, there were love stories and resistance groups. (Farocki, "Commentary," 90)

Photo from Auschwitz (Reproduced in *Images of the World and the Inscription of War*.)

Yet as the photographs show, just as the Algerian women do not necessarily look horrified, the female prisoner does not necessarily smile. To sentimentalize these women in this way is really akin to sentimentalizing the death camps by stating—without further comment—that there were love stories there. Is Farocki here directly contradicting his earlier statement in *Images of the World and the Inscription of War* that "the success of the TV series 'Holocaust'—which aims to depict vividly suffering and dying, . . . turns it into kitsch"?[33] He seems himself at risk, in these three voice-overs involving women, of producing precisely such kitsch, indeed of reproducing the problematic in/visibility he exposes in his account of the IG Farben/Auschwitz photographs. True, what is now at issue explicitly—and hence self-reflectively—is more a matter of vision of gender than of the vision of military surveillance. Still, why does Farocki include such a potentially sentimental narrative and ascribe it to a female voice? Perhaps he does so—or can be interpreted to do so—precisely to disrupt any assumption that viewers know what these images mean. An essay film is supposed to make its audience doubt and think. By spotlighting the tension between the visual and the audible, Farocki makes alternative narratives—opposed narratives, even—possible and perhaps necessary.[34]

33. Farocki, "Commentary," 81.

34. This more or less un/decidable and im/perceptible effect is further enhanced by an ever-so-slight tinkling of classical European piano music in the background. Viewing

The photographs are of Berber women who have been photographed by the military police because they are suspected criminals—more precisely, "terrorists" carrying bombs. Gillo Pontecorvo's 1966 pseudodocumentary, *Battle of Algiers,* dealt sympathetically with a similar theme, showing Algerian women in the Casbah who disguise themselves as Europeans so that they may pass through French checkpoints to plant bombs in the European part of the city, while Algerian men veil themselves like traditional Muslim women to escape detection by the French.[35] More than Algerian, however, the photographed women's faces in Farocki's film are primarily the faces of the (female) enemy, actual or potential: fatales being femmes.[36] Through his montage, Farocki links these singularly unhorrified faces to present-day German police photographs of wanted suspects (women—one composite photo bears an uncanny resemblance to Ulrike Meinhof—or men disguised as women) and then moves back again to the two photographs of women in Auschwitz. Whether "Jew," "Algerian," or "German," it is suggested that they are all someone's enemies. They are also all females, it is true, but they primarily evoke facing an in/visible enemy in a world of violence and terror—in/visible because that world has been historically and culturally en/gendered as a male sphere. At once female and hostile, the "inappropriate/d other" appears here to be particularly dangerous because it surfaces not where one expects it but where one does not.[37] We also begin to grasp why the German police photograph of a wanted woman is computer enhanced into a male face. It is almost as if the suspected female "terrorist" was changed into a male to better identify her as the enemy other—traditionally a military, male other. As Susan Sontag and Paul Virilio proclaim, to photograph is—potentially—to kill.[38]

Farocki's treatment of the Algerian women, this musical sound track weaves its way in and out here, too, as if to recall not only the history of the cinema (that is, silent films without audible verbal interpretation and/or misinterpretation) but also the subliminal hegemony of the (here aural) West over the (here visible) Orient. This would be an ironic reversal of Trinh T. Minh-ha's remark, following Foucault, that in the West the power/knowledge effect resides primarily in the visual ("The World as a Foreign Land" [1989], in Trinh, *When the Moon Waxes Red: Representation, Gender, and Cultural Politics* [New York: Routledge, 1991], 189).

35. *Battle of Algiers,* dir. Gillo Pontecorvo (screenplay Franco Solinas), 35mm, 120 min., Igor Films, Algeria, France, and Italy, 1965. This film had a huge impact when it appeared and was censored in many countries.

36. For an important psychoanalytic approach to the femme fatale in cinema, see Mary Ann Doane, *Femmes Fatales: Feminism, Film Theory, Psychoanalysis* (New York: Routledge, 1991).

37. On the concept of "inappropriate/d other" in this sense, see Trinh T. Minh-ha, ed., *She, the Inappropriate/d Other* (special issue of *Discourse* 8 [fall–winter 1986–87]).

38. Susan Sontag, *On Photography* (New York: Doubleday, 1973); Paul Virilio, *War and Cinema: The Logistics of Perception* (1984; trans. Patrick Camillor [London: Verso, 1989]).

Still, women are the carriers of bombs in Farocki's film—as in the actual battle of Algiers and in the movie *Battle of Algiers.* And women had done so earlier in Auschwitz, as Farocki will presently show. It is also worth noting that the "revolutionary" Algerian women are shown unveiled, perhaps as a symbolic allusion, Farocki's as well as the women's, to their rejection of the pre- and postcolonial and/or Islamic oppression of women in Algeria. But the absence of the veil also suggest the women's refusal of public invisibility and of the resulting sexual mystery and appeal.[39] In that sense, Farocki might have wanted to link the veil motif with another group of women terrorists—Gudrun Ensslin and Ulrike Meinhof—and so to protest against the relentless mass media branding of these women as whores, lesbians, PLO trainees, and so on.[40] (Indeed, *As One Sees* directly refers to Meinhof with the inclusion of a popular magazine's cover story on her.) This linkage is not surprising because, as demonstrated earlier, the overdetermined layering of the enemy body with "female" and "oriental" sexuality seems to cut across many cultures and times.[41]

Then there is the story of the Auschwitz women. Three rhythmically inserted sequences show a series of handwritten numbers on a slip of paper. On the first two occasions, viewers are offered what turn out to be false leads, seeming to link the numbers with military reconnaissance or with electronic image manipulation. The numbers flash on the screen without voice-over commentary, but the visual context suggests some semantics even though we do not see yet their precise historical meaning. Only near the end of the film is this series of numbers explained retroactively

---

39. For the classic work on the intricate dialectic between repressive and liberatory aspects of native cultures in the context of revolutionary situations generally and in Africa specifically, see the work of Frantz Fanon, including *The Wretched of the Earth* [1961], preface by Jean-Paul Sartre, trans. Constance Farrington (New York: Grove Press, 1978). On the ambivalent attraction to and fear of veiled women, see Doane's ongoing work, beginning with "Film and the Masquerade: Theorizing the Female Spectator" [1982], reprinted in *The Sexual Subject: A "Screen" Reader in Sexuality,* ed. John Caughie and Annette Kuhn (New York: Routledge, 1992), 227–43.

40. For a detailed investigation into representations and constructions of terrorism in German culture and cultural theory, see Matthew T. Grant, "Critical Intellectuals and the New Media: Bernward Vesper, Ulrike Meinhof, the Frankfurt School, and the Red Army Faction" (Ph.D. diss., Cornell University, 1993).

41. In literature, the image of the Vietnamese woman as simultaneously a prostitute and a terrorist is a common international theme. See my *Vietnam Protest Theatre: The Television War on Stage* (Bloomington: Indiana University Press, 1996). Today a similar problematic of veiling and unveiling emerges in the so-called *Vermummungsgesetz*—the prohibition of veils or masks in German demonstrations and, in France, schools. The specter of anyone, perhaps women especially, as a potential terrorists who might be called in/visible is haunting now for many people, male and female.

(that is, after the audience has begun to assimilate them in/visibly): the female voice-over explains that they were

> coded messages from Auschwitz prisoners who belonged to a resistance group. They set the date for an uprising. . . . With explosive devices made from powder that women had smuggled out from the Union Munitions factory, they set fire to the crematorium.[42]

Without these women, neither terrorism nor resistance would have been possible. They, at least, attempted actively to do what the combined might of Allied bombers could not—or would not—accomplish: stop the horror.[43]

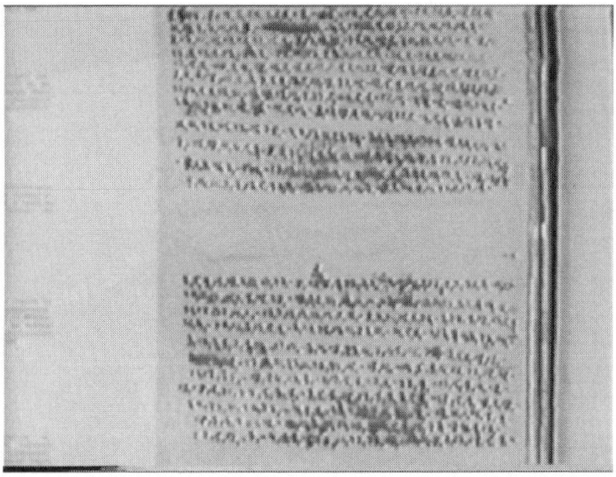

Photo of camp writings. (Reproduced in *Images of the World and the Inscription of War.*)

Thus, women are allowed access—into history and into Farocki's film—precisely because they are in/visible. But does the female voice-over problematize or reinforce this point? Silverman's *The Acoustic Mirror* contains a helpful analysis of the role of the female voice in feature films. She deconstructs "the classic cinema's rigorous 'marriage' of voice to image" and explores the "ironic distance between the female voice and her

42. Farocki, "Commentary," 92. One of these women was Roza Robota, whose photograph in the U.S. Holocaust Memorial Museum is captioned to assert that she was responsible for smuggling out the explosives that resulted in the October 7, 1944, demolition of a small part of the Auschwitz crematorium. She was executed for her "crime" on January 1, 1945.

43. This issue has by no means been settled; indeed, in the U.S. Holocaust Memorial Museum it is raised once again with the supporting evidence of letters by members of Jewish organizations addressed to British and U.S. heads of state, pleading for the bombing of the camps and the train lines; the rejections of these demands are also displayed.

filmic 'stand-in.'"[44] On these grounds, the voice-over in the essay film *Images of the World and the Inscription of War* would also be "a voice 'apart,' in both senses of that word—a voice which asserts its independence from the classic system, and which is somehow a part of what it narrates."[45] As critics have pointed out, German male directors have often used a male voice-over to undermine female characters and women's issues—a voice that "takes on the guise of a meta-character, offered up unproblematically for audience identification, smoothing over the real contradictions of the film's form in order to displace attention upon false contradictions taken to represent impossible obstacles to political consciousness or action."[46] However, switching the gender of the voice-over from male to female does not necessarily solve the problem of biased presentation.[47] Part of the problem in *Images of the World and the Inscription of War* is that Farocki's audible woman is never made visible: she is literally disembodied, ventriloquizing for a Farocki whose hands, at least, are visible in the film. It may be that the problematic of the political tension between the in/visible and the in/audible is not wholly under Farocki's conscious control but rather is part of his own political unconscious. Furthermore, the accompanying soft piano music acts in tandem with the female voice as a parallel suture: another way of seaming the movie together in terms of its seeming gendered content, or semes. Here again, a direct link can be made back to the written essay, for as Adorno observes, "the essay approaches the logic of music, that stringent and yet aconceptual art of transition."[48] As in a Hollywood feature film, that nondiegetic music signals moments of special significance, producing an "acoustic mirror": in this case, a replication of the audiovisual, acutely en/gendered

44. Kaja Silverman, *The Acoustic Mirror: The Female Voice in Psychoanalysis and Cinema* (Bloomington: Indiana University Press, 1988), 168.

45. Silverman, *Acoustic Mirror,* 131.

46. B. Ruby Rich, "She Says, He Says: The Power of the Narrator in Modernist Film Politics" [1983], in *Gender and German Cinema: Feminist Interventions,* vol. 1, *Gender and Representation in New German Cinema,* ed. Sandra Frieden, Richard W. McCormick, Vibeke R. Petersen, and Laurie Melissa Vogelsang (Providence, R.I.: Berg, 1993), 151. On male voice-overs undermining female characters, see, for example, the analysis of Alexander Kluge's mis/use of male voice-over in Miriam Hansen, "Cooperative Auteur Cinema and Oppositional Public Sphere: Alexander Kluge's Contribution to *Germany in Autumn,*" *New German Critique* 24–25 (fall–winter 1981–82): 36–56, where Hansen argues that the status of Kluge's male narrator is never radically questioned. Building on this argument, see further Rich, "She Says, He Says," 143–61.

47. Various male directors other than Farocki use—wittingly or not—a female voice-over to deflect possible criticism expressing feminist perspectives. Indeed, this has become something of a trend in recent documentaries, exemplified by the English version of Ray Müller's *The Wonderful Horrible Life of Leni Riefenstahl* (1993).

48. Adorno, "Essay as Form," 22.

montage. But, of course, not all of the montage serves gender issues, and its contribution to the film's intelligence has more general political effects. In that sense the question now becomes, what exactly are its in/visible and in/audible countercultural politics?

III. Political In/Visibility, In/Audibility

This secret but ultimately driving meaning of *Images of the World and the Inscription of War* is articulated by one of the strongest structuring leitmotifs that Farocki incorporates into his film: a series of images of camouflage and concealment that conjure the coexistence of two interfacing worlds—one visible, the other invisible. At the most manifest level, this problematic jibes easily with the film's relatively explicit discourse on what is visible and what escapes detection. Examples abound: most tragically, the Allies failed, within the regime of visibility, to see at the level of visuality precisely what they had photographed at the level of vision—the Auschwitz death camp in the immediate vicinity of IG Farben. Or veils are made to conceal the identities of Algerian women from the male gaze. Or more mundanely, European women apply makeup to beautify their looks under the gaze of men, and so on, just as buildings and landscapes are camouflaged during wartime to avoid destruction, and so on. Yet this entire discursive level is really only thematic. It points to the lack of reliability of signs and/or to the rupture between signs and reality and the takeover of the latter by the former in an age of spectacularization, a society of spectacle, a pertinent but somehow insufficient lesson. In a film that centers so much on concealment and disguise, viewers also want to know what Farocki is hiding, consciously or not. Is there a camouflaged political text? *Images of the World and the Inscription of War* may be conforming to political rhetoric, where if one talks about the presence of hidden meanings, then a good possibility exists that one is putting one's money where one's mouth is, that one is not merely constating but also performing an act of political im/perceptibility.[49]

As a political filmmaker, Farocki had a history of situationist activism,[50] and *Images of the World and the Inscription of War* logically both conceals and reveals his strong censure of West Germany—a censure directed not merely against its Nazi past but also against its postwar political developments. When the narrator remarks that "after the war the IG Farben company took another name, as some SS men also did,"[51] Farocki

49. See, for example, Leo Strauss, *Persecution and the Art of Writing* (1952; Chicago: University of Chicago Press, 1988).

50. See Elsaesser, *New German Cinema,* 82.

51. Farocki, "Commentary," 87.

purposefully—or instinctively—uses what classical rhetoric called *sigetics,* the argument from silence: viewers want to know these other names, yet the film fails to mention them: One reason for the silence may be pragmatic. Farocki uses parts of other projects—sequences from technological films or documentaries, including the clip of the Dior model being made up[52]—to help finance his essay films, which largely owe their careful montage to all these premanufactured images. To name what IG Farben has turned into—a rather small "secret"—might be disingenuous, counterproductive, or even economically suicidal for future films of this *Verbundsystem* heritage. After all, such companies were Farocki's bread and butter, and it would be foolish overtly to implicate them, to bite the hand that feeds him.

But there is more, of course. There is Farocki's own reference, mentioned earlier, to advertising montage as related to Soviet film practice—a blueprint of a more general pragmatic strategy.[53] Farocki is surely aware that in contemporary neocapitalism, technology and industry have so pervaded the public sphere that it is virtually impossible to avoid dealing with them—and with their im/perceptibility. What in modernist times counted as self-reflection tends to become in today's Jamesonian postmodern condition the way in which "culture acts out its own commodification."[54] *Images of the World and the Inscription of War,* too, must act out cultural commodification but can also work to subvert it (much as Adorno had claimed for the role of the essay). Hearing that IG Farben now flies under another name, Farocki's viewers are invited to find out what that name is, if they don't know it already, or, if they do, to wonder why this knowledge is concealed here. Three major companies have evolved out of IG Farben: Bayer, Hoechst, and BASF, which produces the kind of videotape on which one can view and hear *Images of the World and the Inscription of War.* These names, an anthropologist might say, are the "public secret" at

52. When Farocki intercuts *Images of the World and the Inscription of War* with the long sequence of this woman being made up (in all senses) and, in effect, being disguised, his female voice-over comments, "Women paint themselves to be beautiful," even though a man is clearly doing the work (see also Farocki, "Commentary," 88). To be sure, there are other possible interpretations of this scene. For example, I would prefer to read it (also) as an allusion to the aforementioned scene in Pontecorvo's *Battle of Algiers,* when Algerian militants make themselves up as Europeans to conceal their identity and then plant bombs.

53. The dictum of Dziga Vertov is illustrative in this regard: "Kino-eye is the documentary cinematic decoding of both the visible world and that which is invisible to the naked eye" ("From Kino-Eye to Radio-Eye" [1929], in *Kino-Eye: The Writings of Dziga Vertov,* ed. and intro. Annette Michelson, trans. Kevin O'Brien [Berkeley: University of California Press, 1984], 87).

54. Jameson, *Geopolitical Aesthetic,* 5.

the basis of social/cultural mimesis, in/audible and in/visible.[55] And Farocki's film functions as an act of understated—im/perceptible—resistance to that culture, since as he puts it, in the face of the increasingly global "development in production techniques, [which] excludes me and shuts me out, . . . my only means of defense is to make films on this topic. I make films about the industrialization of thought."[56]

The concrete, specific, topical aspects of German politics that underlie and motivate the general censure in *Images of the World and the Inscription of War* are introduced in the penultimate image sequence of the film. Rhetorically speaking, this is an effective location for such a message, since the beginning or end would be too obvious. (Commentators on texts produced under censorship, such as Leo Strauss, theorize that most explicit political messages are rarely concealed at the easily visible positions but rather somewhere nearby.) Farocki's female voice-over sends the following message:

> In 1983, as the number of atomic weapons in the Federal Republic of Germany was to be increased again, Günter Anders recalled the failure to bomb Auschwitz and demanded: the reality must begin: "The reality must begin. That means: the blockading of all entrances to the murder installations which permanently persist must be equally persistent. Let us destroy the possibility of access to these weapons." To the atomic weapons.[57]

This is obviously part of Farocki's message. But it is not only thematically but also formally and aesthetically coded, like the numbers used by the Auschwitz resistance group. And, like the pleas for Allied bombing of the railroads leading to Auschwitz, this statement calls for the destruction of train lines, this time the tracks that lead to the atomic weapons placed in

55. See Michael Taussig, *Mimesis and Alterity: A Particular History of the Senses* (New York: Routledge, 1993), esp. 83–86. Taussig argues that "the 'origins' of mimesis lie in art and politics and not in survival" and that mimesis in effect is the "nature" that cultures use to produce second nature to maintain various types of social control, including the means of public secrets and various forms of aesthetic semblance. For Adorno, "under the essay's gaze second nature recognizes itself as first nature," in part because "the essay has something like an aesthetic autonomy that is easily accused of being simply derived from art, although it is distinguished from art by its medium, concepts, and by its claim to be a truth devoid of aesthetic semblance" (Adorno, "Essay as Form," 5, 20). I argue that the essay film as practiced by Farocki attempts to continue this properly Enlightenment tradition by bringing it up to technocultural speed, whatever the limitations may be.

56. Harun Farocki, "The Industrialization of Thought," *Discourse* 15 (spring 1993): 77.

57. Farocki, "Commentary," 92.

Germany by the Allies, especially the United States (partly responsible for not bombing the death camps). In an article that contains part of the text of *Images of the World and the Inscription of War,* Farocki says as much, in some detail.[58] But in his essay film, this political message is at once most explicit and most in/audible and in/visible when Farocki shows his own hand literally inscribing (à la Astruc), with a crayon or pen, his call to action on the inmate Alfred Kantor's drawing of a locomotive bringing prisoners to their death in Auschwitz.

Alfred Kantor image with Harun Farocki's handwriting. (Video caption from *Images of the World and the Inscription of War.*)

Farocki twice writes, "Den Zugang blockieren!" (Block the access routes!). Offering a first version of a "political anamorphosis," Farocki

58. See Harun Farocki, "Reality Would Have to Begin," trans. Marek Wieczorek, Thomas Keenan, and Thomas Y. Levin, *Documents* 1—2 (fall–winter 1992): 136–46; originally published as "Die Wirklichkeit hätte zu beginnen," in *Fotovision: Projekt Photographie nach 150 Jahren,* ed. Bernd Busch, Udo Liebelt, and Werner Oeder (Hannover: Sprengle Museum, 1988). This text, written about the same time as Farocki made the *Images of the World and the Inscription of War,* contains much of the film's basic narrative text. Farocki starts with a quotation from Anders ("reality would have to begin") and then immediately offers the following commentary, which is later dropped from the film version: "Nuclear weapons stationed in the Federal Republic of Germany arrive by ship in Bremerhaven where they are put on trains, whose departure time and destination are kept secret. About a week before departure, Army aircraft fly the entire length of the route and photograph it. This status report is repeated half an hour before the train is to pass, and the most recent set of images is compared with the first set. Through their juxtaposition one can discern whether any significant changes have occurred in the interim. If, for example, a construction vehicle has recently been parked along the tracks, the police will drive to or fly over the spot to investigate whether it is providing camouflage for saboteurs. Whether such sabotage has been attempted is not made public" (136).

depicts his inscription at an unnatural angle—making it harder to see yet still visible. By similar reckoning, the entire *Images of the World and the Inscription of War* is itself the "inscription of war" (*Inschrift des Krieges*) alluded to in the title: a more or less concealed, more or less im/perceptible instruction about waging war against nuclear might, much as *Battle of Algiers* was viewed as a manual for waging underground urban war.

To be more precise, Farocki's film proposes a double war of position and maneuver: tactically and immediately, blockade the trains! But Farocki is well aware that massive surveillance by the military-industrial complex will make such blockades almost impossible, though nonetheless necessary. Hence his recourse to a second form of warfare in and as *Images of the World and the Inscription of War* itself: a more strategic and long-term action. It involves another anamorphosis, almost subliminal and quite independent of perspective: images showing the use of hydropower in opposition to nuclear power. This contrast provides the underlying reason for the otherwise inexplicably recurrent and redundant image of the Hannover water-research laboratory. The accompanying female voice-over notes—but only once, near the beginning of the film—that "the motions of water are still less researched than those of light."[59] This is a remarkable acknowledgment of the power of science and technology in a film that is—ostensibly—critical of their impact on today's culture. Perhaps Farocki trusts that labs such as the Hannover plant, given enough financial and public support, will someday come up with alternatives to nuclear energy. For the rest of the industrial companies for whom Farocki must make documentaries, he is employing the *Verbundsystem* against itself, attempting to accomplish, what the situationists might have called its *détournement,* Brecht its *Umfunktionierung.*[60] Not far away, one might imagine, is the im/perceptible affirmation of direct action up to and including what others would call terrorism.

Paradoxically, Farocki's attempt to use the subliminal anamorphosis of the im/perceptible may be seen as contradicting the enlightenment aspect of his project, which demands complete disclosure. Much of his ultimate political strategy thus risks remaining obscure while being grasped as emotionally subversive. Noting in 1983 that "film as a form of intelligence is Farocki's own guerrilla war,"[61] Elsaesser declined to make any more specific the form such warfare might take, either in Farocki's work or more generally in cinematic practice, criticism, and theory.

59. Farocki, "Commentary," 78.

60. On Brecht and Farocki as different but also related types of political filmmakers, see Elsaesser, "'*It All Started with These Images.*'"

61. Thomas Elsaesser, "Working at the Margins: Two or Three Things Not Known about Harun Farocki," *Monthly Film Bulletin* 50, no. 597 (October 1983): 270.

On a more general note, it is worth quoting in that respect filmmaker and theorist Trinh T. Minh-ha. Attuned to the aesthetic, economic, and historical as well as the (sexual) political, she writes about documentaries as one might write about an effective essay film:

> A documentary aware of its own artifice is one that remains sensitive to the flow between fact and fiction. It does not work to conceal or exclude what is normalized as "non-factual," for it understands the mutual dependence of realism and "artificiality" in the process of filmmaking. It recognizes the necessity of composing (on) life in living it or making it. Documentary reduced to a mere vehicle of facts may be used to advocate a cause, but it does not constitute one in itself. . . . Meaning can therefore be political only when it does not let itself be easily stabilized, and, when it does not rely on any single source of authority, but rather empties it, decentralizes it.[62]

The dual task of criticism, similarly, is, on the one hand, to resist overly stabilizing the meaning of an essay film like *Images of the World and the Inscription of War* and/or to reducing it to its advocacy. But, on the other hand, it is equally important to resist the overdecentralization of (possible) political messages that would thus become ineffective, and, in that sense, im/perceptible. In spite and because of its multilayered, self-reflective quality generating solipsisms and contradictions, Farocki's essay film does have a relatively decidable political message—indeed, is ultimately quite agitational in intent. Keeping alive the old agitprop tradition under postmodern conditions, it transcends the simply modernist version of political cinema, informing the omnibus production *Germany in Autumn* by a hyperconscious attention to self-reflexivity. Conversely, its acute awareness of the political nature of its message contrasts with other self-reflexive films that are more oriented toward problems of audiovisual media and are best represented by the essay films of Wim Wenders.

62. Trinh T. Minh-ha, "The Totalizing Quest of Meaning" [1990], in *When the Moon Waxes Red* 41.

CHAPTER 4

Global Politics, Cinematographic Space: Wenders's *Tokyo-Ga* and *Notebooks on Cities and Clothes*

> The author has never, in any sense, photographed Japan. Rather, he has done the opposite: Japan has starred him with any number of "flashes"; or, better still, Japan has afforded him a situation of writing. This situation is the very one in which a certain disturbance of the person occurs, a subversion of earlier readings, a shock of meaning lacerated, extenuated to the point of its irreplaceable void, without the object's ever ceasing to be significant, desirable.
>
> —Roland Barthes, *Empire of Signs*

> All of a sudden, on the turbulent streets of Tokyo, I realized that a valid image of this city might very well be an electronic one, and not only my sacred celluloid images. In its own language, the video camera was capturing this city in an appropriate way. I was shocked. A language of images was not the privilege of cinema. Wasn't it necessary then to reevaluate everything? All notions of identity, language, images, authorship? Perhaps our future authors were the makers of commercials or videoclips, or the designers of electronic games and computer programs. Fuck!
>
> —Wim Wenders, *Notebooks on Cities and Clothes*

> Small fragments of war enshrined in everyday life.
>
> —Chris Marker, *Sans soleil*

One of the founding members of New German Cinema and responsible for the resurgence of German film in the 1970s, Wim Wenders is arguably the only German filmmaker to have consistently made feature films both critically acclaimed and commercially viable on the world market. He remains perhaps the most respected German filmmaker to command the popularity and the capital to advance what is left of film avant-garde into the postmodern age.[1] For most critics and historians, he stands on an equal or comparable footing with successful popular directors such as Dorris Dörrie, Fassbinder, Herzog, Schlöndorff, von Trotta, and Peterson. However, Wenders's feature films are but one side of his filmic production; equally successful, albeit with less mass appeal, are his essay films.

Wenders calls his brand of essay film a "diary," and he seeks inspiration less from the essay film nurtured in the Soviet Union or Germany than in France and especially the work of Jean-Luc Godard and Chris Marker.[2] Wenders is not the only German feature film director to cultivate nonfiction filmmaking as an alternative to feature film production. Both Fassbinder and Herzog, among others, have also experimented with mixing documentaries and features, sometimes in a single hybrid film.[3] But no other director has stated as bluntly as Wenders that his essay films, while a favored type of practice, are also his film theory.[4] To be sure, he has also produced a respectable body of critical writings that stand as texts in their own right,[5] but they are often quite problematic: at once jazzily accessible, glittering with hyperbole, yet difficult to follow logically. The search for a

1. Among Wenders's earlier films, *The American Friend* (1977) made him famous, followed by his first Hollywood feature, *Hammett* (1982). His more recent, better-known, and successful films include *Wings of Desire* (1987), *Until the End of the World* (1991), *Faraway, So Close!* (1993), *Lisbon Story* (1995), and *Buena Vista Social Club* (1999). *Wings of Desire* is one of only two films (the other is Ridley Scott's *Blade Runner*) to be analyzed by David Harvey in the first systematic attempt to find the articulation between postmodern culture and the global political economy of postindustrialism (see Harvey, *The Condition of Postmodernity: An Inquiry into the Origins of Cultural Change* [Oxford: Blackwell, 1989], 308–23 ["Time and Space in the Postmodern Cinema"]). Wenders also plays an axial role in the major philosophy of cinema developed by Gilles Deleuze (see Deleuze, *Cinema 1: The Movement-Image,* trans. Hugh Tomlinson and Barbara Habberjam [1983; Minneapolis: University of Minnesota Press, 1986], 5, 22, 101; Deleuze, *Cinema 2: The Time-Image,* trans. Hugh Tomlinson and Robert Galeta [1985; Minneapolis: University of Minnesota Press, 1989], 76–78, 136).

2. Both Marker and Godard have turned away from film to embrace video and digital production, paralleling but in a more extreme way Wenders's interest in new media. Their combination of investigation into forms of image reproduction and the interplay of different media, as well as their political slant, particularly impresses him.

3. See, for example, Fassbinder's *Beware of a Holy Whore* (1970) or Herzog's *Fata Morgana* (1968–70).

4. Wim Wenders, "Ein Gespräch mit Wim Wenders" [1989], in Reinhold Rauh, *Wim Wenders und seine Filme* (Munich: Wilhelm Heyne, 1990), 253.

5. The best known is no doubt *The Act of Seeing: Texte und Gespräche* (Frankfurt am Main: Verlag der Autoren, 1992), esp. 57–93, reprinting his "Die Wahrheit der Bilder" (1989), on the influence of painting on his early films. In addition, see, in English, Wim Wenders, *Emotion Pictures: Reflections on the Cinema,* trans. Sean Whiteside and Michael Hofmann (1986; London: Faber and Faber, 1989); Wim Wenders, *The Logic of Images: Essays and Conversations,* trans. Michael Hofmann (1988; London: Faber and Faber, 1991).

stable meaning in Wenders's writing is thus best carried out in coordination with a viewing of his films, especially the essay films. Following his advice, students should read between his lines—whether printed, projected, or digitalized—and match the various readings.[6]

Such readings are facilitated by Wenders's steadfast dedication to essay films, technically or thematically linked to full features. Throughout his career, he has spent a great amount of energy and resources on producing these filmic essays, usually following a feature fiction, like a self-consciously reflexive and reflective echo or a reworked section of painter's canvas.[7] The 1977 classic *The American Friend* was followed by the 1980 essay *Lightning over Water: Nick's Film;* the 1982 feature *Hammett* by both the mixed genre *The State of Things* and the essay *Reverse Angle* (the same year); the 1984 feature *Paris, Texas* by the 1985 essay *Tokyo-Ga;* the 1987 feature *Wings of Desire* by the 1989 essay *Notebooks on Cities and Clothes,* in turn followed by the feature *Until the End of the World* (1991). Recent features have included *Faraway, So Close!* (1993), *Lisbon Story* (1994), *The End of Violence* (1997), and essay films have included *Night and Day* (1990) and *Trick of Light* (1995, on the occasion of film centennial). And finally, his popular nonfiction film *Buena Vista Social Club* (1999) may be said to have synthesized the two practices together in one film. The progression from one work to the next varies; it may be relatively smooth, showing maturation rather than a transition, or it may take the form of a break, but it always creates a gap. In these gaps, as well as in more conscious and contrived gaps between the lines of each essay film, lie Wenders's theories and messages that his writings leave somewhat vague.

More closely than most of his fellow German filmmakers, Wenders seems attuned to the main political, technological, and artistic (r)evolutions of his time. Born in 1946 under the immediate impact of the postwar American occupation, he has always been hyperconscious of his overdetermined background and situation: his direct, generational link to National Socialist aggression, the Holocaust, and their legacy; his deeply

6. According to Wenders, "The television image 'writes' itself: it is no isolated image but rather builds itself up line by line. Therefore, I have attempted to make a film that is to some extent to be read 'between the lines'" ("Die Revolution ohne Wahrheitsanspruch" [1990], in *Act of Seeing,* 90).

7. Wenders freely acknowledges how much fine art influences his filmmaking and how initially he came to filmmaking through his painting. For example, he referred in 1989 to his early films as "paintings, not with paints and canvas but rather with a camera. I modeled myself more on painters than directors" ("Die Wahrheit," 57). He also continues to photograph as well as to produce what he calls "electronic paintings," which include reproductions of images of "memories" and "dreams" depicted in *Until the End of the World.*

ambivalent relationship to American popular and technoculture (which, he says, has both "colonized" the European "unconscious" and saved him from "becoming a lawyer"); his struggle to break out of this German-American double bind by opening himself up to what Fredric Jameson calls the "geopolitical aesthetic," which for Wenders refers not merely to the romance countries of Europe but also to the aboriginal culture of Australia and, above all, to Japan.[8] As a country characterized by new technologies of image production, Japan exerted a special fascination. *Tokyo-Ga* (1985) and *Notebooks on Cities and Clothes* (1989), separately but particularly taken together, yield a revealing picture of Wenders's concerns and hopes in regard to new media. Wenders's "between the lines" is either surreptitiously or overtly ideological, dealing with the problematic of the simulacrum, the connection between everyday life and re/presentation, and the im/possibility of such imaging to release the tension between internationalism and nationalism. Wenders's essay films certainly allude to these ideological moments but do not adequately process them: they form an in/visible and in/audible blind spot in an otherwise extremely self-reflective film genre.

I. *Tokyo-Ga,* or, from Metropolis to Electropolis

> The whole of Japan is a pure invention. There is no such country, there are no such people.
>
> —Oscar Wilde, "The Decay of Lying: An Observation"

By Wenders's own admission, *Tokyo-Ga* came at a crisis point in his directing career that was never totally resolved: the film was informed by a nexus of intersecting problems that had haunted him in particular and film history in general.[9] *Tokyo-Ga* was first filmed in Tokyo in 1983—after *Hammett* (and Wenders's misadventures in Hollywood and his dispute with Coppola, depicted in *Reverse Angle*)—but it was edited and produced in 1985 after Wenders's last American film, *Paris, Texas.* Wenders acknowledges that *Tokyo-Ga* was crucial technically for his use of voice-over narration: "If I'd never made *Tokyo-Ga* after *Paris, Texas,* then I wouldn't have dared to do that thing with voices in *Wings of Desire.*"[10] More generally, *Tokyo-Ga* marks the moment in his life when he stops

8. From Wenders's 1976 film *Kings of the Road,* 35mm, 176 min.; Fredric Jameson, *The Geopolitical Aesthetic: Cinema and Space in the World System* (Bloomington: Indiana University Press, 1992).

9. *Tokyo-Ga,* dir. Wim Wenders, Gray City, New York; 1985.

10. Wenders, "Ein Gespräch," 248.

looking obsessively and almost exclusively to America (and Hollywood) and turns back to Europe, more specifically to Germany, for his identity and for the locus of his films. But surprisingly perhaps, this return to the Old World also entangles him (as it has many Europeans from Oscar Wilde to Roland Barthes and beyond) in things "Japanese." Thematically, *Tokyo-Ga* is a hybrid work that combines four topics: (1) an homage to Japanese director Yasujiro Ozu; (2) a study of Tokyo and Japan; (3) a rather disillusioned and sometimes paradoxical reflection on the nature of film and on the production, meaning, and consumption of images; (4) a commentary on what had been for Wenders the greatest threat to the cinema—the technology of TV, MTV, and video.

II. (Re)Searching Ozu

The most immediate subject of *Tokyo-Ga* is Yasujiro Ozu (1903–63), arguably the most distinguished and certainly most prolific Japanese filmmaker. To make a film about another filmmaker was by no means new territory for Wenders: his 1980 essay film, *Lightning over Water,* recorded the final days of Nicholas Ray, and both Ray and Samuel Fuller have figured prominently in other Wenders films, such as the 1977 feature *The American Friend.* Wenders, who was born on the day of Japanese capitulation to the United States in World War II, began to shoot his film in Tokyo in 1983, on the twentieth anniversary of Ozu's death. According to Youssef Ishaghpour, *Tokyo-Ga* "is a funereal commemoration" in technological terms and Wenders's Eastern complement to his Western vision informing *Lightning over Water.*[11]

The re/search for Ozu took Wenders not only to "real" Tokyo and its periphery but also to the Tokyo of Ozu's films. The film evokes both the artist's role as mediator between the real city and its filmic images and the city's role as mediator between these images and the imagined identity of the artist. Wenders shot the footage for *Tokyo-Ga* when he visited Tokyo for the 1983 Japanese-German Film Week. He intended to film a diary covering one week but ended up staying a fortnight and did not edit the footage until two years later. The resulting film shows approximately seven "days" in and around Tokyo. This temporal lag—between what may be regarded as the search for empirical or realistic filming and a more interventionist and formalistic research during the editing stage—is curi-

11. Youssef Ishaghpour, "L'État des choses: Wenders: Hammett, L'État des choses, Tokyo Ga," in *Cinéma contemporain: De ce côté du miroir* (Paris: Editions de la Différence, 1986), 167.

ously masked in *Tokyo-Ga.* In general, editing seems to be downplayed. Thus, while Wenders extensively interviews Ozu's main male lead and cameraman about Ozu as director, Wenders strangely neglects to address Ozu as editor. It is as if Wenders wanted (viewers) to ignore Ozu the constructor for the sake of Ozu the seer and, in the process, exorcise Wenders's powers as editor. Wenders claims to have gone to Tokyo to try to recapture the city that was the topic of Ozu's films, but, after the two-year lag, he participates in the process by which cinema aestheticizes and hence distorts or at least appropriates topical reality. In fact, from the beginning of *Tokyo-Ga,* Wenders calls into question the validity of what he is or was attempting to do, admitting (in the manner of Susan Sontag) that if he had not looked at Tokyo through the lens of his own camera, he might have remembered it better.[12] He confronts one of the main problems/themes of the essay film: its uneasy interface between an objective image of reality and the subjective message or narrative meaning conveyed through montage.[13]

This perspective helps to explain why Wenders chose Ozu as the focal point of *Tokyo-Ga.* Ozu was not a personal acquaintance of Wenders, as were Fuller and Ray; Wenders discovered Ozu's films only relatively late, during a trip to New York City in 1973. Yet Ozu became one of the most important filmmakers for Wenders—indeed, by his own admission, maybe the most important. For, if Wenders "so much appreciated Ozu" because he learned from his predecessor, in the spirit of essay films, "that refusing to explain things was right and that you could explain them well enough by just showing them."[14] Another reason for this fascination derives from the appeal of the underlying theme of most of Ozu's films: the urban filmic landscape in general and that of Tokyo in particular, to which Wenders

12. "But I can't help but thinking: If I had been there without the camera, I'd now be able to better remember." Wim Wenders, *Tokyo-Ga: A Filmed Diary* (Berlin: Verlag der Autoren, 1985), 8. See Susan Sontag, *On Photography* (New York: Doubleday/Anchor, 1977), which critics have quipped might have been more accurately titled "Against Photography."

13. This problem (more evident in film than video) of first recording and then editing an experience—be it real or imagined—and rendering it visible in the form of an image is further explored in *Until the End of the World* (1991); there, through advanced technology, humans' most subjective imaginary—dreams—is recorded during sleep; this terra incognita, every bit as strange as the view of earth from the space station seen through Claire's eyes at the end of the film, is then transposed technovisually so that it can be objectified, manipulated, and—theoretically at least—made available to universal vision.

14. Jan Dawson, "An Interview with Wim Wenders" [1967], in *Wim Wenders,* Jan Dawson, trans. Carla Wartenberg (New York: Zoetrope, 1976), 10.

will return in *Notebooks on Cities and Clothes.*[15] As he states in a voice-over at the beginning of *Tokyo-Ga,* "Ozu's films always tell the same simple stories, of the same people, in the same city of Tokyo."[16]

In the voice-over of the edited film, Wenders adds that these stories span "over forty years." These multiple stories are told over and over again, as if their retelling could capture, via a kind of repetition compulsion that struggles to manage and stage some unstated—perhaps unrepresentable—trauma, what a first telling could not. The repetitions attempt to capture both the unrepresentable essence of Ozu's vision of the city and its people and the essence of the city's fascination for Wenders. Chronologically, Ozu's career encapsulates most of the formal and technical evolution of cinema. He made fifty-four films: some silent, some black-and-white, and finally some in color. In this sense, for Wenders, Ozu is indeed metonymically—if not literally—cinema, and exploring his art becomes an exploration of the nature of visual technology in general, an archaeology not only of its past but also of its potential.[17]

Because Ozu has had such a long career without breaks or apparent crises, he has been accepted as the father of Japanese cinema, or even (for the reasons just given) as the father of cinema tout court. He stands as a paternal figure providing a continuity of cinematic practice that was so notably absent in post–World War II Germany. There have been two main stages in the exodus of German film directors from Germany: first, during the Weimar period, when directors such as F. W. Murnau were bought up by Hollywood and moved to the United States; and second, during the Third Reich, when many Jewish or left-wing directors, such as Billy Wilder, were forced to flee. With some exceptions, those directors who remained in Germany during the Third Reich were discredited. Thus, in German cinema there were no representative father (as well as mother)

15. I cite from the soundtrack of *Notebooks on Cities and Clothes* (Aufzeichnungen zu Kleidern und Städten), dir. Wim Wenders, 35mm, 80 min, Road Films, Berlin, 1989. For a slightly different text, see Wenders, "Aufzeichnungen zu Kleidern und Städten" [1989], in *Act of Seeing,* 111. This text differs from the soundtrack in several ways, including the absence of the remarks of Yohji Yamamoto, Wenders's interview subject. Later, in *Tokyo-Ga,* Wenders asserts that he seeks his images in the "chaos" of Tokyo.

16. See also Wenders, "Tokyo-Ga," in *The Logic of Images,* 60. This text, which apparently served as a draft script for the film, does not always correspond exactly to the voice-over in the final version. Citations to the film voice-over will be *Tokyo-Ga;* citations to the written text will be "Tokyo-Ga." While the difference between these two texts is undoubtedly significant in other contexts, it is not necessary to take account of it here.

17. For a useful article on Ozu's influence on Wenders, see Kathe Geist, "West Looks East: The Influence of Yasujiro Ozu on Wim Wenders and Peter Handke," *Art Journal* 43 (fall 1983): 234–39. Remarkably, Geist wrote her piece before Wenders made *Tokyo-Ga.*

figures to whom to look up or back.[18] In this filmic generation without fathers, Ozu filled such a role for Wenders. No doubt there are other ideological implications of latching onto a figure of continuity after World War II, but they do not seem to have been extensively discussed by film historians, and the jury on Ozu's ideological commitments remains out.[19] Furthermore, Wenders does not raise that question, let alone answer it—neither in *Tokyo-Ga* nor elsewhere.[20] This failure may be viewed as *Tokyo-Ga*'s major "symptomatic silence," its "determinate absence."[21] As a result, viewers will be more or less satisfied with Wenders's tendency to make elusive (not to say evasive) statements.

Ozu always used only one camera lens to shoot his films—a 50mm. This aesthetic strategy led directly to Wenders's experiments with lenses in Tokyo, most notably to try to replicate the shot of a street in Shinjuku that often appears in Ozu's films. First shot with a standard 35mm lens, the street looks strange, even though that lens most closely approximates the normal visual field of the unaided human eye. Then Wenders refilms the street, like Ozu, with a 50mm lens with straight telephoto effect, and the street bursts to special life, even as the lens distorts normal vision by further reducing the field of depth to an almost photographical two-dimensional plane. That new vital image, Wenders sadly acknowledges, is neither the street's nor his own: it belongs to Ozu. And yet it somehow looks less strange, closer to nature, than the image yielded by the normal 35mm "eye/I." As Peter Beicken and Phillip Kolker suggest, "the son—by

18. This explains perhaps why Wenders turned, at least initially, to American auteurs such as Samuel Fuller or Nicholas Ray. (At one point in his career, Wenders had imagined Fritz Lang as a kind of father figure.) By instructive contrast, Fassbinder found a major source of inspiration in Douglas Sirk (or Detlef Sierck, as he was known in Germany before his emigration).

19. Ozu's political position during World War II is not clear. He was sent to Singapore to make propaganda films for the Japanese regime. (His *There Once Was a Father* won a 1942 prize for the best propaganda film.) In Singapore, he saw many captured American films and was particularly impressed by *Fantasia* (1940, Disney) and *Citizen Kane* (1941, Wells). Ozu later became a soldier and eventually landed in an Allied prisoner of war camp. For contrasting views of Ozu's relationship to Japanese fascism, see Joan Mellon, *The Waves at Genji's Door: Japan through Its Cinema* (New York: Pantheon, 1976); David Bordwell, *Ozu and the Poetics of Cinema* (Princeton: Princeton University Press, 1988), esp. 282–95.

20. See in this regard Jameson's incisive critique of Wenders for not having followed through on his postmodern pretensions, instead leading viewers "into a phantasmagoria of the perceptual fragmented present no less somber and insulated than the classical solipsism and anomie reserved for the traditional individualistic centered subject" (*Geopolitical Aesthetic,* 166–67).

21. These terms are (loosely) derived from Louis Althusser and Étienne Balibar, *Reading Capital,* trans. Ben Brewster (London: NLB, 1977), 13–40; Althusser, *Lenin and Philosophy and Other Essays,* trans. Ben Brewster (New York: Monthly Review Press, 1971), 229–42.

the act of changing a lens—becomes the father. . . . Wenders finds a father, seems almost to see from behind his eyes, but realizes that, finally, the patriarch's images are not his own."[22] What exactly is happening technically at such filmic moments? Objectively, Wenders appropriates and then discards the image produced by Ozu's eye, replacing it with Wenders's own.[23] He approximates the Bloomian category of epigonal misprision (that is, creative mis/appropriation), known as "daemonization," whereby the "later poet opens himself to what he believes to be a power in the parent poem that does not belong to the parent proper, but to a range of being just beyond that of the precursor."[24] By a similar act of re/creative misprision, the epigone Wenders starts *Tokyo-Ga* with the credits and opening footage of Ozu's *Tokyo Story* (1953).[25] Wenders then inserts his own footage of *Tokyo-Ga* before splicing back to the end of *Tokyo Story* and terminating with his own credits. Thus, Wenders both frames and appropriates Ozu's work but leaves open the question of how far he goes beyond it,[26] what he creates in the interface between the given and the invented—that is, how *Tokyo-Ga* functions as an essay film.

Ozu's unquestioned mastery of his chosen cinematographic medium brought him to a level of formal perfection that eventually generated a new fashion in filmmaking, especially in Japan. In a similar vein, Wenders seeks a personal form that would somehow break with tradition (fashion) and yet would also succeed, like Ozu's films, in showing the continuity of

---

22. Robert Phillip Kolker and Peter Beicken, *The Films of Wim Wenders: Cinema as Vision and Desire* (Cambridge: Cambridge University Press, 1993), 89. This is a major leitmotif of their work; see esp. chap. 1, "The Boy with the Movie Camera: Biography, Historical Background, Student Films."

23. In *Until the End of the World,* Wenders appropriates both Ozu's main actor, Chishu Ryu, and that same Shinjuku street shot.

24. Harold Bloom, *The Anxiety of Influence* (London: Oxford University Press, 1973), 15. Of course Bloom's six categories are never completely distinct, and in Wenders's relationship to Ozu, one finds contaminating evidence, for example, of "tessera" (completion of the work of the precursor) as well as of "kenosis" (discontinuity with the precursor).

25. Wenders is hardly alone in his fascination with *Tokyo Story.* David Bordwell and Kristin Thompson note that it "was the first Ozu film to make a considerable impression in the West." Also interesting, in light of Wenders's disruptive narrative technique in *Tokyo-Ga,* is Bordwell and Thompson's thesis that "instead of making narrative events the central organizing principle, Ozu tends to decenter narrative slightly. Spatial and temporal structures come forward and create their own interest. Sometimes we learn of important narrative events only indirectly; an ellipsis occurs at a crucial moment" (*Film Art: An Introduction,* 3d ed. [New York: McGraw-Hill, 1990], 329). Returning to the notion of the "determinate absence" in Wenders's confrontation with Ozu's wartime past and political ideology, one might say that this problematic is present in *Tokyo-Ga* after all—but only, paradoxically enough, indirectly, in its ellipsis.

26. Of course, this is an appraisal of a technical problem, not a moral judgment. There is no value—necessarily, in and of itself—in being original.

tradition wrought by post/modern society. In a 1973 interview, just after having discovered Ozu in New York, Wenders explains, "The importance of Ozu for me . . . was to see that somebody whose cinema was also completely developed out of the American cinema, had managed nevertheless to change it into a completely personal vision. So Ozu was the one who helped me, and who showed me that it was possible to be colonized, or imperialized, in such a way that you really accepted the language. I mean, for me, there is no other language, no other film language. . . . I'm not even sure you can still call it an American one, but it was made in America at least."[27] Wenders sees Ozu as the archetypal artist who had no choice but to operate under the same ambiguous sign of Hollywood influence as did Wenders yet carved out a powerful original film style or language. No wonder he served Wenders as both an adopted precursor and role model.

Wenders's equivocal relation with America has not been limited to matters of Hollywood and cinematographic language. He has long been plagued by the anxiety resulting from the continued American presence and influence in Germany, much like the anxiety felt by Japanese with regard to the American occupation of their country. As Wenders formulated most laconically and notoriously in *Kings of the Road* (1976), "The Yanks have even colonized our subconscious." Or, as he explained in an interview that same year, "The American army was still here, and it still is. . . . But the fact that U.S. imperialism was so effective over here was highly favored by Germany's own difficulties with their past. One way of forgetting it, and one way of repression, was to accept the American imperialism."[28] In some never fully articulated way, as a film coming out of one former Axis power, *Tokyo-Ga* reflects via Ozu on the film history of another Axis power that turned submission through appropriation to liberation through subversion.

III. Images/Simulacra/Hyperreality: Tokyo and the Postmodern World

> The real is not that which can be reproduced, but that which is always already reproduced. The hyperreal.
>
> —Jean Baudrillard, *Simulations*

Tokyo-Ga is not merely about Ozu but also ostensibly about the modern city of Tokyo and, by extension, modern civilization in general. As recaptured by Wenders, Ozu's films show the transformation of life in a Japan

27. Dawson, "Interview," 8.
28. Dawson, "Interview," 7.

that was changing from a preindustrial to a modern society.[29] In *Tokyo-Ga,* Wenders adopts the debatable proposition that the decline of national identity is necessarily linked to, and coterminous with, the dissolution of the nuclear family. This leads him to the second subtext of *Tokyo-Ga:* its discourse on contemporary civilization, marked, in Tokyo, by the technology of image production and reproduction.

What specific images strike Wenders as he wanders through Tokyo on the mission to capture the ostensible Japan of Ozu's films, or the "trace" of that Japan, as Wenders's voice-over expresses it? The most significant sequences show a world dominated by mass media images, artificial signs of an alienated hyperreality suggesting an overall loss of essence and the related loss of an unmediated vision or meaning of reality. *Tokyo-Ga* seeks not merely to document and/or to construct the surface consciousness of a ritualized Japan but also to problematize the distinction between document and filmic invention on which the Hamburg Declaration and Kracauer's film theory depended.

On his first "day" of the edited film, Wenders shows the pachinko parlors, an apocalyptic picture of sets of pinball machines (shot not only with establishing shots but also with extreme, abstracting close-ups). Rows of Japanese men play the machines endlessly, losing themselves in the game as if wanting to escape reality (or rather move from one reality into another) by a process of prosthetic self-reification, transforming themselves into tiny mobile spheres. In contrast to American gambling culture, winning is not the primary goal here—though winning coupons can be exchanged for money, both legally and on the black market. Wenders's voice-over notes that pachinko first appeared after World War II, "when the Japanese people had a national trauma to forget." Pachinko thus evokes how Ozu could remain both caught up in the hegemony of Hollywood and yet somehow retain or produce his own identity and style. Wenders's words serve as a reminder of his national origins in postwar Germany, which also has massive traumas to work through, to repress, to suppress, to forget, and perhaps to reenact. Young Wenders was fascinated with the pinball machines introduced by the conquering GIs, in tandem with their films, during their early colonization of the German—and

29. This transition in Japan is roughly parallel to German industrialization, which, in the global and European context, came significantly later than in England and France. Thus, the shock of the new was greater in Japan than in countries where the transition had been more gradual. Many Japanese intellectuals recorded this shock in the 1920s when they returned from travel and study in Germany (where they had gone precisely because of this perceived parallel) to find a Japan they hardly recognized (even after a leave of what was in some cases only a few years). The returnees became torn between Western and Eastern values, and this crisis cut across ideological lines: some became Marxists, others Heideggerians.

global—unconscious. The intuition of a symbolic triad of Wenders's world begins to take shape: Japan, Germany, and the United States, the three dominant industrial postwar powers, both victorious and defeated. Wenders is fascinated because Ozu's "films show the slow decline of the Japanese family and the collapse of national identity," a fascination that is legitimated by the feeling that these films "don't do it by pointing aghast at the new, American, occidental influences, but by lamenting the losses with a gentle melancholy as they occur,"[30] losses experienced by Germany and the United States as well. The paradox that Barthes noted about pachinko—"a collective and solitary game"[31]—can be applied to the problematic of the film medium as Wenders views it.

Another repetitive sequence showing broader cultural units and contrasts occurs on the third "day" of *Tokyo-Ga,* when Wenders films a five-tiered driving range where Japanese men, for hours on end, hit hundreds upon hundreds of golf balls. In contrast to an American driving range, it does not matter where the balls go or even if they are hit. What counts is the ritual performative gesture of swinging the golf club, the mediatized image of doing the right, or fashionable, thing. Wenders's voice-over notes that in some of Ozu's later films, there are similarly ironic comments on golf and its transformation into pure form, since the concrete goal of getting the ball into a hole has been either forgotten or actively rejected. Both Ozu and Wenders have severed golf as it is usually understood—a sport traditionally in which players compete against both other players and nature—from its original purpose and metamorphosed it into a self-referential set of visual gestures, its Zen or satori. Once again, as in pachinko's ritual metamorphosis of the gain-oriented pinball machines, the original Western model has been transformed into something uncannily familiar yet radically different and other.

On the fourth "day," Wenders films the manufacture of wax reproductions of restaurant dishes. These expensive simulacra of food are displayed in the windows of Japanese restaurants as a sort of concrete menu where one can appreciate perfectly formed sandwiches, salads, and noodles. They are consumed visually, though not otherwise—an ironic and self-effacing commentary on the relation of vision to more primary bodily functions and needs. The creation of fake food in Japan has become a highly technical and lucrative craft, an art shunning realistic connections to the reality it claims to represent. Wenders is allowed to film the entire, quasi-artisanal production process in the surprisingly low-tech and pre-Fordist factory, with one notable exception: the lunch break, when real

30. Wenders, "Tokyo-Ga," 35.

31. Roland Barthes, *Empire of Signs,* trans. Richard Howard (1970; New York: Hill and Wang/Noonday Press, 1982), 27.

fast food is brought in and consumed. Thus, the only live moment—biological incorporation—eludes, or is forbidden to, the camera's eye. In a sense, manufacturing seductive, deceptive dishes for the eye of the consumer is not dissimilar from filmmaking. The creation of fake food starts with real food that is fixed with artful means, just as real life is artfully fixed on celluloid before it becomes cinematic images. The materialist-modernist slogan *man ist, was man ißt* (one is what one eats) becomes a postmodern—but still materialist—*man ist, was man sieht* (one is what one sees).[32]

Following a "day" four interview with Herzog and an aborted trip to the Japanese version of Disney World, arguably the icon of all simulacra, "day" five takes Wenders to a public park on a rainy Sunday afternoon. The park is invaded by groups of Japanese teenagers gathering around boom boxes that emit different forms of music. Each group is dressed in costumes corresponding to a specific musical style. Here is fashion as aural-visual simulacrum: in one corner, the young people play music from the rebellious 1950s (Elvis); in another corner the music is Blondie, from the '70s; still another machine plays 1960s rock; and so on. (Few filmmakers know Western popular music better than Wenders.) There are dance lessons, posing and fashion lessons, and so forth. Everyone attempts to reproduce the images—the signs and subcultural style—of borrowed models, primarily American or, more accurately, seemingly American.[33] What is thus produced is a form of cultural history or a simulation of history. For the Japanese students, who go to the park without parental consent,

32. This moment in *Tokyo-Ga* seems to confirm a thesis about postmodernism developed by Japanese media critic Takayuki Tatsumi. With reference to the cyberpunk novels of William Gibson, Tatsumi describes the "postmodern paradox," in East and West alike, as a situation in which "the perceiver literally becomes the perceived." For example, "Gibson's Chiba City may have sprung from his misperception of Japan, but it was this misperception that encouraged Japanese readers to correctly perceive the nature of postmodernist Japan. In short, the moment we perceive cyberpunk stories which misperceive Japan, we are already perceived correctly by cyberpunk" ("The Japanese Reflection of Mirror Shades," in *Storming the Reality Studio: A Casebook of Cyberpunk and Postmodern Science Fiction,* ed. Larry McCaffery [Durham: Duke University Press, 1991], 372).

33. In the park Wenders finds a group of people who, as the voice-over says, "don't let the rain stop them from *being an American.*" The humor of this scene, at least for some viewers, depends on the debatable assumption (which also seems to be Wenders's) that the young Japanese are merely imitating things American; in fact, however, they are (also) appropriating American images (among others) for the sake of what Dick Hebdige called counterhegemonic style (*Subculture: The Meaning of Style* [London: Methuen, 1979]). For some of the cultural-political implications of style in this sense, see Greil Marcus, *Lipstick Traces: A Secret History of the Twentieth Century* (Cambridge: Harvard University Press, 1990); Jon Savage, *England's Dreaming: Anarchy, Sex Pistols, Punk Rock, and Beyond* (New York: St Martin's, 1992).

this activity constitutes a form of rebellion, but this rebellion is ritualized in the form of reproduced styles, and their music is pure form, like pachinko, the driving range, and perhaps even film itself. That formalizing process, of course, could also mirror the American model since, in the United States, the same music, once a sign of rebellion, similarly ended up coopted and commodified.

The film raises an old question for art: how much is reality, and how much is artifice? (What is real and what is Memorex?) Are we supposed to envision all of the modern world—especially Japan, Germany, and the United States—whether filmed or not, as merely a derived spectacle or simulation, a Baudrillardian or Debordian nihilistic universe, a televisual projection? Wenders's *Tokyo-Ga* surely reflects a basic fascination with spectacles in a society where mass-produced images, disseminated as commodities, lose connections to reality and become valued and consumed only for their own sake as images. Yet at the same time, Wenders the filmmaker contributes to this multiplication of images and feeds off them, incorporating them in various senses of the word. Whether Wenders's critique of spectacularization reflects adequately on this semiparasitical relation remains a troubling and unresolved question in *Tokyo-Ga.*

Wenders's images of Tokyo, Japan, and the modern world may be taken at their face value as images of reality, believing that, however aestheticized, spectacularized, and distorted, they reflect or express a real Tokyo and evoke a real world. But one could also conclude that Wenders's sequences are not true images of Tokyo but are only arbitrarily selected and edited, without any basic regard for reality, that they are only attractive spectacles to entertain viewers. This is but one of several points where *Tokyo-Ga* opens up onto its third main theme: a reflection on the nature of film and its images. Wenders leaves unresolved the problem of reality, which is displaced by the obsessive self-reflexivity of a medium that, from its inception, has increasingly posed the question of reality.

IV. Film and Images

> What counts is that the mobile camera is like a *general equivalent* of all the means of locomotion that it shows or that it makes use of—aeroplane, car, boat, bicycle, foot, metro.
>
> —Gilles Deleuze, *Cinema 1: The Movement-Image*

Wenders's partly mimetic problematic is rooted in his initial decision to give his film about Ozu the form of a documentary.[34] Unlike the earlier

34. Wenders, "Ein Gespräch," 248.

Lightning over Water, which he states is a "movie without any rules,"[35] a documentary is supposed to be governed by rules of realism and verisimilitude. Logically, then, Wenders subtitles *Tokyo-Ga* a "filmed diary" and, through editing, he organizes clear day/night sequences as if they took place over a week, whereas in actuality they stretched over two weeks of footage. He intended the film, he claims, "just to take a look without wanting to prove anything"[36]—a traditional claim for realistic objectivity. In the same spirit, *Tokyo-Ga* displays several manifestly objective documents: actual sequences from one of Ozu's films, *Tokyo Story;* black and white photographs of Ozu at work with his crew; and four interviews in contemporary Tokyo. Two of these are with Western filmmakers, Werner Herzog and Chris Marker, and two with Japanese closely associated with Ozu, actor Chishu Ryu and cameraman Yuharu Atsuta. These documentary images help to persuade viewers of the documentary veracity of all of *Tokyo-Ga:* if what they show is somehow obviously true, Wenders's remaining images of Tokyo and his vision of the post/modern world must also be so.

At the same time, however, with a perversely iconoclastic (and sometimes iconophobic) pleasure, Wenders inserts multiple references to the misleading nature of all cinematographic statements: Japanese, German, American, or whichever. From this metafilmic perspective, *Tokyo-Ga* appears as a film about films rather than a film about reality (or rather about the rest of reality, since obviously film is part of reality), a filmic practice both defined and confined by cinematographic illusion.[37] In addition to the scenes from Ozu's *Tokyo Story,* Wenders's film contains a clip from John Ford's *She Wore a Yellow Ribbon* in which John Wayne stands without emotion in a cemetery—in a sequence Wenders saw on the TV in his hotel room during his first night in Tokyo. The images of Wenders's Tokyo "diary" may offer an illusion of the, or a, "real" Tokyo, but they also—and primarily—reflect real/illusory images of Ozu's cinematographic Tokyo.

There are other ways in which Wenders grafts his own discourse onto Ozu's images, down to specific icons. The most meaningful among them is no doubt the train. Images of trains and subways travel across the screen throughout Tokyo-Ga. (The omnipresence of trains in Tokyo is also captured by Marker in *Sans soleil.*)[38] It is well known that each of Ozu's films

35. Wenders's voice-over commentary in *Lightning over Water.*

36. Wenders's voice-over commentary in *Tokyo-Ga.*

37. This serves as a reminder of Jameson's thesis that "in the postmodern, autoreferentiality can be initially detected in the way in which culture acts out its own commodification" (*Geopolitical Aesthetic,* 5).

38. *Sans soleil,* dir. Chris Marker, 35mm, 100 min., Argos Films, Paris, 1982.

includes an image of a train viewed as a symbol or allegory of modernity.[39] Wenders opens his documentary with a shot of a traditional train excerpted from Ozu's *Tokyo Story* and matches it graphically with his own shot of a contemporary bullet train. For Wenders, the function of the train as the allegory of mechanized modernity and the seemingly irrevocable alteration of the quality of life is not limited specifically to Japan; it is a universal sign of modernism. His Tokyo merely represents yet another hyperreal instance of what is always already occurring globally. In this sense, like Mike Davis's Los Angeles, Tokyo is an imaginary future archaeological site.[40] Wenders's Japan is a self-consciously imaginary construction, "faraway, so close," like Barthes's Japan: "Though in no way claiming to represent or to analyze reality itself (these being the major gestures of Western discourse) [I can] isolate somewhere in the world (*faraway*) a certain number of features (a term employed in linguistics), and out of these features deliberately form a system. It is this system which I shall call: Japan."[41]

In fact, the train, the quintessential modern form of transport, may also have appealed to Wenders, and before him to Ozu, because the effects of train travel on territorial and national identity, simultaneously integrating and fragmenting, are remarkably similar to those of international cinema. Walter Schivelbusch claims that railways in the nineteenth century abolished traditional notions of space, destroyed boundaries, and reconfigured the here and now. At the same time, according to Schivelbusch, "when spatial distance is no longer experienced, the difference between original and reproduction diminishes."[42] The same disorientation and/or confusion may result from filmic experiences that collapse spatial dimensions even faster than do the images of reality—viewed like frames of a film—through the windows of a moving train. In response to the question of why there are so many trains in his films, Wenders explains, "Ozu has trains in almost all of his films too. . . . The locomotive with all of its

39. This allegorical connection has been pointed out often, including by Walter Benjamin, *Das Passagen-Werk,* ed. Rolf Tiedemann (1934–40; Frankfurt am Main: Suhrkamp, 1982); Frances D. Klingender, *Art and the Industrial Revolution,* ed. and rev. Arthur Elton (1947; Frogmore, U.K.: Paladin, 1975); Lynne Kirby, *Parallel Tracks: The Railroad and Silent Cinema* (Durham: Duke University Press, 1997); as well as earlier and in films by Dziga Vertov (*Man with a Movie Camera* [1929]) and Walter Ruttman (*Berlin, Sinfonie einer Großstadt* [1927]).

40. See Mike Davis, *City of Quartz: Excavating the Future in Los Angeles* (London: Verso, 1990).

41. Barthes, *Empire of Signs,* 3.

42. Walter Schivelbusch, "Railroad Space and Railroad Time," *New German Critique* 14 (spring 1978): 35.

wheels simply belongs to the cinema. It's a piece of machinery like the cine-camera. They are both products of the nineteenth century, the mechanical age."[43] But on this point his film produces a more adequate film theory than does his rather disjointed attempts at theorizing.

Thus, on "day" two, Wenders films a long, remarkable sequence of the Tokyo metro, focusing on the train windows as they go by: they look exactly like celluloid frames, each window an individual frame. The sequence provides an apt illustration for Deleuze's thesis in *Cinema 1* that, in a certain kind of cinema exemplified by Wenders, there is a direct link or "translation" between a film frame and the view from the window of a moving vehicle: "One might conceive of a series of means of translation (train, car, aeroplane . . .) and, in parallel, a series of means of expression (diagram, photo, cinema). The camera would then appear as an exchanger or, rather, as a generalized equivalent of movements of translation."[44] Just as Ozu's films show the deterioration of Japanese culture in the age of the train, so Wenders's films record a similar continuous deterioration, in the age of cinema, but with an increasing pessimism and concomitant nostalgia. Wenders's Japan of the 1980s is informed by both the most striking display of high tech and by the persistence of premodern tradition—as well as the most traditional vision of ritualized modern society.[45] In the same spirit of double allusion, the train in the framing shots refers not only to modernity—that is, a real outside world—but also to the train in the Lumière brothers' first film at the birth of cinema. It refers to the analogous visual experience provided by the aforementioned view from the moving windows and—by a further play on reality versus art—to the very consciously composed documentary image of the Lumières' train, filmed and edited at an angle rather than head-on.

All these explicit or implicit allusions clearly position *Tokyo-Ga* within the tradition of a self-referential cinematographic aesthetic practice—another feature of the essay film. Wenders argues that "in the instant when one puts a camera on a tripod and looks through it, three generations of filmmakers, or indeed four, have already done so."[46] One enters into the technohistory of film, whether consciously or not. As Bill Nichols remarks, "the documentary effect, as it were, turns us back toward the historical dimension and the challenge of praxis with a forcefulness borne of the text's almost tangible bond to that which it also represents *as though*

43. Wim Wenders, "Film Thieves" [1982], in *The Logic of Images,* 35.

44. Deleuze, *Cinema 1,* 4–5.

45. Something like this paradox has been noted by many 1980s writers and directors, including novelist Jay McInerney and Ridley Scott (*Black Rain* [1989]).

46. Wenders, "Ein Gespräch," 255.

for the first time."[47] It is in the site of precisely this "as though" that Wenders's (re)produces his images.

The quasi-historical, quasi-self-referential dimension at stake borders on the problematic of the history of the film. Besides the train, it involves various narratives placed in Tokyo and, of course, Tokyo itself. Entailed here is a tension between two city sites, Ozu's and Wenders's, which is particularly perplexing because, to continue citing Nichols, "documentary operates in the crease between the life as lived and the life as narrativized."[48] As Pier Paolo Pasolini noted, between lived experience and its narrative there always stands edited montage or pastiche. And so *Tokyo-Ga* must be seen as a filmed narrative pastiche that tests the truth of another filmed narrative, *Tokyo Story.* Both refer to the same rather jaded reality: Tokyo. The title, *Tokyo-Ga,* can mean something like *Tokyo, n'est ce pas? Tokyo, nicht wahr?* or *Oh, yeah, Tokyo, right?* Yet Tokyo's own reality is invisible in the film; it can only appear and be critiqued in an artistic form. The act of filming present-day Tokyo shifts it into the past.[49]

What, then, is the city narrative in *Tokyo-Ga,* and what symptomatic images and technologies does it highlight? Wenders's stated purpose was to see whether he "could still detect any traces of the time (of Ozu's films), whether there was anything left of that work, images or even people, or if too much had changed in Tokyo and in Japan in the twenty years since Ozu's death."[50] He is searching for present evidence of an assumed former true statement about or image of Tokyo—a truth that is created by the artful work not only of his own making or of Ozu's but of a camera and its edited trace. Wenders assembled his visual memory of Tokyo largely from frozen images in the text of Ozu's films. This use of stills may be related to Raymond Bellour's notion that in film, the use of nonmoving images opens up a space for self-reflection, not only on the movies but on the act of viewing the movie: "By creating distance and another time, the photograph allows me to think in the cinema. It allows me to think the film as well as the very fact of being in the cinema. In short, the presence of the photograph allows me to cathect more freely what I see. It helps me (a little) to

47. Bill Nichols, "Questions of Magnitude," in *Documentary and the Mass Media,* ed. John Corner (London: Edward Arnold, 1986), 111.

48. Nichols, "Questions of Magnitude," 111. "It, like the historical fiction, presents the question of how to figure the body, the structure, or present the person situated in history within a text situated as narrative" (114).

49. The "narrator transforms the present into the past" (235). Pier Paolo Pasolini, "Observations on the Sequence Shot," in *Heretical Empiricism,* ed. Louise K. Barnett, trans. Ben Lawton and Louise K. Barnett (Bloomington: Indiana University Press, 1988).

50. Wenders, "Tokyo-Ga," 60.

close my eyes though they keep on being open."[51] Indeed, Bellour has noted that the use of still photographs is a constitutive feature not only of essay films but also of essay videos because it is a way of allowing "the image to think," not merely to slow down time but also to stave off death.[52] Toward the end of Tokyo-*Ga,* like viewers of a striptease, the audience finally gets to see Ozu after first being shown his grave. This revealing image is accessed through a series of black-and-white photographs of the master shooting and directing films, including *Tokyo Story.*

A basic paradox that underlies *Tokyo-Ga*—and Wenders's essay cinema more generally—is that, as a documentary, it seeks a goal that cannot be reached and yet must be sought, an objective truth about a reality that is always subjectively perceived and thus always elusive as truth. In search for a more or less post-Romantic closure, Wenders's visit to Ozu's grave is symbolic of that paradox: on the gravestone he finds no name, only the Chinese character *mu,* which, as Wenders explains, means emptiness or nothingness. "We are nothing," the Romantic poet Hölderlin had written in *Hyperion* (a text known to Wenders), "what we seek is everything."[53] This absence of closure, inscribed on the opaque black rock of Ozu's headstone under the guise of formal closure, understandably troubles Wenders. For him, his voice-over says, nothingness cannot exist; only reality can exist and be perceived, recorded, and edited into a film. One can never film nothingness but only suggest it, as it were, by a real reference to an absence and/or an artificial reference to a presence. Wenders's search for Ozu leads to such a suggestion of determinate absence: a gravestone inscription that is real but refers to a nothingness, which cannot, by definition, be represented. Similarly, all cinema's search for reality is figured by images that may in some sense be real and artistically striking but can only suggest a reality without any objective reliability. In that sense, *Tokyo-Ga* displays a particularly deep tension that underlies all recent Wenders films, both essays and features: a tension between images of a porous reality that can only be hinted at and images of a clearly artistic representation of reality that seems omnipresent. For Wenders, the distinction between image and narrative, between feature and essay film, becomes porous, threatening to collapse completely.

---

51. Bellour as cited by Stojan Pelko in "Punctum Caecum; or, Of Insight and Blindness," in *Everything You Always Wanted to Know about Lacan (But Were Afraid to Ask Hitchcock),* ed. Slavoj Žižek (New York: Verso, 1992), 107.

52. Raymond Bellour, "Zwischen sehen und verstehen" [1990], in *Schreiben Bilder Sprechen: Texte zum essayistischen Film,* ed. Christa Blümlinger and Constantin Wulff (Vienna: Sonderzahl, 1992), 63.

53. Wim Wenders, "Das Wahrnehmen einer Bewegung" [1988], in *Act of Seeing,* 47.

This complexity underlies even the most "documentary" features of the film—that is, the interviews that are expected to document reality by recording an authentic human presence and voice. The first is with Ryu, an actor who played in most of Ozu's films. Strangely, Ryu almost always acted out characters much older than he was himself. He describes himself as being a blank page, a tabula rasa—almost like his master's gravestone, though he dare not say it—that was completely empty until Ozu filled it with instructions. Ryu's filmed testimony, supposed to assist the search for truth, paradoxically implies that his filmed statements always involve deception because of their artificial nature and that the author of that deception was the greatest realist filmmaker: Ozu. Ozu, who except for trains, rarely shot outdoors, re-created reality within his studio with a painstaking mix of artificial elements. The Ryu sequence also evokes Wenders's shooting and later editing *Tokyo-Ga,* including his presence in the film as voice-over (his hands also appear on occasion) so that this aural—not visual—presence has an obvious suturing function as a kind of master narrative. Wenders never refers to editing as a vital part of Ozu's filmmaking, raising the painstaking process only in later recollections, where Wenders notes that *Tokyo-Ga* "made me realize that editing a documentary is a much more complicated business than editing a feature film. . . . The editing took months; it got out of all proportion to the filming."[54] With these words, Wenders problematizes his relationship to the problem of representation by alluding to his technique.

The second interview on "day" five is with Werner Herzog and may be viewed as emblematic for Post/New German Cinema—an allegory of its aesthetic, political, historical limits and future potentialities. The two filmmakers meet for a conversation atop the Tokyo Tower, a simulacrum of the Eiffel Tower.[55] Herzog complains that there are no longer any "pure and clear and transparent images" left to film in Tokyo or, for that matter, in the familiar modern world.[56] His only chance as a filmmaker, Herzog

54. Wim Wenders, "Le souffle de l'ange" [1987], in *The Logic of Images,* 107.

55. A number of meetings/encounters between Herzog and Wenders have taken place: in 1976 in Düsseldorf, for the collaborative essay film *Chambre 666,* and so on. They have become almost expected.

56. Whereas Herzog puts the search for images in aesthetic, optical, and metaphysical terms (purity, clarity, transparency), Wenders uses terms that are epistemological and pragmatic. Thus, speaking of Ozu, he writes, "Never before or since has the cinema been so close to its true purpose: to give an image of man in the twentieth century, *a true, valid and useful image,* in which he can not only recognize himself, but from which he can learn as well" (Wenders, "Tokyo-Ga," 60, 64). Herzog comes across as a rather naive Cartesian, Wenders as a savvy Kantian. Herzog apparently did not much like this moment in *Tokyo-Ga.* Furthermore, Wenders discarded Herzog's type of image by the time of the 1975 film *Wrong Move.* At the end of the film, the protagonist goes to the top of a mountain, expecting a storm or a moving aesthetic experience—but, as the voice-over says, nothing happens.

insists, would be to join the space shuttle, go into a war zone, climb to the top of a mountain and see something really new.[57] For Herzog, pure images entail extreme risk, even to the point of death, not only theoretically but in the actual shooting of films (and at least one actor has died during his shooting process). But even as Herzog decries the lack of potential images in Tokyo, Wenders's camera begins to pan surreptitiously over the various images that Tokyo supplies for his film; his apparent interest putting the lie to Herzog's fret, which appears as naive, anachronistic, nostalgic, modernist, even premodern. At first glance there is a "Mexican standoff" between two giants of New German Cinema: Herzog, who stands for a cinema of purity but finds virtually no more real images to film; and Wenders, who stands for a cinema of immersion and finds too many images of too many cultures in which to revel. Yet at the same time, Wenders is seen struggling less with Herzog himself than with a certain "Herzog effect"—the continuing search for modernist and premodernist authenticity in a resolutely postmodernist condition, mistrustful of master narratives or even all narratives. To this day, Wenders still problematizes this search, to the point of killing it off again and again in the act of imaging it.

The Herzog interview is immediately followed, on "day" six, by a very fleeting encounter with Marker. This easily overlooked meeting takes place in a bar bearing the name of one of Marker's best-known films, *La Jetée* (1962), a "feature" film consisting entirely of still photographs that asks a basic question that Wenders takes up three decades later in *Until the End of the World:* can the unconscious be captured in a photographic image? Marker's influence should not be underestimated, and at the beginning of *Tokyo-Ga,* Wenders alludes to *Sans soleil,* another of Marker's films. Marker's protagonist writes, "I remember, I remember a January in Tokyo, or rather I remember the images I filmed in January in Tokyo. They have replaced my memories, they are my memories. I wonder how people remember who don't film, who don't photograph, who don't use tape recorders." Wenders's version of this comment in *Tokyo-Ga* is, "I no longer have the slightest recollection. I recollect nothing whatsoever. I know I was in Tokyo. I know it was in the Spring of 1983. I know I had a camera with me and I did some filming. I have the pictures, they have become my memory. But I think to myself: if you'd gone there without a camera, you would remember more."[58] The appraisal of memory, recorded for Marker but subjective for Wenders, echoes the tension between the documentary and creative poles of the essay film. Marker's

57. Herzog seems to have at least partially realized his dream during the 1991 Gulf War when, in his *Lectures in Darkness,* he filmed the war-ravaged Near East against the soundtrack of classical music, including Wagner.

58. Wenders, "Tokyo-Ga," 60–61.

presence in *Tokyo-Ga* shows that Wenders imputes to Marker a privileged status, so that the film—an explicit tribute to Ozu—offers also an implicit and troubling tribute to Marker as photographer, essayist, image maker, and subject. Like the workers eating their lunch in the wax food factory, Marker does not allow himself to be photographed, except for one eye. Like the one eye of the painter Derwatt (actor-filmmaker Sam Fuller) in *The American Friend,* this is the monocular eye of all artists working in two dimensionality, unlike binocular "natural" vision.

The last—and most technically oriented—interview, on *Tokyo-Ga's* seventh "day" (the day on which one is allowed to rest, creation having been completed), presents Atsuta, Ozu's cameraman. Under Ozu's guidance, Atsuta simplified the technique of visual expression, shooting only with a 50mm lens camera fixed at the eye level of someone sitting on the floor, on the ground, or even lower. He recalls that Ozu objected vehemently to the use of any different lens or position, holding that this supposedly simple shooting technique enabled him to get images that were both epistemologically or ontologically true and formally and technically flawless—in other words, images that disclosed a deeper order in a chaotic world out of order and joint. Atsuta suggests that Ozu's vision of reality only appears truthful, that its perfection results from a particular filming style, from artifice. In response, Wenders experiments by switching lenses and, as a result, agrees. It is implied that shooting techniques are always a personal matter yet are impersonal to the extent that they are historical and technological—a matter of an individual, sometimes idiosyncratic personality, projecting its vision on actors, cameramen, even objects. Atsuta's interview ultimately leads to a requestioning of the nature of filmed reality: yes, there are real streets in Tokyo, and, yes, they must be filmed so that cinema can keep them and itself alive; but the filmed images of these streets reflect as much self-concerned art as reality. When carried to a decadent extreme, this obviously self-reflecting (but also perhaps onanistic, solipsistic, or cannibalistic) notion of cinema as art that feeds on itself accounts for Wenders's admiration for the craftsmanship of great film auteurs such as Ozu.

V. Television and National Politics

> Television is poison ivy of the eyes.
>
> —Wim Wenders, *Reverse Angle*

It is up to the viewer today to recall or imagine what sort of allegory could be represented by Japan in the mid-1980s, before the general collapse of East Asia's economy. As one of the world's wealthiest and, at least on the surface, most stable countries, Japan offered fascinating features: soaring real estate values, buying and selling of works of art at outrageous prices, extensive education and recreation programs, a fully socialized and integrated workforce, various models for foreigners who wanted to get rich quickly, and masses of Japanese tourists who seemed to circulate internationally, as ubiquitous as the Japanese products that were spreading throughout the world marketplaces, workplaces, recreation sites, and homes: computers, televisions, cameras, video recorders. Through vertical and horizontal integration, companies like Sony and Panasonic not only provided the technological means for the production and reproduction of images but also networks to control and determine the distribution and consumption of these images. The total picture was fascinating but threatening in its implication for art. Japan largely epitomized postmodern civilization, but not all aspects of that civilization met with approval, at least not from Wenders.

One feature of this cultural hegemony that Wenders particularly disliked, even feared, at least initially was television, which he considered a technological evil. In 1989 he had few doubts: "In principle, I believe that television is unbearable—it is naked fascism [*der nackte Faschismus*]."[59] For a long time television was viewed as the competitor and eventual destroyer of cinema (though that has not come to pass), which may explain Wenders's mighty ire born partly from despair. For Wenders, television could only stifle the viewer's already fragile creativity. Arguing in 1989 that "the great thing about rock 'n' roll" is that it could suggest for listeners a "collective dream," Wenders complained that, with the advent of MTV, "today each song is already supplied with the dream, so that one can no longer supply it with images. They already come with it."[60] Ironically, this diatribe against MTV and, by extension, the "new" TV in general is informed by the same traditionalist or modernist arguments that defenders of literature used to attack cinema at its inception for ostensibly murdering imagination.

TV is omnipresent in *Tokyo-Ga* (not only visibly but invisibly as mood) in the form of commercials in the background; in shop windows along the streets; on the screens in Wenders's hotel room, in taxicabs, and so forth. TV has forcefully intruded into Wenders's films, insinuating its supposedly malevolent, totalitarian, fascist presence into every nook and cranny of filmed everyday life. As if resigned to this cultural invasion, Wenders at the same time begins to show an appreciation for video.[61] In the 1989 *Notebooks on Cities and Clothes,* he goes into some length about

59. Wenders, "Ein Gespräch," 240.

60. Wenders, "Ein Gespräch," 238.

61. Indeed, Wenders was one of the first of New German Cinema directors to ensure that all of his films were distributed in video format, thereby helping to promote his commercial success.

the advantages of video over film. In 1993 he agreed to make music videos for the Irish rock group U2. And he made it possible to receive *Until the End of the World* and *Faraway, So Close!* as MTV—with the result that the film's sound track has had greater commercial success than the film itself. Nonetheless, in the mid-1980s Wenders's hostility toward TV and MTV were unambiguous, leading him to declare in *Tokyo-Ga* that "every shitty television set has become the center of the world."[62]

The globalization of the networks contributed a new geopolitical dimension to Wenders's on-and-off crusade. He notes that among the three great Western powers to which *Tokyo-Ga* refers, only two—Japan and the United States—are linked in the unholy alliance to TV. As he states in *Tokyo-Ga,* though the Japanese build the most and best television sets, these sets show American images that are becoming the "center of the world." Here, Wenders returns to his old theme, the cultural hegemony of America, the imperialist expansion of American culture throughout the world. But, Wenders's practice undermines his ideology. There could be many practical reasons why Wenders would narrate *Tokyo-Ga* in English—and American English, at that. But there is no particular explanation of why no mention is ever made (either in the film or in the credits) of who translated the Japanese interviews. On the one hand, Wenders says he knows no Japanese; on the other, he uses his disembodied Americanized voice to mediate what is being said to non-Japanese audiences. Is Wenders thereby participating in a baneful linguistic hegemony, or is he trying to gain power over that hegemony by appropriating its language as his own?[63] His suturing voice-over is extremely controlling and authorial, and though he may pretend to show something without explaining anything, this voice betrays the ambiguity of his project.

Thus, for Wenders, film—in contrast to television—may help subvert American hegemony. In the Reinhold Rauh interview, conducted in 1989, just before German reunification, Wenders offers a vision for the future of cinema that links it directly to a future integrated and independent common European market. In a united Europe, cinema could become a standard-bearer for European culture, just as television is for Japan and America:

---

62. It is ironic, therefore, that after the credits of *Tokyo-Ga* end—those of Ozu and those of Wenders—the last words that appear on the screen before it goes blank are these: "Commissioned by Westdeutscher Rundfunk."

63. Wenders's English-language voice-over has become something of a signature in his essay films. It also appears in *Lightning over Water, Reverse Angle,* and *Notebooks on Cities and Clothes.* Therefore, it comes as a surprise to hear Wenders's contemplative voice in his native German in *Report from Hollywood* (1982), directed by Edward Lachman.

> Film is in fact a vanguard for the European idea of 1992. Films today are coming out of different European countries and being made by colleagues and means from three, four different nations, in which they are also being seen. . . . And even as form, as language, film is the only trans-European culture [*übereuropäische Kultur*] that we have today.[64]

As yet another defender of *Kultur,* Wenders wants (his) cinema to become part a modernist project for European unity and *Gemeinschaft.* He will undertake that project in earnest immediately after *Tokyo-Ga* with *Until the End of the World* and *Lisbon Story* (1995), the latter of which constitutes a truly European production.[65]

VI. *Notebooks on Cities and Clothes;* or, The Germany-Japan-France Axis

In 1989 Wenders justified and legitimated film by linking it to the high culture of literature and painting, claiming that literature, and perhaps also painting, is likely the only thing that can save something like inwardness.[66] Only by alluding to or re-presenting this interiority, this inner experience, might the camera—might Wenders's films—momentarily acknowledge their own limits and place their vision, as in a painting, both personally and historically.[67] Wenders came to filmmaking by way of painting, and the idea of a painted image more original than film has haunted him ever since.[68] The notion of originality and its interface with modern technology of production (rather than [Benjaminesque] reproduction) seems to worry

64. Wenders, "Ein Gespräch," 260.

65. In *Until the End of the World,* Wenders visits all the countries that figured in his earlier films. But he also moves beyond Europe and the United States to the Australian outback. A certain primitivism is thus added into the pot.

66. Wenders, "Ein Gespräch," 241.

67. "But for a filmmaker, Vermeer is the only painter there is. He's really the only one who gives you the idea that his paintings could start moving. He'd be the ultimate cameraman, the ultimate top-notch cameraman. Ozu's are the only film images I can think of on a level with Vermeer's painting" (Dawson, "Interview," 23). In *Until the End of the World,* Wenders at one point re-creates a Vermeer painting when Claire captures the image of the daughter and granddaughter.

68. Wenders is not alone in problematizing the relationship between painting and cinema, Jean-Luc Godard has long incorporated classical images from great masterpieces into his films. For important discussions of the problematic relationship between film and painting (though not about Wenders specifically), see Raymond Bellour, ed., *Cinéma et peinture: Approches* (Paris: Presses Universitaires de France, 1990).

and confuse Wenders. He celebrates Polaroid technology because it involves no negative, only an "original." In his 1989 *Notebooks on Cities and Clothes,* he suggests that digital imaging may provide the only true images of the postcontemporary future, precisely because there is no original. Conversely, he shot *Notebooks* in both the traditional 35mm and the new format of the (then hated) video.[69] Although *Notebooks* provides ample evidence of Wenders's antipathy to television and video, his fascination with the world of the simulacra and the power of audiovisual media to replicate (if not redeem) reality, with or without originals, belies this antipathy and moves him to confront several technocultural forms in his work, including high-definition television.[70]

The Paris (Pompidou) Centre National d'Art de Culture originally commissioned *Notebooks* in 1988 as a film about fashion and the fashion industry. This was not an exceptional occurrence: many European essay films were (and still are) financed by government and/or industry through a system of industrialized rationalization and cooperation that Harun Farocki calls *das Verbundsystem*—a nexus of economic and political interests that financially support nonfiction cinema and yet, in turn, are often critiqued by it. Wenders claims to have accepted the offer because, as his voice-over explains, "this film would give me the opportunity to meet somebody who had already aroused my curiosity—someone who worked in Tokyo." And the resulting film ostensibly focuses on the Paris- and Tokyo-based high-fashion designer Yohji Yamamoto.

Wenders clearly had also other goals in mind since Yamamoto, like Ozu, is not the only topic of *Notebooks.* No doubt the decision to focus on a single designer, not the whole industry, allowed Wenders to pursue the problematic of authorship in this, the age of the death of the author. And the very pointed reference to Yamamoto's association with Tokyo suggests that even before Wenders started working on the film, he intended to make it a companion piece to *Tokyo-Ga.* The shared Japanese nationality of the two apparent protagonists is meaningful by itself, and the common evocation of Tokyo draws attention to significant thematic features, which in *Notebooks* manifest a conscious striving for both for continuity and change, two of Wenders's preoccupations.

The least innovative of these themes, in terms of Wenders's previous practice, stresses the nature and the role of the city, exemplified by Tokyo but also possibly by Paris, always floating in Wenders's imaginary background as the site of the metamorphosis of the modern into the postmodern world. In that sense there is no break between *Tokyo-Ga* and *Note-*

69. This no longer seems to be an issue: Wenders recently shot *Buena Vista Social Club* entirely on video.

70. See Wim Wenders, "High Definition" [1990], in *Act of Seeing,* 94–99.

books. Both can be dubbed "city films" and placed in the international tradition of Walter Ruttman's *Berlin, Symphony of a Great City* (1927), Dziga Vertov's *Man with a Movie Camera* (1929), and Marker's *Le joli mai* (1962). Wenders's fascination with the metropolis recalls Siegfried Kracauer's theory that film enjoys a generic connection to modern urban life because of the "medium's primordial concern for actuality."[71] In a 1991 address to Japanese architects, "The Urban Landscape," Wenders updated but hardly modified this theory:

> Film is an urban culture. It was called into life toward the end of the 19th century, and came to fruition together with the metroplexes of the world. Cinema and the cities grew up together, entered into maturity together. Film is witness to the development in the course of which the powerful cities of the turn of the century became the bursting and hectic cities of millions today. Film is witness to the destruction of two world wars. Film has seen the skyscrapers and the ghettos grow, it has seen the rich get richer and the poor get poorer.[72]

Wenders would agree with Kracauer that cinema is particularly apt to capture (and redeem) the physical reality of everyday life, "whose composition varies according to place, people and time."[73] That both Japanese and German cities endured massive destruction and reconstruction in the twentieth century cannot have escaped Wenders. Additionally, the concept of everyday life is extremely important to Wenders, and his fascination with protean daily existence may be said to echo Maurice Blanchot's notion that the everyday is the site of a creative contradiction involving the familiar, "the insignificant . . . without truth, without reality, without secret but perhaps also the site of all possible signification."[74] Located outside the texts of standard cinematographic fiction (or fantasy), Wenders similarly perceived that space between the lines as the preferred site of possible, rather than stable, images and meanings—that is, in the cinematographic economy of the essay film, as opposed to the strict documentary.

There is little doubt indeed that for Wenders the filmmaker, the accelerating new everyday life must have been primarily marked by the progress of the visual culture, which, as Jameson observed, was experiencing a paradigmatic shift from (high modernist) cinema to (postmodernist)

71. Siegfried Kracauer, *Theory of Film: The Redemption of Physical Reality* (1960; Princeton: Princeton University Press, 1997), 71–72.

72. Wim Wenders, "The Urban Landscape" [1991], in *Act of Seeing,* 116.

73. Kracauer, *Theory of Film,* 304.

74. Maurice Blanchot, "Everyday Speech" [1959], in *Everyday Life,* ed. Alice Kaplan and Kristin Ross (special issue of *Yale French Studies* 73 [1987]: 12–20), 12, 14.

television and video. The multiplication of relatively cheap and easy-to-operate video cameras was changing the way the general public was manipulating and receiving images.[75] The long-debated notions of authenticity, originality, production, and reproduction had to be reexamined, as did the special role of cinema in the new visual configuration. *Notebooks* pursues the most obsessive issue in Wenders's postmodern films: the problematic survival of the cinema in a time of video's explosive technological and commercial success. The tension between films and videotapes and the surprising thematic and structural exploitation of that tension form the most stimulating, most dynamic, and perhaps most controversial aspect of *Notebooks.*

For different reasons, and with different impacts, Wenders devotes extensive treatment to at least two topics in the film: haute couture as an obliged topic, a mirror of the fate of cinema, and a telling point of convergence of sociological, technological, and political aspects of the postmodern world; and the emerging international geopolitical aesthetic that encompasses Japan, Germany, and France. These two themes are interrelated, and while the first one—the fate of the cinema—clearly is the most pervasive and closest to Wenders's heart, the other one offers an essential key to understanding Wenders in the New World. More clearly than in *Tokyo-Ga,* where Wenders somehow eludes a definite commitment to political and social causes that his images seem to conjure, his treatment of fashion and global techno-aesthetics in *Notebooks* finally expresses with determination what happens in those areas of everyday life.

VII. Film versus Video Revisited

> Everything changes. And fast. Images above all change faster and faster, and they have been multiplying at a hellish rate ever since the explosion that unleashed the electronic images, the very images that are now replacing photography. We have learned to trust the photographic image; can we trust the electronic image? With painting, everything was simple, and each copy was a copy, a forgery. In film it began to get complicated. The original was a negative—without a print, it did not exist. Just the opposite—each copy was the original. But now with the electronic image and soon the digital, there is no more negative and no more positive, the very notion of the original is obsolete, everything is copy, all distinctions have become arbitrary.
>
> —Wenders, *Notebooks on Cities and Clothes*

75. For an insightful analysis on the ways in which not only video but cable programming have affected filmic production, see Timothy Corrigan's *A Cinema without Walls: Movies and Culture after Vietnam* (New Brunswick, N.J.: Rutgers University Press, 1991).

In terms of cinematography, the most obvious—perhaps most striking—and most surprising feature of *Notebooks* is its systematic alternating use of the two "enemy" media: film and video. This was the second major film that Wenders shot in both 35mm and video. In the first, *Lightning over Water* (1980), economic pressures rather than genuine free choice forced Wenders to have recourse to video and its haphazard, cold images. He resented what he viewed as a video contamination of his film, parallel, and allegorically identical, to the cancer that was consuming the body of his friend, Nicholas Ray. "Because it was a film about sickness," Wenders noted later, "within the film the video images seemed to me like a sickness," a particularly deadly "poison ivy of the eyes."[76] He had no well-considered ideological or artistic reasons for the mixed technique, no revision of his long-standing dislike for the new medium.

All that changed with *Notebooks.* For the first time, Wenders decided seriously to come to terms with video and, discarding past judgments, to work it through creatively, looking for a positive instead of negative relationship with film, and finally combining the two media in an innovative production. The resulting work was, he confides, "more than merely a little bit of gaming," because "it allowed me to make everything more or less by myself."[77] In a somewhat paradoxical way, he seemed to discover, with relief and joy, that the same video that he had condemned as lacking artistic impact could now enable him to keep on playing the author's role, practicing authorship in the form of affirmed identity and control. Wenders intended *Notebooks* to redeem video but to do so as film—or, rather, as an equal partner to film in the combined final product. The careful alternation between these media shaped *Notebooks* in the same way that the structure of film sequences shaped *Tokyo-Ga.* Wenders's personal style comes through in an idiosyncratic rhythm of both media and intramedia cuts that accentuates some of his basic ambiguities.

Notebooks opens with a "snow screen" of a video or TV screen, the credits displayed against it rather than written on it. After the credits, the screen remains as backdrop, and Wenders's voice-over is heard in English as the corresponding typewritten words are displayed. This is a long monologue about the crisis of identity in modern cities and clothes. After several minutes of this simultaneous audio and visual text, a seemingly arbitrary cut suddenly occurs, revealing an independent image: from the

76. Wenders, "Die Wahrheit," 70; *Reverse Angle: NYC March '82,* dir. Wim Wenders, 35mm, 17 min., Gray City, New York, 1982. *Lightning over Water* also expresses a certain moral crisis for Wenders in that he was not present as promised to witness and record the moment of his close friend's death, having gone away on business to finance his next feature film.

77. Wenders, "Die Wahrheit," 70.

backseat of a moving vehicle appears both the road in front and, closer, a small handheld TV screen. The video image on the inserted screen shows Tokyo streets, while on the spectator's left side are projected 35mm film images of the streets of Paris. The European Paris is associated with the older medium of film and the Asian Japan with the newer medium of video. As the vehicle moves on toward and around Paris on the Périphérique (circular bypass), logos appear on buildings: Sony, Pentax, and other brands of imaging technologies, all Japanese. The opening shots of the film thus announce its hybrid video/cinematic nature and its ambivalent inter/national, trans-technological matrix.

This strategy informs the entirety of *Notebooks,* which is spliced together from sequences shot in 35mm film and in video. The implementation two media illustrates Wenders's theory of image production. In a major subtext of the film, Wenders investigates video not only in the present but proleptically, in the not-so-distant future, attempting "to grasp what is approaching us."[78] He now acknowledges that video, firmly identified as part of everyday life, is here to stay and that he must come to terms with it for both pragmatic and aesthetic reasons. As he put it in 1990, "more people look at video than they see films on the screen," and, therefore, "one simply has to give up this deadly enmity [*Todfeindschaft*] and accept video."[79] *Notebooks* systematically alternates between interviews with Yamamoto, shot in 35mm on the outside terrace atop the Centre Pompidou, and video interviews conducted in Yamamoto's Tokyo studio. The binary polarization persists—Paris = film and Tokyo = video—but there is also a global synthesis achieved in Wenders's total film presented as film. In other words, under the appearance of balance, the scales remain formally weighted against the old enemy, video, framed and swallowed by the film as cinema.

Thanks to Wenders's complex technique, the two media are never entirely separate. From the credit sequence on, their images are often superimposed (metaphorically, poetically) and/or side by side (metonymically, realistically); in some cases, they are even tripled or quadrupled on a single screen. For example, at some points, the spectator/listener is treated to four different images and sounds at once, originating in four different spaces and time periods that are sometimes in sync with the everyday of haute couture but often are out of it. The content of these images tends to be less significant than their formal play, though there are important exceptions. A typical instance of such a technical manipulation is a collage sequence of Yamamoto's Parisian fashion show (to which the film's fea-

78. Wenders, "Die Wahrheit," 71.
79. Wenders, "Die Revolution," 91–92.

turelike narrative builds): 35mm footage occupies the top third of the screen, while the right- and left-hand sides return to interviews with Yamamoto in Paris and in Tokyo.[80] Wenders might have intended such an intricate *mise en abîme,* or "displacement mapping," to assert his own dominant position as filmmaker above and beyond the filmic status of his favorite fashion designer. What remains unclear is the semantic content of this play, even if there is no other meaning to it than another wink to a videotized revolution without truth claim. Such an obvious manipulation of overdetermined images, their intense spatiotemporal compression, requires and eludes a storylike narration, a problem to which Wenders returns repeatedly in his oeuvre.[81]

Notebooks often depicts a small video viewing/editing screen held in Wenders's hand so that the spectator momentarily experiences his point of view—indeed, "is" his point of view. This is one of many stylistic and formal explorations of the technological possibilities that the cohabitation of the main imaging media (film, video, TV) can offer. In the film, Wenders even concedes certain advantages to video:

> I felt like some monster making this film, working like [Yamamoto] in two different languages and using two essentially different systems. Behind my little 35mm movie camera I felt as though I were manipulating something ancient or perhaps classic. Yes, that's the word. Because my camera only takes 30m roles of film, I was obliged to reload every 60 seconds; therefore I found myself more often behind

80. Such multiple images are a familiar trope in art history as the "gallery painting" (a genre that depicts all the paintings in a patron's collection, sometimes including the frame painting) and are today a favored object of digital manipulation, which creates "a paradoxical picture gallery produced by repeatedly mapping an image into foreshortened rectangles" (William J. Mitchell, *The Reconfigured Eye: Visual Truth in the Post-Photographic Era* [Cambridge: MIT Press, 1993], 176).

81. For Wenders, the video format was never designed solely for commercial production: from its inception, artists have used video. As several critics have pointed out from different angles, video artists have always understood theirs to be a problematic medium, pitted with and against not only film but also television. And this is one of the problems that Wenders appears to be tackling, though often as if he were the only one. See further David Antin, "Video: The Distinctive Features of the Medium," in *Video Culture: A Critical Investigation,* ed. John Hanhardt (Layton, Utah: Peregrine Smith Books, 1986), 147–66. Antin argues that it is "unwise to despise an enemy, especially a more powerful, older enemy, who happens to be your frightful parent. So it is with television that we have to begin to consider video, because if anything has defined the formal and technical properties of the video medium, it is the television industry" (149). See also Doug Hall and Sally Jo Fifer, eds., *Illuminating Video: An Essential Guide to Video Art* (New York: Aperture Foundation, 1990), esp. Kathy Rae Huffman, "Video Art: What's TV Got to Do with It?" and Maureen Turim, "The Cultural Logic of Video."

> my video camera, which was always ready and allowed me to capture Yohji's work in real time. Its language was not classic, rather efficient and practical; the video images even felt more accurate sometimes, as if they had a better understanding of the phenomena before the lens, as if they had a certain affinity with fashion.[82]

The notion of video's "real time" to which Wenders alludes is problematic, not only because he once thought, with Kracauer, that real time in the urban everyday was the province of cinema. The deeper conceptual problem is that, whether made for film, video, or TV, real time evokes a metaphysics of presence and leads to the misrecognition that an image can exist somehow in an undetermined, auratic, nonmediated, nonmediatized, nonedited form.[83] Video's apparent affinity for real time and space has moved some theorists to link video not only to postmodernity, as does Jameson, but also to a high-modernist project in that it "was to create artistic forms responsive to the dynamic changes of industrialization," including "video's ability to spatialize time and temporalize space as potentially a means to continue the dissection of the apprehension and meaning of an event."[84] In *Notebooks* Wenders relates this problematic of video to the ephemeral transcendence of space and time shared with the world of high fashion.

This doesn't mean that video's pragmatic advantages have persuaded Wenders to place it above or alongside film in all areas of his work. Fashion sequences come out well in video, but in a parallel, 35mm documentary shots of the urban landscape of Paris and Tokyo interspersed throughout *Notebooks* exist as transition or suturing devices, the seams of his filmic texture. They display a rich array of long shots, wide-angles, close-ups with a zoom lens, and so forth—in short, a personal encyclopedia of filmmaking with a virtuosity that Wenders's video doesn't match. Wenders's video imaging, despite its claim to access real time, is not very accomplished. The sound bars are often visible; the tracking is slightly off; the verbal text lags behind the image; the cuts are too abrupt; the video text reveals its seams, unlike both Yamamoto's garments and Wenders's films. Is this rather crude representation of video technology—which is capable of being extremely sophisticated—intentionally rooted in prejudice, or does it reflect Wenders's failure to master the new medium in the years since *Lightning over Water.* Or is the point to foreground video as a medium against its "natural" tendency to conceal its nature.

---

82. Wenders's voice-over commentary in *Notebooks on Cities and Clothes.*

83. For a critique of this assumption, see Richard Dienst, *Still Life in Real Time: Theory after Television* (Durham, N.C.: Duke University Press, 1994).

84. Turim, "Cultural Logic," 338–39.

The pure film sequences in *Notebooks* primarily weave the narrative of everyday city life. Wenders candidly shows, in neo-Kracauerian terms, that only film can (still) redeem the real—a process that determines not only the end result seen but also how it was produced. As Wenders says in "Revolution without Truth Claim,"

> Everything that I liked of my preliminary video images [*Videoaufzeichnungen*], I recorded again on film. "Video" is here redeemed by "film" [*hier in "Film" hinübergerettet worden*]. I would never, ever use video if it were then possible to make only videos.[85]

He has continued to repeat such assertions in other essays.[86] Indeed, Wenders remains committed to the high-modernist aesthetic and ethical project to redeem the urban everyday in and through film. Video serves that main project only as a first stage—a first draft, as it were—of the filmic redemption. In addition to its direct affinity with fashion, video enables Wenders to capture private scenes that would normally be inaccessible to the more intrusive film camera. Video's forensic aspect is particularly useful for surreptitious surveillance. People become more easily used to the presence of the video camera than to the movements of an entire film crew, and, as Wenders observes,

> Slowly, almost in spite of myself, I began to feel comfortable working with the video camera. With the Eyemo [film camera], I always felt like an intruder. She made too much of an impression. The video camera impressed and disturbed no one; she was just there.[87]

85. Wenders, *Act of Seeing*, 92.

86. See, for example, Wenders, "Die Wahrheit," 70.

87. Wenders's voice-over commentary in *Notebooks on Cities and Clothes*. This reference to the camera as feminine is similar to the remark in *Tokyo-Ga* by Ozu's cameraman, who refers to his camera as his girlfriend—both men sexualize the camera. One also notes that both Yamamoto in his clothing and Wenders in his film are in the business of "fashioning a female body." According to Jane Gaines, "One can draw a useful analogy between the photographic representation of woman and the everyday adornment of her body," but although "this analogy between cinema and costume as representational systems—the comparison between two different mediators which construct 'woman'—may be fruitful, the parallel also calls our attention to something significantly different about cinematic representation and woman's dress as self-representation" ("Introduction: Fabricating the Female Body," in *Fabrications: Costumes and the Female Body*, ed. Jane Gaines and Charlotte Herzog [New York: Routledge, 1990], 1–2). The film industry has worked closely with the fashion industry—the former often promoting, exhibiting, and to a certain extent advertising the products of the latter—creating perceived needs as well as satisfying them. For a discussion of the connections among classic Hollywood cinema (especially MGM), consumer culture,

During this voice-over, the entire screen shows a video image—indeed, the only overtly gaming image in the film: inverted shots, people laughing without narrative motivation, and so on. Wenders attempts to capture in that way the effervescent behind-the-scenes world and everyday life of the fashion system. For that purpose video suffices, since, in fashion, there is no need for professional actors or even professional filmmakers—a situation that, were he to use a film camera, would have countered his pretension to redeem reality by film.[88]

At the beginning of *Notebooks,* Wenders, cited as an epigraph to this section, projects an apocalyptic vision of future video and other electronic media that do not have a negative or print (like film): for them, the idea of an original or a copy (even a copy of a copy) has become nearly obsolete. Now "all distinctions have become arbitrary"—a dizzying (and financially limiting) prospect for filmmakers. Where can a stable meaning be located, let alone the redemption that Wenders claims he is trying to find and show in his films? Perhaps this question cannot be answered in terms of video's power, because it obviates crucial technical difference: for Wenders, video is ethically irresponsible, not redemptive.[89] "Video," he wrote in 1990,

> has actually something "irresponsible" about it and is to that extent is exactly comparable to the phenomenon that I have investigated, namely fashion [*Mode*]. That is to say, my film images about fashion were presumptuous or hybrid attempts "to say" something about it.

---

and fashion, see Charles Eckert, "Carole Lombard in Macy's Window," in *Fabrications: Costume and the Female Body,* 100–121.To be sure, current Hollywood films are no longer such an exclusive vehicle of the promotion of haute couture. That function is rivaled by video and the Internet. For example, Norma Kamali exhibits her line on video, much like MTV, and there is a publication entitled *Video Fashion Monthly.* Willingly or not, Wenders's *Notebooks* participates in this project, for the film captures in video format a fashion show and advertises Yamamoto's work.

88. This ability to capture the private everyday may explain why one of America's most popular television genres endlessly replays "American home videos," ostensibly democratizing and somehow even immortalizing often excruciatingly boring personal, mundane lives. Virtually anyone can be video producer, though the jury is still out on the results. This has led pop musician Peter Gabriel to convince the Reebok Foundation to distribute inexpensive video cameras to the Third World for the recording of human rights abuses, although the Rodney King case offers cause for pessimism about the long- or even short-term effects of such videotaping. Farocki's *Videogram of a Revolution* contrasts the official film version of the Romanian revolution with that produced by citizens with video cameras.

89. "A film negative can be manipulated, but the truth claim that one grants to photography is still justified. But this is no longer so in a digital television image: the image as such is no longer a bearer of truth" (Wenders, "Die Revolution," 93).

> By contrast, video was an appropriate, heuristic attempt merely "to show" something.[90]

The distinction between "showing" and "saying" resonates with Walter Benjamin's methodology in his *Passagenwerk.* Wenders's peculiar version encourages a closer look at what he says and shows about fashion.

VIII. Film and Fashion

> Filmmaking is a much more moralizing act than making clothes.
>
> —Wim Wenders, "Die Wahrheit der Bilder"

First there was a simile: video is to clothing as film is to haute couture. *Notebooks,* in an apocalyptic reading, records the fall of both film and haute couture, their expulsion from their paradise, the urban milieu. Not any urban milieu, but only its incarnation in the modern city or metropolis. For Wenders, the world of haute couture seems to be as foreign to everyday life and its manufactured clothes as is his cinema, the author's cinema to video. The industry of haute couture is limited to the narrow zone where clothing becomes more than necessity as its use value shades into the symbolic value of a sign.[91] It is the site where creative production is perceived to belong both inside and outside the everyday. Haute couture, like film, thus can carry various meanings made of representations that are added to the mechanical nature of its material making.

What motivated Wenders's interest in haute couture? The Centre Pompidou's proposal was the anecdotal trigger. Wenders's voice-over in *Notebooks on Cities and Clothes* claims that his spontaneous initial response when asked to make the film was, "Fashion, I'll have nothing of it . . . I'm interested in the world, not in fashion." To thus separate fashion from the world seems now a bit disingenuous or naive—after all, fashion is surely part of the world and is quite symptomatic of the modern urban culture. One may recall the French etymological tie between *modernité* and *mode.*[92]

90. Wenders, "Die Revolution," 91.

91. On the importance of symbolic value as a crucial supplement to use and exchange value, see Pierre Bourdieu, *Outline of a Theory of Practice,* trans. Richard Nice (1972; Cambridge: Cambridge University Press, 1977), esp. 171–83. On sign value, see Jean Baudrillard, *For a Critique of the Political Economy of the Sign,* trans. Charles Levin (St. Louis: Telos Press, 1981).

92. This link was seen by Charles Baudelaire in "Le peintre de la vie moderne" and was later taken up by Georg Simmel and many others. For a detailed history of fashion and its ties to the world of modernity, the urban landscape, and so forth, see Elizabeth Wilson, *Adorned in Dreams: Fashion and Modernity* (1985; Berkeley: University of California Press, 1987).

Fashion has long been related directly to modern urban life and the power centers of its geopolitical aesthetic: Milan, London, New York, Paris, Tokyo. Catching up to this common insight and his professional interest in modernity, Wenders's rather disjointed voice-over records a change of mind that led him to film *Notebooks:* "Why not examine [fashion] like any other industry, like the movies, for example: maybe fashion and cinema had something in common." And so, together with other goals, his project gains one more objective: to compare and contrast fashion not with the world but with film and thus demonstrate once again cinema's mission as a register of life.

The "anxiety of influence" that informed Wenders's previous work continues to haunt *Notebooks,* but in disguised form. The ghost to be exorcised this time is the highly political Soviet filmmaker Dziga Vertov. In a sense, the subtitle of *Notebooks*—the articulation of cities and clothes—was forged already in Vertov's *Man with a Movie Camera.* That 1929 documentary chronicled a single day in Moscow through the eyes of a cameraman filming the postrevolutionary capital from dawn to dusk.[93] A self-reflexive essay film on the art of filmmaking, it elaborated Vertov's theory of the "kino-eye," in many ways an inspiration for Wenders. Whereas in *Tokyo-Ga* Wenders explicitly duplicated certain shots of Ozu to celebrate and to re/see through the master's eyes, in *Notebooks* he acknowledges Vertov only tacitly in two allusive shot sequences. First, there is a replication of the famous Vertov shot of the movie camera standing alone as the central protagonist of (the) film. Then, and more significantly, Wenders's voice-over states that making a film is like being a seamstress, which evokes Vertov's repeated shots that crosscut from his wife editing film footage to Muscovite factory women working at their sewing machines. Both film and clothing manufacture, it is implied, start with material (celluloid or cloth) that needs to be fashioned (tailored or edited) into something for public consumption. In opposition to Vertov, Wenders states this parallel in artisanal rather than industrial terms, which, for him, entails a certain distance between human and machine: "Form and material. The same old dilemma and ritual as with old handicrafts: take a distance [*Abstandnehmen*], look, approach again, grasp, touch." Thus, Wenders inscribes a major contrast to Vertov between the lines. In the Soviet filmmaker's case, the factory production of clothing marks the transition from artisanal to industrial mechanization and Tay-

93. While similar to Ruttman's *Berlin, Symphony of a Great City,* Vertov's film differs significantly in being an investigation and exposition of filmmaking. The personage of the cameraman is constantly foregrounded, showing the audience how certain shots are obtained. To that extent, *Man with a Movie Camera* closely parallels Buster Keaton's 1928 feature film, *The Camera Man.*

lorization by and for the masses, just as film is produced for them by a collective. Clothes are made and represented in their most essential form: as items of necessity and use, not, as in the case of haute couture, as a luxury, as fashion. The historical context has changed and so have the patrons—the Centre Pompidou replacing the communist Soviets.

And yet the Centre Pompidou's motivations in urging Wenders to make a film about fashion may have been influenced by another communist institution: the French Communist Party (PCF). During 1988–89—on the cusp of the bicentennial of the French Revolution—there occurred an attempt in Paris to wrest of high fashion from its elitist status and bring it to the people. This project was undertaken by a most curious coalition: the French communists and a French designer at least as well known as Yamamoto—Yves Saint Laurent. The result, in September 1988, was a huge open-air fashion show at the Fête de l'Humanité, hosted by the PCF for its members, its leftist friends, and the fraternal communist parties of the world. Some 50,000 people attended. The Fête de l'Humanité, an annual festival that combines political speeches, membership drives, and exhibits with a food fair and amusement rides, might be the Parisian reflection of the glory that used to be the Third International. Saint Laurent, portrayed to the public as an obsessively reclusive figure, was relatively left-wing for his industry and had close associates in or near the PCF. In fact, he was one of first haute couture designers to market off-the-rack fashions, his pret-a-porter line having a trickle-down effect for the general public. His 1988 show was unprecedented in introducing a new collection to the public before "le tout Paris" of haute couture.

The PCF announced that this event was intended to open up an ideological debate about the role of fashion, especially high fashion, in a time of scarce resources.[94] The Communist Party press anticipated accusations that high fashion is a waste of time and money when most of the world desperately needs basic essentials; that luxury is a sin when there is global and local poverty; that fashion constructs a false image of women, enticing them to conform to a patriarchal-capitalist model unattainable for the vast majority both physically and financially; and that fashion contributes to the principle of marginal dissatisfaction that motors commodity capitalism, meaning that fashion creates false needs and makes people dissatisfied with their lives but does so only in non- or counterrevolutionary ways that fold people back into the commodity culture of the society of

94. Unfortunately for posterity, the most detailed and interesting features of the ensuing lively debate, which took place at the fête the day after the fashion show, were not transcribed on the pages of *L'Humanité,* the party daily. But I am very grateful to Serge Cantó, head of documentation of *L'Humanité,* for providing me with all available research materials.

spectacle. On the positive side, the party anticipated that fashion is a utopian projection of what everyday life—integrating aesthetics and work—could be under communism; that fashion gives people something beautiful with which to compare their workday life, thus making them want to change it, a gap between the ideological and the real (Louis Althusser) that communist parties can exploit; and that communism needs to become less puritanical and ascetic, to loosen up and to understand people's fascination with luxury and wealth, a fascination found in genuinely popular discourse that ought to be neither ignored nor monopolized by the Right and Center. Despite dissenting voices, especially on the feminist Left, the PCF came down (more or less officially) on the positive side of the argument. After all, it had sponsored the event. "Let us forget for one evening," *L'Humanité* suggested, "that the most expensive dresses of the greatest French couturier are only a dream for nearly all women, and let us appreciate the fact that the great art form and spectacle of couture is being offered to the public for the first time."[95]

Just how Wenders's film fits into this larger sociocultural discourse must remain conjectural. The intellectual climate in Paris would have prompted the left-leaning Centre Pompidou to give its own spin to a cultural debate that was being promoted by the PCF and thus would bring Wenders into the discussion. The debate in the press was more complex than the arguments sketched out in Wenders's film. What, precisely, are the links in Wenders's *Notebooks* among film, haute couture, and leftist ideology? Wenders associates filmmaking and fashion as artisanal productions because both require *Abstandnehmen,* "taking a distance," which, in John Fiske's words, "is a key marker of difference between high and low culture, between meanings, practices and pleasures characteristic of empowered and disempowered social formations."[96] In empowered culture, that distance serves to minimize social differences "in favor of transcendent appreciation or aesthetic sensibility with claims to universality."[97] It is ironic but understandable that residues of that transcendent appreciation can be found "even" on the pages of *L'Humanité,* which proudly proclaimed, "in France, fashion is an art. Our great couturiers are painters and sculptures."[98]

Yet the appeal of universal aesthetic sensibility satisfied neither the PCF's nor Wenders's need for social justification. *L'Humanité* reminded its readers about the presence of workers behind the scene: "While celebrating fashion as art, we do not forget its economic dimension (paid

95. *L'Humanité,* September 2, 1988.
96. John Fiske, *Power Plays, Power Works* (London: Verso, 1993), 154.
97. Fiske, *Power Plays,* 154.
98. *L'Humanité,* September 2, 1988.

work) and still less the workers of haute couture, who are the artisans so indispensable for the creation of beauty," and Saint Laurent's show was transformed into "an homage to the workers of haute couture," contributing to PCF's expected "workerism."[99] More surprisingly, this politicoeconomic dimension also forms a part of Wenders's vision. He too feels compelled to show that the world of fashion is work, just like other forms of artisanal labor, but he channels this seemingly left-wing concern with the workers to support the cause of cinema and its workers. To be sure, he remarks on several occasions that the work of Yamamoto's staff "had just begun, they worked way into the night, after the show they would immediately go back to work." *Notebooks* spends much time showing the labor of producing fashion in Yamamoto's studio and getting it ready for the Paris *défilé*—the same event for which Saint Laurent was preparing. Wenders uses video to capture that work but crosscuts from scenes of collective fashion production to film editing tables, evoking a metaphysics of presence in which everyday artisanal work becomes inseparable from a higher final product, whether film or fashion. The homage to fashion and film workers turns into a celebration of making art—with textile or celluloid.

But nothing is straightforward with Wenders. Assuredly, it is video that records the interior world of fashion, providing as it were, its mise-en-scène. A video image discloses what Wenders claims is the most unusual moment in his film: a collective shot of workers' hands at the cutting table vigorously shaping and executing fashion designs: an extraordinarily privileged, almost literally redemptive instant. Indeed, without apparent irony, he dubs the owners of these hands the "guardian angels" of Yamamoto's artistry. But because this privileged image is captured by a video camera held in Wenders's hands, one is left wondering of whose art these two hands are the guardian angels. Is it Wenders himself, with video the ideal medium for a redeeming auteur? Is this a return to a modernist figure of the mighty creator? Not quite, but then not quite not either. For, despite his auteurism, Wenders views the loss of a working collective in negative terms. He is not willing to betray the filmic community and its workers for video, even as he himself is propelled into using it as a forerunner of the televisual technoculture of the next century. Torn between nostalgia for the artisanal artistry of cinema and the quasidocumentary rawness of video, suspended between the past and the future of the essay film, Wenders seems a little confused:

> And Cinema. This discovery of the 19th century, this beautiful art of the mechanical age, this language of light and movement, made of

99. *L'Humanité*, September 2, 1988.

> myths and adventures, those of love and hatred, of war and peace . . . are all these supposed to remain behind by wayside? And all these craftsmen [*Handwerker*], behind the camera, behind the floodlights, at the editing tables, are they all supposed to learn new jobs? Would there ever be an electronic craft [*Handwerk*], a digital craftsman?[100]

Wenders seems to be haunted by the prospect of an eventual demise of cinema, and one particularly telling shot lingers on his editing table, standing empty and unused.[101] If, for Wenders, the idea of collectivity in production is being increasingly eradicated through technological "advances," this does not mean that its informing tension disappears in his work. His more or less productive oppositions between film and video, individuality and collectivity, are *aufgehoben* in *Notebooks* as a new version of another old opposition for him: that between national and international identity. It is here that *Notebooks* fashions its final most disturbing link between the representation of everyday life and the perceived necessity for its (filmic) redemption.

IX. National Identity, Mourning, *Geschichte*, Everyday Life

> In its most extreme form, [cloth society] is a society in which values and exchange alike take the form of cloth. . . . In a cloth society . . . cloth is both a currency and a means of incorporation. As it changes hands, it binds people into networks of obligation. The particular power of cloth to effect these networks is closely associated with two almost contradictory aspects of its materiality: its ability to be permeated and transformed by maker and wearer alike; its ability to endure over time. Cloth thus tends to be powerfully associated with memory. Or, to put it more strongly, cloth *is* a kind of memory.
>
> —Peter Stallybrass, "Worn Worlds: Clothes, Mourning, and the Life of Things"

100. Wenders's voice-over commentary in *Notebooks on Cities and Clothes.* Critics have long remarked on the ostensibly narcissistic aspect of video: see, for example, Rosalind Krauss, "Video: The Aesthetics of Narcissism" [1978], in *Video Culture,* ed. Hanhardt, 179–91. As Turim has pointed out, "Early attempts to define video's cultural logic then posited a directly socially determined logic on the one hand (the antitelevisual vocation of video) and one internally determined logic, narcissism, that itself was soon posited as overdetermined by social conditions" ("Cultural Logic," 337).

101. This image is reminiscent of Vertov's *Man with a Movie Camera.* Of course, as a way of contrasting Hollywood production and the independent European avant-garde style, Wenders already had shown, in *Reverse Angle,* three separate editing rooms used for his first and last Hollywood feature, *Hammett.*

The matrix of geopolitical references surrounding Wenders's work gives it an aura of internationalism: The French government commissioned Wenders, a German filmmaker, to make a film about a leading Japanese fashion designer, but almost the entire filmic text is in American English. Thus, the nationalistic aspect of *Notebooks* has not received much attention, and Wenders's well-deserved reputation as a transitional artist has not been questioned. Yet a particularly important interview with Yamamoto is disturbing and even provocative. The setting, on the outside terrace of the Centre Pompidou, serves as an advertisement for the Centre, evoking its function as international shopping mall and museum—temple of the muses, guardian of recent world art, and commodifier of its simulacra.[102] During this interview, Yamamoto's past, and by extension that of Japan, suddenly creates a false note in what may be the single most fascinating—but also problematic and "undecidable"—shot sequence in *Notebooks*. The sequence is composed of two related but distinct parts, an image track and a sound track that are complexly interwoven, the sound track (subdivided into voice-over and music track) bridging different spaces not only in Paris but also in Tokyo.

The crucial sequence is rooted in a preceding sequence that begins in a pool hall in Paris, where Wenders and Yamamoto play pool while Wenders interviews Yamamoto in English about his work and his past. Before the dialog proper begins, Wenders's voice-over states that he is wearing a Yamamoto shirt, which, along with matching jacket, is the first haute couture item he has purchased and which fits not merely like a second skin but like "armor" that can protect sensitive or vulnerable organs. At one point, the conversation touches personal matters, with Yamamoto mentioning in passing that his father is dead. With this remark, Wenders cuts immediately to the Centre Pompidou. The dialogue is now in Japanese with English subtitles (and a nondiegetic sound-track music that is stereotypically "Oriental" and "mournful"), but the voice track is so cleverly edited that the language change is barely noticeable. The designer says that his father wasn't a professional soldier but was drafted during the war. "In fact," Yamamoto's translated voice continues,

> he had to go to war against his will, . . . and he died. His buddies were prisoners in Siberia. When I see the letters they wrote, when I read them, and when I think of my dead father, I realize that the war is still raging inside me. There is no postwar for me. What they wanted to

102. On the connections among film, museums, shopping, and fashions, see Anne Friedberg, *Window Shopping: Cinema and the Postmodern* (Berkeley: University of California Press, 1993).

> achieve, I am doing for them. It is a role I feel compelled to play. So that everything I have done so far, I did by accident. I really feel I am floating. When I think of my life, the first thing that comes to mind is that I'm not fighting this battle alone. I think it's the continuation of something else.

In the exact space between the last two sentences—the caesura between "this battle alone" and "I think it's the continuation of something else"—the film cuts again without warning from Yamamoto's face against the backdrop of Paris sky and buildings to a landscape that only gradually becomes identifiable as Japan. Still in 35mm, with the same "mournful," "Oriental" music bridge, the camera picks up a bit of the sky that could be anywhere, pans down over modern buildings that could also be almost anywhere, and then pans further down, finally showing, nestled in the shadow beneath some international-style buildings, a small group of distinctly Japanese single-family houses—an architectural flashback to pre–World War II Japan or its modern simulacrum. This enclave of traditional dwellings surrounded by modern urban landscape seems the formal equivalent, in Wenders's conceptual world, of a chiasmatic imaging reversal. It constitutes an architectural version of a film sequence contained within video sequence, reflecting the constitutive tension in Wenders between the traditional (film) and the new (video), all of which are still contained by 35mm film. The music becomes increasingly inaudible, and another cut occurs: this time to Yamamoto's Tokyo studio, where Wenders's voice-over changes the topic to the problem of signing one's work—that is, affixing a personal signature to a collective product (Yamamoto uses Western script to sign his name). Then the music sound track trails off at last into silence.

This formal tour de force (achieved by the apparent seamlessness of sound and image track) distracts from both the scene's explicit meaning and its implicit ideology. The visual cut moves viewers not merely from Paris to Tokyo but also away from Yamamoto's extraordinary suggestion that fashion—his fashion, at least—is somehow a "continuation of something else" after World War II, much like Baron von Clausewitz's bon mot, "Politics is the continuation of war by other means." Yamamoto echoes an earlier discourse in Japan that demanded "overcoming the modern," which meant the industrial West. This slogan has been serving since the late 1930s as an ideological legitimization for imperialist aggression and war.[103] Many postwar Japanese writers and thinkers also have called

103. For a comparison of the popular response to the war experience in Germany and Japan, see Ian Buruma, *The Wages of Guilt: Memories of War in Germany and Japan* (London: Penguin, 1994).

for a continuing struggle against the West "by other means," including what writer Hayashi Fusao called the "One Hundred Year War in East Asia." Yamamoto's confession that he is continuing what his father was doing in Manchuria—and died for—seems to be an attempt to advocate a modernity independent from Western imitation and models.[104] That purchasing, wearing, and viewing Yamamoto's haute couture (which relies on Western elements) would accomplish this goal is a bizarre notion, but apparently it is exactly what Yamamoto means.

Yet in *Notebooks,* Wenders does not make explicit or even remark on the startling implication that the everyday world of fashion could continue a fascist war by other means. He may show but does not say; it is left to viewers to connect the dots. The overlay of the musical score here serves as a nearly subliminal suture over potentially embarrassing semantic visual and voice-over gaps.[105] Of course, Wenders's choice of music is always significant: he picks (and markets) his sound tracks very carefully. He generates his narratives through his musical score as much as from his fascination with still images (*Bilder*). Music rarely merely represents what Wenders shows, it also has the capacity to produce what he shows and what he does not show. But what semantics or ideologies are specifically sutured over by the "Oriental" music? What is the political in/visible and in/audible of *Notebooks?*

The key interview over the musical score takes place in Japanese; Yamamoto's national identity is thus foregrounded (indeed interpellated) by his voice and by "his" music. Yet in an earlier interview at the Centre Pompidou, speaking in English, Yamamoto states in no uncertain terms that he does not feel any national identity but rather an identity linked to a city, especially Tokyo or Paris. If he is a citizen of anything, he says it is a city, not a country. He adds that this increases his sense of being "irresponsible," a feeling he claims to enjoy.

But loyalty to a city does not promote a blind irresponsibility, as patriotism does. In the 1991 essay "The Urban Landscape," Wenders

---

104. I am indebted to Harry Harootunian for this crucial information and point. For the American viewer, Yamamoto's name is tangled up in a further field of references, recalling Isoruku Yamamoto (1884–1943). An admiral in the Japanese navy during World War II, he headed the combined imperial fleet in 1941 and masterminded the strike on Pearl Harbor. After being killed in action, he became a national hero and remains so in many quarters to this day. I have been unable to determine if the two Yamamotos are related.

105. Throughout the history of sound cinema, the music track has served an ideological function (in direct analogy to the Wagnerian *Gesamtkunstwerk*). See Caryl Flinn, *Strains of Utopia: Gender, Nostalgia, and Hollywood Film Music* (Princeton: Princeton University Press, 1992); Theodor W. Adorno, *In Search of Wagner,* trans. Rodney Livingston (London: New Left Books, 1981), 100. See further Theodor Adorno and Hanns Eisler, *Composing for the Films* [1947], intro. Graham McCann (London: Athlone, 1994).

admits that "cities cannot tell any stories [*Geschichten*]"; however, he adds, "they can tell us something about HISTORY [*GESCHICHTE*]." He continues,

> Cities can bear their history [*Geschichte*] in themselves and show it, they can make it visible or they can conceal it. They can open up eyes, exactly like films, or they can close them.[106a]

The notion of *Geschichte* is essential to grasp Wenders's unformulated position on Yamamoto's bizarre implication about fashion and war and on the related problems of city versus national identity, film versus video, and something once called fascism. It is important not to forget that issues of national identity, history, war, memory, and guilt were debated heatedly in the public sphere in West Germany just a few years prior to the making of *Notebooks* in the infamous *Historikerstreit* (historian's debate) of 1986.[107]

The over- or underlayering of music in *Notebooks* breaks outs temporarily from the strict documentary interview mode and switches into the narrative/interpretative mode of the essay film. This imbrication of fact and narrative spotlights the duplicity inhering in the German word and concept *Geschichte.* In spite of—even because of—its double meaning as both "lived history" (Ranke's *wie es eigentlich gewesen*) and "story" (Voltaire's "pack of tricks played by the living on the dead"), filmic *Geschichte* remains for Wenders a way of redeeming everyday life. Previously, at the time of *Reverse Angle* and *Tokyo-Ga,* he thought that pure images were what mattered, but he learned to rue it in "The Urban Landscape."[108] Now, in *Notebooks,* the *Geschichte* surrounding images is dominant, much as the film surrounds the video. Wenders's real subject in *Notebooks* is less the fashion designer Yamamoto than the latter's *Geschichte:* his father, World War II, and its afterlife. But this raises a basic question: what is Wenders's ideological subject, his *Geschichte,* and how should they be read between the lines?

---

106. Wenders, "Urban Landscape," 124.

107. For a clear analysis of the debate, see Dominick LaCapra's *History and Memory after Auschwitz* (Ithaca: Cornell University Press, 1998), esp. chap. 2, "Revisiting the Historian's Debate: Mourning and Genocide."

108. "I've learned from mistakes: the only protection from the danger or the sickness of self-satisfied image [*Bild*] is the belief in the primacy of history [*Geschichte*]. I've learned that each image only possesses truthfulness in relation to a figure [*eine Figur*] within history. Whenever images take themselves too seriously, so I've discovered, they reduce and weaken the figure. And a story [*eine Geschichte*] with weak figures possesses no energy. Only the *Geschichte* of figures grants each individual image its believability, it 'gives a moral' to the story, to use the jargon of an imagemaker" (Wenders, "Urban Landscape," 121).

When Wenders purchased the shirt and jacket in preparation for his meeting with Yamamoto, he immediately felt "self-identity with myself for the first time," protected from and indeed "armored" against the world, yet also felt incorporated into the fashion world of a foreign artist. This uncanny feeling, and the outfit that triggered it, says Wenders, "came from faraway, from the past: this jacket made me remember my childhood, the feeling 'father' was tailored into it. . . . The jacket was the direct translation of this feeling." Only after this admission does Yamamoto begin to talk about his dead father and his work on fashion as a continuation of his father's war. Perhaps, at one level of psychology, it is not all that surprising that the memory of a father, or some other person to whom one is close, is evoked at such moments.[109] Put in Wenders's "historical" terms, Yamamoto's clothing forces Wenders, its new wearer in *Notebooks,* to ask how much *Geschichte* he could allow a jacket and a shirt to transport—to transport across time and space from the older generation's Japanese war to Hitler's war? How much of that *Geschichte* was a Nazi past?

Later in the film, Wenders is intrigued that both he and Yamamoto share the same favorite book of photography, August Sander's *People of the 20th Century* (which has fascinated many critics, including Benjamin, Barthes, Sontag, and John Berger).[110] Yamamoto claims that he draws nearly all of his fashion inspiration from Sander's photos, which were intended to be visual "archetypes," "to represent every possible type, social class, sub-class, job, vocation, privilege."[111] Like the clothing they inspired, these photographs have the power to last longer than human life,

109. The context of the epigraph for this section was Stallybrass's experience of wearing the jacket of a deceased friend.

110. August Sander, *Menschen des 20. Jahrhunderts* (Munich: Schirmer/Mosel GmbH, 1980); Benjamin, "Short History of Photography" (1931), reprinted in *Classic Essays on Photography,* ed. Alan Trachtenberg (New Haven: Leete's Island Books, 1980), 199–216; Roland Barthes, *Camera Lucida: Reflections on Photography,* trans. Richard Howard (1980; New York: Noonday Press, 1981), 34–38; Sontag, *On Photography,* 59–63; John Berger, "The Suit and the Photograph," in *About Looking* (New York: Pantheon, 1980), 27–36.

111. Berger, "Suit and the Photograph," 27. Interestingly, the photograph by Sander that interests Berger most—three peasant men in suits—appears also in *Notebooks.* Yamamoto and Wenders discuss the image in the designer's Tokyo studio because the photograph has so influenced his current line of men's clothing. Also, in light of Wenders's ambivalent relation as filmmaker both to still photography and to video, see Turim's thesis that "video . . . seems to look nostalgically back at the modernist heritage of photography. . . . Video, then, exists simultaneously in a space of cultural lag and premonition, through which it strives to articulate a meaningful interaction with the present" ("Cultural Logic," 339). And so, too, does fashion, in terms of retrofashion and nostalgia feature films, both of which are commercially very lucrative. In Berger's words again, "A past style in clothes often looks absurd until it is re-incorporated into fashion. Indeed, the economic logic of fashion depends on making the old-fashioned look absurd" ("The Suit and the Photograph," 31).

preserving for Yamamoto and Wenders the memories of fathers and their not-so-distant world war. The (male) bond forged in Japan and France between Yamamoto and Wenders, between a (Japanese) fashion designer and a (German) filmmaker, is strengthened by their parallel inherited legacy. This uncanny (in/visible, in/audible) bonding links in the political unconscious of *Notebooks* the two main fascist Axis powers of World War II, Germany and Japan—also two economic and technological superpowers of the 1980s—showing what could be the future culture. The same linking is involved when, looking at the Japanese's collection of photographs, Wenders's video camera lingers over an image from the German 1920s: a "body culture" photo of women posed like petals of an open flower, their arms raised to the sky. Anticipating the body cults in Nazism, this image once again serves as a reminder of the main concealed signified of the film: Germany. Wenders shows us in this manner—between the lines—the role of his suppressed national identity as German, but he does not say anything about it. Yamamoto's remark could be rephrased as a question: Is this irresponsible? No matter what the answer, it is the everyday life not only of postwar Japan but also of Germany and France that, in Marker's *Sans soleil* "enshrines fragments of war."

More than his feature films, Wenders's essay films make visible and audible a deep anxiety about the course charted by the postmodern geopolitical aesthetic. They exemplify in that sense what the Russian formalists called the "canonization of the junior branch," the cultural mechanism by which a minor or avant-garde genre becomes a leading representational medium of major or mass-cultural events. While Wenders's overall cultural anxiety may be widely shared around the world, he gives it a special German stamp as he frets obsessively about the future of German creativity—specifically German filmmaking—threatened not only by the United States (Hollywood) but also by France (for example, Marker's films, which significantly anticipate Wenders's dual ambivalence about Japan and video) and Japan (Ozu's films and the fashion industry that thrives in a society of the simulacrum). Like so many other German intellectuals across the political spectrum, Wenders states in his 1991 "Reden über Deutschland" (Discourses on Germany) that

> our salvation in this currently so unredeemable country is the German language [*unser Heil in diesem zur Zeit so heillosen Land ist unsere Deutsche Sprache*]. It is able to draw distinctions, is precise, sharp, and cautious all at once. It is rich [*reich*]. . . . It is everything that this country no longer is, not yet again is, perhaps never more can be.[112]

112. Wenders, *Act of Seeing,* 198.

Reading these lines and between them, one hears an echo of the (West) German national anthem on a ghostly sound track; after all, the original lyrics for the *Deutschlandlied* were written in the middle of the nineteenth century, a time when the German language *was,* in a significant sense, the German nation. More disturbing, Wenders seems dangerously close here to the cliché (in the popular mass culture but also in Heidegger and beyond) that Germans (and by extension the expanding German nation) are especially blessed with "die heilige deutsche Sprache." It now seems that his cosmopolitan and internationalist filmic project is being supplemented, if not replaced, perhaps only momentarily, by a project that is specifically national and linguistic. It is significant that Wenders's first postunification film, *Faraway, So Close* returns to Berlin. This return is singular, and recent Wenders films have featured diverse global locations from Portugal to Cuba. Throughout all of Wenders's filmic projects there remains a creative tension between solipsistic fascination for his art and interest in social reality. Wenders works in a filmmaking context codetermined by other essay filmmakers, including Ulrike Ottinger and Marcel Ophüls, whose work contains equal concern for the possibilities of creativity within the geopolitical aesthetic; however, leaving their travels to foreign regions behind them, they now return to a unified Germany.

CHAPTER 5

Reunification in a Decentered Lens: Ottinger and Ophüls

> To the foreigner cursorily acquainted with the pattern of German life who has even briefly traveled about the country, its inhabitants seem no less bizarre than an exotic race. A witty Frenchman has said: "A German seldom understands himself. If he has once understood himself, he will not say so. If he says so, he will not make himself understood." This comfortless distance was increased by the war, but not merely through the real and legendary atrocities that Germans are reported to have committed. Rather, what completes the isolation of Germany in the eyes of other Europeans, what really engenders the attitude that they are dealing with Hottentots in the Germans (as it has been aptly put), is the violence, incomprehensible to outsiders and wholly imperceptible to those imprisoned by it, with which circumstances, squalor, and stupidity here subjugate people entirely to collective forces, as the lives of savages alone are subjected to tribal laws. The most European of all accomplishments, that more or less discernible irony with which the life of the individual asserts the right to run its course independently of the community into which he is cast, has completely deserted the Germans.
>
> —Walter Benjamin, "One-Way Street"

> This liquidation of the Other is accompanied by an artificial synthesis of otherness—a radical cosmetic surgery of which cosmetic faces on faces and bodies is merely a symptom. For the crime is perfect only when even traces of the destruction of the Other have disappeared. With modernity, we enter the age of the production of the other. The aim is no longer to kill the other, devour it, seduce it, love it or hate it, but, first, to produce it. It is not longer an object of passion, it is an object of production. Perhaps, in its irreducible singularity, the Other has become dangerous or unbearable, and its seduction has to be exorcised?
>
> —Jean Baudrillard, *The Perfect Crime*

I. Introducing Walls on the Möbius Strip

> And then Humpty Dumpty spoke to Alice:
> "In winter when the fields are white,
> I sing this song for your delight;
> In spring when woods are getting green,
> I'll try and tell you what I mean;
> In summer when the days are long,
> Perhaps you'll understand this song;
> In autumn when the leaves are brown,
> Take pen and ink and write it all down."
>
> —Lewis Carroll, *Alice in Wonderland*

Marcel Ophüls recites these lines early in his *November Days: Voices and Paths* (1990). Attempting to comprehend postreunification Germany, pen and ink may be hardly sufficient. Not only has the prototypical "wall jumper" Humpty Dumpty plummeted, not only has the Wall itself collapsed, but the walls between all the media that produce and/or document such occurrences are increasingly fluid, and any referential truth-content becomes difficult to grasp. This chapter is concerned with film's early response to the events from the autumn of 1989 into 1991, commonly depicted by the media as the fall of the Wall or the fall of communism. I will focus particularly on the way German reunification and European integration—and their social, economic, and cultural ramifications—have been viewed, in the sense not only of passively reflected, as through a lens, but also actively produced for possible revision and hence in the lens. In this case, video and filmmakers peripheral to world cinema as defined by mainstream producers, directors, distributors, and audiences are in different ways addressing and to some extent embodying problems of alterity or otherness, through and in which they project the images and sounds of reunification.

At least since Vietnam ("the television war"), most world events have been thoroughly "recorded," "frozen," "captured," and so forth, in a multimedia memory bank available for future generations to peruse, review, and relive as "history." It is not entirely clear however, whether the public is entirely convinced that anything it sees on television is really real. The media coverage of German reunification and its aftermath falls under a general ambivalence and undecidability that is not necessarily reassuring. Alternative filmmakers and video makers feel compelled to confront the differences between fact and fiction, documentary and feature, as alive as possible when these differences matter most through their shaping of the events they are reporting.

Two metaphors illustrate vividly the complexity of that task. The first is offered by a voice-over in Harun Farocki's and Andrei Ujica's *Videogram of a Revolution* (1992), made with images and sounds video recorded by Romanian citizens during the December 1988 uprising:

> Camera and event. Since its invention, film has seemed destined to make history visible. It has been able to portray the past and to stage the present. We have seen Napoleon on his horse and Lenin in the train. Film was possible because there was history. Almost imperceptibly, like moving forward on a Möbius strip, the side was flipped. We look on and have to think, if film is possible, then history too is possible.

The metaphor of the Möbius strip clarifies the title of the film by revealing its deep ambiguity: not only videograms about a revolution, or videograms produced by a revolution, but also vice versa: a revolution produced by videograms. The second metaphoric key can be found in McKenzie Wark's narrative of the process by which the Berlin Wall was penetrated psychologically and ideologically by the mass media (the cause) before it came down as material object (the effect):

> While the physical wall was ever-present, information blew through like radiation, slowed down but unstoppable. East Germans, the bearers of oppressive social relations, were also the bearers of an unbearable contradiction between the physical space with its rudimentary divide running at its most sensitive spot between the Mitte and Tiergarten districts of Berlin, and the spectacular shopping-arcade landscape beyond the mirror of West German television. Whereas in West Germany television holds up a specular mirror to the social relations of capital and those who bear them, to East Germans it was a mirror to pass through into an enchanted land. They imagined a real world behind the mirror which their Western counterparts have grown used to assuming is just an image. So they passed through the mirror, and redrew the map. The remaking of the real, of course, has yet to catch up.[1]

For, television the fall of the Wall was merely one epiphenomenal event: nothing happened except a significant rise in the ratings and advertising

1. McKenzie Wark, *Virtual Geography: Living with Global Media Events* (Bloomington: Indiana University Press, 1994), 61. As perceptive as many of Wark's insights are, others are insensitive and condescending: "Television attracted East German viewers like flies to shit" (56).

revenues for nonfiction programming. The cause-effect relationship of event-reporting was reversed, since, in one sense, television caused the Wall to fall. At the same time, however, a countercultural tendency was necessitated to shatter the asymmetrical, one-way mirror of East/West television production, consumption, and exchange and to delay as long as possible the remapping or remaking of a real, already determined by the mass media. That counter tactic—deconstructive, destructive, and delaying—was implemented by an alternative—or Other—nonfiction cinema (or video) that was irreducibly within the media and yet resolutely against the media. Rather than merely viewing the fall of the Wall either simply from above (governments and victors) or simply from below (common people and vanquished) the most significant filmmakers—including Ottinger and Ophüls—projected reunification from a point of view of otherness vis-à-vis the mass media.

To be sure, any reporting of events in Germany in the autumn of 1989 could not escape the multiple technocultural pressures that had been subverting distinctions between reality and illusion, truth and fiction. Yet a certain hegemonic vision tended to emerge from even the most equivocal or misleading signs. During those heady November days, globalized television networks—CNN, ARD, CBS, BBC, ZDF, TELE1—transmitted the same bright images and sounds of the fall of the Berlin Wall. A worldwide audience ostensibly became united in its consumption—its illusion of coproduction—of the collapse and attendant funeral of socialism and communism and the coterminous triumph of liberal democracy.[2] On the surface, these overdetermined and largely unprocessed political developments were registered and transmitted by means of relentless repetition—as if they were phenomenologically unmediated and required no analysis. The replay of the same series of images produced a veritable closed economy of the audiovisual archive: East and West Germans dancing in euphoria on the Wall; its dismantling by hand; lead-belching Trabis passing unhindered through former checkpoints; unchecked consumption of bananas. A single week witnessed the transformation of the democratic—indeed, still communist—slogan *Wir sind das Volk!* (We are the people!) into the chauvinistic, nationalist slogan and performative speech act *Wir sind ein Volk!* (We are one people!).[3] Projected to the world out of Ger-

2. For data about the media's role in transmitting the events before, during, and after the *Wende* as well as a critique, see Geoffrey Nowell-Smith and Tana Wollen, eds., *After the Wall: Broadcasting in Germany* (London: BFI, 1991); Wark, *Virtual Geography,* esp. 47–94.

3. As Stephen Brockmann has noted, "The mere change from the definite to the indefinite article implied the move from a revolution based on democratic principles to a revolution based on ethnic togetherness, a shift from demos to ethnos" ("Introduction: The Reunification Debate," *New German Critique* 52 [winter 1991]: 6). *Volk* means both "people"

many's extreme uncertainty and upheaval, in a situation that was by no means as clear as it was imagined to be, was a simulacrum composed of unified images and sounds of clarity, decisiveness, and above all optimism—all tempered by uncanny anxieties just beneath the audiovisual surface. If doubts lingered about the reality of the events, "one only had to go to a department store where the edited and packaged media highlights of these historic moments were available on video cassette almost immediately."[4] Genuine ambivalence, hesitation, and contradictions were rarely shown or heard explicitly. It was the necessary task and fate of alternative artists to pry open the im/perceptible anxieties between the lines in ways that are at once unconsciously uncanny and consciously canny, both under and out of the ultimate control of audiences and directors alike.

The mass media that most fully embraced unification, instantly seeking to represent it live, were video and/or film.[5] Within weeks of the collapse of the Wall, two short films appeared, *Leipzig in Autumn* and *The New Look Wandlitz,* although in both cases production had begun earlier. In 1990 a veritable explosion of films occurred, including Ulrike Ottinger's three-hour *Countdown.* The following year, the number of films continued to grow—no longer just German productions such as Sibylle Schönemann's *Verriegelte Zeit* (Locked-up Time, 1991) but international as well. Major nonfeature directors soon joined the 1990–91 fray: among the most notable were Ophüls with *November Days,* Chris Marker with *Berlin '90,* and Jean-Luc Godard with *Germany 90 Nine Zero.*[6] Godard's title was particularly significant, alluding to Roberto Rossellini's seminal post–World War II feature film, *Germany Year Zero.* If it was given to fiction film circa 1945 to mark an epistemic break in the history of cinema at the end of the hot war, it was now nonfiction film's turn to initiate a similarly epochal shift at the end of the Cold War circa 1989, projecting visual

---

and "nation," and the notorious populist-nationalist connotations of the untranslatable adjective *völkisch* are often not far away. The evolution of *Wir sind ein Volk!* should be especially noted. In World War I the national slogan had been "Ein Volk, ein Reich, ein Gott!" (appearing, for example, on soldiers' belt buckles), and in Hitlerian Germany it became "Ein Volk, ein Reich, ein Führer!"

4. Michael Hoffman, "The Unity Train," in *After the Wall,* ed. Nowell-Smith and Wollen, 66.

5. There was a response in other genres, of course, especially theater, with its ability quickly to convert onto stage what was happening in the streets and boardrooms. See, for example, Rolf Hochhuth's *Wessis in Weimar,* Elfriede Jelinek's *Totenauberg,* and Botho Strauss's *Schlusschor.* For a discussion, see my "Staging Re/Unification: For and by the West," *European Legacy* 1 (May 1996): 1242–47.

6. Godard in particular has produced a challengingly complex and interesting intervention in this area. See my "Theses on Godard's *Allemagne 90 neuf zéro,*" *Iris* 29 (spring 2001): 117–32.

culture into the coming century. It was not long before more commercial Wall films appeared in Europe and the United States.[7] The first major feature in Germany was Helke Misselwitz's *Herzsprung* (1992)—the name of a town but literally "fissure in the heart"—a somber magical realist look by a former East German at racism and misogyny in the new Germany, which by film's end resembles a Ku Klux Klan–infested American South.[8] The unified Berlin soon came to star in an internationally distributed feature, Wim Wenders's *Faraway, So Close!* (1993), rectifying his critical 1987 image of Berlin in *Wings of Desire* as a city where only angels dared to tread its most radical fissures. Margarethe von Trotta followed with *Das Versprechen* (The Promise, 1994), a disappointingly conventional love story set against the double backdrop of the divided Germany and Europe and the subsequent reunification and integration. There were also indirect or metaphysical allusions to reunification in films ostensibly dealing with another past. Thus, the filmmaker's possible intentions aside, Agnieska Holland's picaresque "true story" *Europa Europa* (1991), an otherwise highly problematic film about the Third Reich and Holocaust, can be interpreted as a considerably more interesting indirect comment about post–Cold War European integration (the best key to the otherwise enigmatic title). *Reunification* is a term as applicable to the interpretation of films as to their production (and exchange or distribution). By the early 1990s, Hollywood and its international surrogates had already begun to close in for the commercial kill in the rubble of the Wall. Nonfeature cinema's challenge was also clear: the event ushering in the next century had to be rescued from its own mass mediatization.

The majority of these earlier and later reunification films tended to be documentaries to one degree or another, their cameras purporting to record the events taking place in Germany with comparatively little or no analysis or accompanying voice-over commentary. Economic constraints might have factored in that trend, since documentaries are generally cheaper to produce than features and can respond more quickly to current events. Some of these documentaries included a personal essay tone motivated by a "true story/I was there" narrative, as in *Verriegelte Zeit.* While emphasizing the stifling and paranoid bureaucratic aspect of the new regime, which allowed little freedom of expression, the majority of these

7. See, for example, *Something to Do with the Wall* (Marilyn Levine and Ross McElwee, United States, 1990). McElwee is best known for his bittersweet documentary/essay film *Sherman's March* (1991).

8. See my "Re/fusing Past and Present: Cinematic Reunification under the Sign of Nationalism and Racism (Helke Misselwitz's *Herzsprung*)," in *Beyond 1989: Re-reading German Literature since 1945,* ed. Keith Bullivant (Providence, R.I.: Berghahn, 1997), 129–52.

films are formally conservative, however, without much interest in original artistry. They tend to reproduce on film, as film, the same dry and one-dimensional control that they attribute to the regime under attack, re-performing aesthetically the totality that they abhor politically. The images appear over and over again, seemingly from a single collective pool or closed economy of signs: the same interviews with former border guards and Stasi informants, the same overall tone and mood imputing to a passive viewer a unified view of what life "over there" was really like. Particularly striking are the long takes and extensive footage of the dismantling of the Wall, which fast became as much a psychological fetish as something physical. As one critic in the *Times* (London) laconically noted, "If you put all the Berlin Wall footage end to end you could cut the country in half again."[9] The film footage was producing a filmic barrier to understanding the one it was replacing; nevertheless, the obsessiveness and recurrence of these film and TV images leads one to question what lies behind this unacknowledged consensus, uniformity, and homogeneity, to ask what suppressed, repressed, and traumatic event was being held at audiovisual bay by being shown and heard in the media. Nonfiction or essay films sought to respond to this historical challenge, a challenge met in very different ways by two filmmakers who also happened to be in some sense mainstream Germany's Others: a self-defined German lesbian Jewish feminist and an expatriate German Jew, working independently of one another in 1990–91. While both share roughly the same ideological position—a more or less leftist critique of the celebration of reunification and of its mass mediatization—less obvious is the *how* of their articulation of politics and aesthetics: Ottinger's reliance on objects and Walter Benjamin's writings, Ophüls's populist turn to musical comedy.

II. Objects as Others: Ottinger's Benjaminian *Countdown* to Monetary Unification

> D day, not 1944 but 1990, was a Sunday. It was a day unlike any other because it was the occasion not of an invasion, but of a *replacement.* The D-Mark, until then only the official currency of the Federal Republic of Germany (FRG), became on this day also the official currency of the German Democratic Republic (GDR). The D-Mark (DM) replaced the Ostmark (OM). The GDR became, thereby, one of a very few sovereign nations that do not issue, and thus does not control, its own currency. . . . D day is a unique event in economic history because the currency replacement occurred not on the basis of the market value of the respective currencies, nor even on the basis of the best economic

9. *Times* (London), November 11, 1990.

> estimate of the relationship of productivity and resources in the two economies, but on the basis of a political agreement.
>
> —Wolfgang W. Fuchs and Berthold Franke, "Decoding the D-Mark"

> But what is being counted here, paid out or sold out? Is an entity being recombined or divided along new lines? What is being counted out and thus pushed to the margins? The arbitrariness of the beginning corresponds to the arbitrariness of the end. But in between there is so much to be recounted.
>
> —Ulrike Ottinger, *Countdown*

The second epigraph to this section comes from the first intertitle of Ulrike Ottinger's 180-minute *Countdown* (1990), which is about what she calls the "first stage of reunification": the monetary unification of the two former Germanys.[10] Most striking to a viewer familiar with Ottinger's oeuvre is this film's minimalist straight documentary character, conveyed by the camera that "objectively" records, seemingly without commentary or voice-over, ten days in Berlin prior to East Germany's adoption of West Germany's currency. This slow pace enables the film to pay extraordinary attention to architectural structures and objects—or what Walter Heynowski and Gerhard Scheumann call "requisites." Conspicuously absent are not only Ottinger's trademarks (fantastically colorful images, lavish costumes and decor, and rejection of linear narrative—this film is chronological) but also her habitual hybridization of genre (the mixing of documentary and feature footage within the same film).[11] Ottinger trained

10. *Countdown,* dir. Ulrike Ottinger, text by Eva Meyer, trans. L. A. Rickels, 35mm, 189 min., Ulrike Ottinger Film Production, 1990.

11. Though Ottinger has made other documentaries, most notably *China—the Arts—Everyday Life* (1985), which served as a (four-hour-plus) sketch for her 1988 feature, *Johanna d'Arc of Mongolia,* her films for the most part avoid facile categorization. Thus, according to critic Janet Bergstrom, Ottinger seeks to blur genre distinctions, bringing "together laments of autobiography, documentary and fiction," with the result that her works "depart from the manner in which these tendencies have been represented in West Berlin's women's films" ("The Theater of Everyday Life: Ulrike Ottinger's *China: The Arts, Everyday Life,*" *Camera Obscura* 18 [1988]: 43). Ottinger reinforces this feature at the beginning of *Johanna d'Arc of Mongolia,* when Lady Windemere asks viewers to consider, "Was it a confrontation with reality or with the imagination. . . . Must imagination shun the encounter with reality? Or are they enamored of each other? Can they form an alliance?" Hence, as critic Brenda Longfellow remarks, the film "is structured around a spectacular alliance of reality and the imagination" ("Lesbian Phantasy and the Other Woman in Ottinger's *Johanna d'Arc of Mongolia,*" *Screen* 34, no. 2 [summer 1993]: 126). With deceptive understatement, Ottinger has said that she is self-consciously pushing the generic limits, taking her point of departure from her critique of the media qua social institution and noting that the "continuing endeavors of the film

in the visual arts as a painter and photographer and had additional aspirations to a career in ethnology; it is quite remarkable just how removed *Countdown* is from Ottinger's earlier films, which come out of the tradition of fantasy and surrealist filmmaking. How different it is from, say, her *Johanna d'Arc of Mongolia* (1988), where, as Janet Bergstrom noted "fantasy and visual opulence predominate over the kind of realism associated with everyday life and vision."[12] *Countdown* records that realism of everyday life that asks the spectator to contemplate what appears, at first viewing, to be the stark appeal of unmediated visual evidence as truth—a convention of the documentary. This interest in quotidian realism certainly underpins Ottinger's chronological countdown of days. *Countdown* reflects an upheaval in Ottinger's cinematic craft, comparable in its radical effect to the impact of German unification on the political scene.

For many years, Ottinger had been considered an enfant terrible among feminist and openly lesbian filmmakers in the German-speaking world, and her films were judged to be inaccessible to mass audiences. However, her *Johanna d'Arc of Mongolia* played to packed houses at the 1989 New York Gay and Lesbian Film Festival and was awarded the Public's Prize that same year in Montreal. More recently, *Exile Shanghai* (1997) chronicles the three great waves of Jewish immigration to China. However, her earlier works were more marginal. The feature *Madame X—An Absolute Ruler* (1977) was an extravagant sci-fi pirate adventure. *Dorian Gray in the Mirror of the Popular Press* (1983) was a demanding and highly ironic postmodern feminist-lesbian meditation on the mass media and the traps of representation, with a lavish decor and costuming (with fashion model Verushka in drag). Other cult hits included *Ticket of No Return* (1979), in which the female protagonist drinks herself to death, and *Freak Orlando* (1981), ostensibly a circus film with a particularly ambitious historical frame of reference (Virginia Woolf's *Orlando*). Those

industry to limit filmmakers and directors to the most narrow stereotyped genre cinema possible cannot be overlooked" ("The Pressure to Make Genre Films: About the Endangered Autorenkino" [1983], in *West German Filmmakers on Film: Visions and Voices,* ed. Eric Rentschler [New York: Holmes and Meier, 1988], 90). In that spirit, Roswitha Mueller points to Ottinger's aesthetic-cum-technological interrogation of the "fixity of oppositions" generally ("The Mirror and the Vamp," *New German Critique* 34 [1985]: 188). Finally, basing her analysis on Ottinger's claim that she is trying to create "a new kind of realism," Longfellow concludes that *Johanna d'Arc of Mongolia* represents a "hybridization of categories in which the distinctions between fiction and documentary begin to break down" ("Lesbian Phantasy," 129). *Countdown* may represent a breakdown of that breakdown. In my terminology, it becomes precisely an essay film after the aporia of oppositions between fiction and/or nonfiction, feature film and/or documentary, biographical and/or autobiographical performance—mediating them, as it were.

12. Bergstrom, "Theater," 43.

familiar with Ottinger's filmmaking history could thus suspect that more would be at stake in *Countdown* than a simple documentation of ten days in Berlin at the end of June 1990. The simplicity of this documentary—in which, she observes, "there is no *mise-en-scène,* so you must have time to see the people and get familiar with them . . . to understand the whole system"[13]—is deceptive, likely intentionally so. This deception stems in part from a primordial tension that underlies all of Ottinger's films, whether obviously fantastic or apparently realistic—a tension that Laurence Rickels describes as "the extended contest of visibility versus invisibility," specifically "the ways that others are reduced to sheer visibility"[14]—and so rendered practically invisible.

One of these Others is essayist Walter Benjamin, who killed himself while trying to flee Nazi Germany and left an indelible mark on postwar German thinkers and artists. In *Countdown,* Ottinger elaborately refers both explicitly and implicitly to Benjamin's essays on Berlin and Germany, subtly metamorphizing these literary texts into a unique audiovisual text. Forming the subtext of an intertextual dialogue, they transform the film from passive documentary into its more volatile etymological root, *docere* (to warn of impending disaster). A crucial undercurrent in that dialogue cuts back and forth from mute objects (dialectic materialism) to Benjamin writings (historical materialism).

Another Other, perhaps more physically visible but somehow excluded from Germany's holistic national self-consciousness, is Berlin—a monstrous political and cultural hybrid. Ottinger's film is not titled *Berlin,* nor is it ostensibly about Berlin. But without Berlin, looming in the dim background, it would be difficult to understand the selection of German unification as a topic of *Countdown.* Why would Ottinger depart from her previous fictional sources (*Dorian Gray, Orlando, Madame X, Johanna d'Arc*) to film a contemporary historical event? Why would a filmmaker informed by feminist issues and sexuality suddenly feel the need to enter into a political/economic debate that is not obviously related to questions of gender and sexual politics? And why, in that process, would she depart from her own tested filmmaking practice? The prestige and the sentimental appeal of Berlin, the inescapable real and symbolic site of reunification, surely offers some explanation. Berlin has always had a special resonance for Ottinger, who used it as the setting for *Ticket of No Return, Berlin Fever* (1973), and *Usinimage* (1987). But Berlin also always held a special aura for artists: in their collective unconscious, it was the dream location of all subversive experiments. The images of Berlin, the Berlin stories, and

---

13. Roby Grundmann and Judith Schulevitz, "Minorities and the Majority: An Interview with Ulrike Ottinger," *Cineaste* 18, no. 3 (1991): 40.

14. "Laurence Rickels Talks with Ulrike Ottinger," *Artforum* (February 1993): 84.

the spirit of Berlin must have coalesced in Ottinger's mind as the necessary (true) background and the satirical inspiration for the challenge of deconstructing its mediatized homogenous surface and exposing the cracks and fissures. Such an experimental project, at least in its formal parameters, has been a consistent strategy of Ottinger's filmic practice.

Countdown opens with the statement that it was filmed in real time in Berlin and its environs during the ten days preceding the unification of currencies on July 1, 1990. The film is shot for the most part in the former East Berlin, but the camera roams back and forth across the old border. The work is divided into ten segments, varying in length from seven to forty minutes, each corresponding to a day of filming. When the film was made, there were still nominally two German sovereign states, but even then the replacement of the Ostmark by the D-mark was commonly viewed (positively or negatively) as the last major enabling act before official national reunification of Germany under capitalist auspices. Both in the film and in reality, a monetary angst reveals and veils a deeper national anxiety—a third haunting Other. According to Wolfgang W. Fuchs and Berthold Franke,

> In Germany, inflation-anxiety is traumatic. It is anxiety in the face of futility, the fear that overnight everything could be shown to have been for naught, something Germans have indeed known. [They] cannot get rid of the deep doubt, even fear, that at some moment the truth will catch up and show that all had been in vain. In German, the word for currency ("*Währung*") is derived from the word for true ("*wahr*"). The more one tries to wave away the haunting truth, the more the energy flows into the fetishization of money (a sign) and its symbol, the currency.[15]

Hence the title *Countdown* evokes this in/visible fear. It projects expectations of and anxieties about a dramatic and explosive event (for example, a missile firing: ten, nine, eight, seven . . .) onto an occurrence in the political economy that—unprecedented though it may be—would hardly seem to offer a good photographic topic. After all, even Eisenstein could not figure out how effectively to film something as abstract—and yet real—as Marx's *Capital* or as capital itself. But a crucial aim of Ottinger's film, however masked, is to expose the myth that a nation-state can be seamlessly sutured through the medium of currency. She wants to "question the perverse logic of granting currency the force to unify."[16] From the per-

15. Wolfgang W. Fuchs and Berthold Franke, "Decoding the D-Mark," *American Journal of Semiotics* 8, nos. 1–2 (1991): 95.

16. Arthur Knight, review of *Countdown, New Art Examiner* 18, no. 9 (May 1991): 55.

spective of capital, of course, it is hardly "perverse"—rather, it is business as usual—to allow money as commodity to "unify" anything. Ottinger's focus on German reunification seeks to critique that sort of relentless normalization.

The notion of a Countdown as a shadow Other of the film helps to clarify and limit Ottinger's possible imputation, quoted in the epigraph to this section, that *Countdown*'s beginning and ending are "arbitrary." Perhaps the historical countdown documented by the film was indeed arbitrary, or perhaps not at all. But for Ottinger surely, both the film and the event are in fact as carefully orchestrated as any countdown. In the film's apparent organization, im/perceptible structures that underlie overall narratives reveal the projections beneath the manifest audiovisual surface. Ottinger's intent is to deconstruct filmically the countdown of history by producing its simulation—or, as Slavoj Žižek might say, its hypersimulation—both in its extravagant promise and in its sheer banality.[17]

Since Ottinger's film is divided into ten segments with the clear teleology of currency reform, the film's beginning and end cannot be totally arbitrary. Even if it could be argued that both beginning and end are somewhat arbitrary, the supporting theme and structures of the segments are not. Each "day" segment is preceded by an epigraph that provides a clue as to how it ought to be read (figuratively and literally), giving the viewers a certain direction if not manipulating their response.

Einsteinturm Observatory. (Video caption from *Countdown*.)

17. See Slavoj Žižek, *Tarrying with the Negative: Kant, Hegel, and the Critique of Ideology* (Durham: Duke University Press, 1993).

Day 1 (June 22, 1990) first shows images of East Germany, focusing on the Einsteinturm Observatory and Institute for Astrophysics in Potsdam (constructed from 1920 to 1924 according to Erich Mendelsohn's design). Entitled "Point in Time/Counterpoint," this introductory segment begins with a self-referential text that draws attention to its filmic nature before eventually invoking Walter Benjamin—native of Berlin—as its silent partner:

> The light of the cosmic source is caught by the upper telescope, reflected and projected into the spectrographic apparatus in the rooms below. "One must create art out of real conditions unfathomable space out of volume and light." Thus, according to Mendelsohn, the inner function of the architectonic organism breaks through to a form which gives material license to recount itself: that it has emerged from the earth or that it has landed, like some outer-space probe. And if one gives oneself enough time to gaze at it, that it is also a strip of film.

The camera moves slowly, tracking the outside structure of the Einsteinturm, like a detective surveying the scene of a crime. There is a conspicuous absence of people—the tower is never penetrated. This uncanny scan of a depopulated panorama produces a pure visual image that, in its materiality and density, in effect tells a long story, albeit with the aid of the epigraph and, later on, a voice-over. An expressionist edifice, the tower rises out of the landscape in marked contrast to contemporary architectural structures—an image that through the slow tracking generates what a phenomenologist might call an eidetic apperception—that is, the vision of a still life invaded by time so that what is seen is never quite static but is simultaneously recollective and anticipatory and hence pregnant with new possibilities. Ottinger's film thus evokes both retroactively (point in time) a lost dream and proleptically (counterpoint) a lost potential. Showing an already obsolete and yet futuristic architectural structure as an alternative to mass media images of Berlin, such as the Brandenburg Gate, Ottinger's film basically conforms to Manfredo Tafuri's provocative thesis that the only reason to study history is to seek alternatives to the present. Designed by a Jew for a Jew forced out of Germany, the Einsteinturm serves as an overdetermined allegory of an alternative history that might have been and might still be but was never allowed to be.[18] In a recent interview,

18. Similarly, in Hélène Cixous's play 1994 *L'histoire qu'on ne connaitra jamais* (The History One Will Never Know) the character of the wandering Jew, Barout, laments that the Germans and the Jews could have made a wonderful history together.

Ottinger states clearly, if somewhat unconsciously, her position on the issue of German guilt: "In Germany the relationship between Jews and Germans was a symbolic one—a love-hate relationship. Thus—and I say this although my mother was Jewish and my family lost relatives under the Nazis—Germany's total loss exceeds the loss of Jewish lives." But she backtracks:

> I am not being cynical. What I mean is this: Jews were so crucial to the development of modernity in Germany, for the evolution of a certain kind of analytical thought, both in culture and in science, particularly in the Twenties and during the period of classical modernism, that losing them meant the loss of an important power in Germany. Then there's the question of dealing with what happened. With the total annihilation of the Jews in this industrial way, Germany stepped over a line. There have been politically criminal acts in history, but this was the first time this line was crossed, and that means that for hundreds of years this problem will have to be dealt with. We are no longer in the realm of Greek tragedy. We have reached something else.[19]

This passage remains problematic in many different ways, not least of which is that Ottinger seems to identify herself as German, although her mother was Jewish. Ottinger makes a connection among Jews, culture, science, and modernity, and she consciously seeks to draw attention audiovisually to the void resulting from the absence of Jews. Though she hardly expects her films to solve this historical question once and for all, Ottinger wants to keep asking such questions for as long as possible.

Following the Einsteinturm scene, Ottinger abruptly cuts to the Jewish cemetery in East German Weißensee, consecrated on September 9, 1880. Here occurs the first explicit citation from Benjamin, drawn from his last major writing, "Theses on the Philosophy of History" (1940), which supplies Ottinger with her intertitle: "Only that writer of History holds the gift of igniting sparks of hope in the past, who is penetrated with the following: the dead too are not safe from the interventions of the triumphant enemy. This enemy has not ceased triumphing."[20] In the original text these sentences are prefaced by a remark that contributes a more militant note to the subtext of the film: "In every era an attempt must be made anew to

19. Grundmann and Schulevitz, "Minorities and the Majority," 16.

20. Or so reads the ungainly translation in the film, departing from Harry Zohn's standard English rendering: "Only that historian will have the gift of fanning the spark of hope in the past who is firmly convinced that *even the dead* will not be safe from the enemy if he wins. And this enemy has not ceased to be victorious" (Walter Benjamin, *Illuminations,* ed. and intro. Hannah Arendt [New York: Schocken, 1940], 255).

wrest tradition away from conformism that is about to overpower it. The Messiah comes not only as the redeemer, he comes as the subduer of the Antichrist."[21] Immediately after Ottinger's text and its evocation of Benjamin, the screen focuses on a close-up of a tombstone. The lens slowly tracks over it before sliding over other tombstones throughout the cemetery. The handheld camera uncannily walks the viewers through the film, serving both as a living eye among the dead and as a dead lens among living memories of the victims. No humans are evident—the only traces of life are leaves, inscriptions on monuments, and, most immediately, the painfully slow movements of the invisible camera. A live voice suddenly erupts on the soundtrack: a man chanting a Hebrew prayer for the dead, with reverberating names of concentration camps—Auschwitz, Bergen-Belsen, Sachsenhausen—and one remembers that the Jews annihilated there died anonymously, without tombstones marking their lives.

Ottinger's choice of the Einsteinturm and the Weißensee cemetery as the opening sequences is far from arbitrary. On the contrary, the juxtaposition of astronomy and Jewishness points again to the work of Benjamin. Benjamin's aphorism "To the Planetarium" in "One-Way Street" (1928) begins as follows:

> If one had to expound the doctrine of antiquity with utmost brevity while standing on one leg, as did Hillel that of the Jews, it could only be with this sentence: "They alone shall possess the earth who live from the powers of the cosmos." Nothing distinguishes the ancient from the modern man so much as the former's absorption in a cosmic experience scarcely known to later periods.[22]

The terrible irony is that Benjamin must be read and Ottinger viewed through the almost opaque filter of the Holocaust: the millions who never had the chance to possess the earth and for whom the powers of the cosmos were the darkened heavens and silent Messiah and God. Ottinger's reference to Benjamin's essay remains cryptic at this stage, although she will cite from "One-Way Street" later in her film. But she creates a hierarchy of spectatorship. Those who know the Benjamin text will begin to approach *Countdown* very differently from those who do not. And viewers familiar with Benjamin might further explore the precise nature of the dialogue between Ottinger and Benjamin, better aware that the Benjaminian

21. Benjamin, *Illuminations,* 255.

22. Walter Benjamin, "One-Way Street" [1928], in *Reflections: Essays, Aphorisms, Autobiographical Writings,* trans. Edmund Jephcott, ed. and intro. Peter Demetz (New York: Schocken, 1986), 92.

context underscores Ottinger's otherwise imperceptible message of political and historical warning.

On this first day of the countdown to the new Germany, Ottinger manifestly shows audiovisual fossils, shells, and traces left after human life has been extinguished, even though life seems peculiarly present in its absence. Fossils, shells, and traces are also central to Benjamin's conception of history. This configuration of tropes, as Susan Buck-Morss notes, "captures as well the process of natural decay that marks the survival of past history within the present, expressing with palpable clarity what the discarded fetish becomes, so hollowed out of life that only the imprint of the material shell remains."[23] Day 1 thus performs a filmic act of mourning and elegy, albeit one that is hardly suggested by the initial perspective of tranquil surface appearances. Ottinger performs Benjamin's challenge to the historical materialist to redeem the past, refusing to consign the memory of the dead to the stories and histories told by their murderers.

Day 2 is entitled "New Permeability. The Waterways." It opens with a liberating boat ride along the canals in and around Berlin, with the camera's trajectory establishing firmly what will be a dominant theme for the remainder of the film: a more or less fluid ability, first by water then by automobile, to move back and forth between the East and the West, whose separation, which persists after reunification, is made visible by the same camera that transgresses it. The inanimate but somehow also live canal sites are as pregnant with history as the Einsteinturm, and Ottinger's camera frames the resting place of Rosa Luxemburg and Karl Liebknecht without identifying them explicitly. From the tourist boat, the audience sees the first live people in the film: tourists captured from the back while looking in the same direction as Ottinger's camera. The viewers are thus sutured into the film with the perspective of interested Others—visitors from another world. This stratagem suggests that Ottinger's point of view—and by extension, the audience's—is as constrained as that of a tourist documenting the newly discovered sights. The camera, now mounted on a car, visits the Bauhausarchiv, the Shellhaus, the synagogue, the Berlin Cathedral—all empty architectural monuments, reflecting an escalation in time and scale from the gravestones in day 1. As the camera passes over the Nikolai Quarter, Bahnhof Friedrichstrasse, Reichstag (particularly resonant with meaning), and the souvenir market, more live people appear in the film, although only in the background and framed by buildings, monuments, sites, and other requisites on which the primary—if ambivalent—focus remains for some time. Their precise significance

23. Susan Buck-Morss, *The Dialectics of Seeing: Walter Benjamin and the Arcades Project* (Cambridge: MIT Press, 1991), 160.

remains unspecified, although they suggest the unbearable weight of history. One might recall another Benjamin reflection in "A Berlin Chronicle" (1932) about how the memories of people from the past "steal along its walls like beggars, appear wraithlike at windows, to vanish again, sniff at thresholds like a genius loci, and even if they fill whole quarters with their names, it is as a dead man fills his gravestone. Noisy, matter-of-fact Berlin, city of work and the metropolis of business, nevertheless has more rather than less than some others, of those places and moments when it bears witness to the dead, shows itself full of dead."[24] The film seems to be in the audiovisual presence of what architect Rafael Moneo (in a very different context) has called "the solitude of buildings."[25] In *Countdown,* empty spaces and depopulated sites are filled with precisely that which can no longer be rendered visible or audible—ghosts of dead people and ideological specters.

Reminiscent of H&S films, the next sequence particularly shows more discarded possessions, relics, or requisites offered as souvenirs—massively overdetermined objects for sale; again they represent the conflation of personal past and political ideology. As viewed by Ottinger, huge buildings, vast sites, and tiny objects become invested with as much lapsed meaning as do people; in a sense they are dereified, granted an uncanny life in the film medium whose dominant tendency is to focus on people, not objects or structures, and to reduce the most complex history to the simplest of narratives.[26] Like Benjamin, Ottinger would have "things" speak not only about their own history but about history tout court. "All those military medals," she observes in an interview, "when you see kilometers and kilometers of them you really understand that the whole military of a country is up for sale."[27] But as the film makes very clear, not only the military is up for sale.

This second day of Ottinger's countdown, marked by the escape (or opening) from the past to the present, offers a first and initially fleeting glimpse of the signifying object par excellence in this particular historical juncture: the Wall, or what remains of it on the eve of monetary unification—the Wall that used to enclose and is now scattered. The Wall has become a thousand shards for sale at souvenir stands, the price of each fragment determined by the quality of graffiti painted on what formally was its western side. The Wall, once a primary Western tourist attraction

24. Walter Benjamin, "A Berlin Chronicle" [1932], in *Reflection,* 28.

25. See Rafael Moneo, *The Solitude of Buildings: Kenzo Tange Lecture, March 9, 1985, George Gund Hall* (Cambridge: Harvard University, Graduate School of Design, 1986).

26. See, for example, Helke Misselwitz's 1992 feature film, *Herzsprung;* Wim Wenders's 1993 *Faraway, So Close;* Margarethe von Trotta's 1994 *The Promise.*

27. Grundmann and Schulevitz, "Minorities and the Majority," 40.

in Berlin, now can be bought and taken home a piece at a time. By the new logic of capitalism, its terrifying use value has been transformed into an exchange value as a curio after its fall. And, as if to stress that point, Ottinger's camera, back on the boat, tracks along the still intact portions of the Wall so that, without evidence of its destruction, one is temporarily interjected back in time to "how it was." But not entirely: on the sound track, very softly but persistently, a steady hammering brings back the present. This hammering functions as a sound bridge long after Ottinger's camera has left the Wall, a bridge not only from the past to the present but also from the present to both a more remote past and an anticipated future—a time of reconstruction when Berlin was filled with the sounds of hammering immediately after its fall during World War II (but before the Wall was built) and a time of construction after the fall of the Wall. In Deleuzean terms, Ottinger would be recording/creating an optical sign, or "opsign," accompanied by a sound sign ("sonsign") to produce a "time-image" capable of breaking the traditional "movement-image" scheme, where what is seen on the screen is immediately extended into an action (as in all classical Hollywood narratives). By contrast, Ottinger seeks to create a "chronosign" in which time is no longer subservient to movement and becomes momentarily (in)visible. Through its double dechronology, the countdown in *Countdown* may be understood not (only) as a teleological movement in space and time, ending with the epiphany of monetary reunification but (also) as a drive to find a radically Other way of perceiving reunification than the one that has been presented by the mass media and their way of seeing and telling.

That Otherness commands day 3, entitled "Trade Nomads." Ottinger finally focuses her camera on living people, involved in selling and buying. In a recent interview, she observed that, in *Countdown*'s Polish market, she wanted to show (bargaining in) the "international language of hand signs" and the time it required her to learn this (foreign) language. More important, in the same interview, she clearly upholds the cause of the Others: "Minorities are a lot more flexible, witty, and active than the majority. Minorities offer solutions to the majority, and that's what my films are about. *Freak Orlando,* for example, is about the history of this relationship between minority and majority, throughout history. But these days, the reception of film has deteriorated to the point where only plot is seen. So people miss these issues in my film."[28] This context explains why *Countdown*'s first main subjects are not Germans. Indeed, it is highly significant that these subjects (associated with objects) consist of all the Others who populate Berlin: Romanians, Sinti, Romani, Poles. They represent the

28. Grundmann and Schulevitz, "Minorities and the Majority," 40.

ephemeral nomads from the East, if not from nowhere, who enter Berlin only to pass through it, never to be at home there. In this regard, the lens becomes an authentic ethnographer or chronicler in the sense developed in the film's literary subtext on minority and majority, Benjamin's "Theses on the Philosophy of History." "A chronicler who recites events without distinguishing between major and minor ones," writes Benjamin, "acts in accordance with the following truth: nothing that has ever happened should be regarded as lost for history. To be sure, only a redeemed mankind has its past become citable in all its moments. Each moment it has lived becomes a *citation a l'ordre du jour*—and that day is Judgement Day."[29] In other words, the responsibility of the chronicler, in film or otherwise, to redeem history with attention to detail risks undermining the larger historical picture.

The figure of the nomad has haunted Ottinger ever since its explicit import in *Johanna d'Arc of Mongolia.* A vital component of Ottinger's efforts to develop her earlier theories of hybridization and one of the various figures that might be called métis, the nomad reflects the nature of her film medium, which can be characterized as a crossbreed. Ottinger frankly admits that she "became quite interested in nomadism" and that for her, "nomad thought is very important."[30] One might recall here Gilles Deleuze and Félix Guattari's theorization of nomadism as a constant moving not only between and within cultures and geophysical spaces but also between and within concepts.[31] The nomadism reproduced in and by Ottinger's cinema is not only territorial but conceptual. Indeed, Ottinger directs her viewers into an overdetermined spectatorial position that adds speculation to unification by showing the potential impact of the new geopolitical entity, not just on Germans but on all Others as well. She moves not only across wide expanses of space and time (from the Einsteinturm to the Turkish market), not only between various forms of discursive practices (from Benjamin's essays to the "international language of hand signs"), but also across a diversity of concepts. She links nomadism with the "Jewish people in particular who, by force of course, nomadized over and over again."[32] This passage is striking in Ottinger's unwitting articulation of the old cliché of the wandering Jew, a figure of the Other without natural ties to a home country or soil.

Before the end of day 3, Ottinger's camera also records immigrants on

29. Benjamin, *Illuminations,* 254.

30. Therese Grisham, "An Interview with Ulrike Ottinger," *Wide Angle* 14, no. 2 (April 1992): 31, 33. See further Grundmann and Schulevitz, "Minorities and the Majority," 41.

31. See Gilles Deleuze and Félix Guattari, *A Thousand Plateaus: Capitalism and Schizophrenia,* trans. Brian Massumi (1980; Minneapolis: University of Minnesota Press, 1987).

32. "Laurence Rickels Talks with Ulrike Ottinger," 87.

Kurfürstendamm, an endless line of Polish buses waiting outside discount supermarkets, the desperate shell and other huckster games, gypsy beggars, who of course evoke once again both the past and the future plight of the Others—the time when the Romani, quintessential cosmopolitan nomads, were exterminated in death camps, a victim status that has yet to be adequately acknowledged, let alone made good. These images force us to look at the Wall—the material counterpoint to nomadism—from still another perspective. Are we to believe that all these nomadic peoples in a post-Wall Germany are (and will be) in any way more free to move than before? Ottinger does not presume to answer this question, as the camera consistently avoids eye-line matches from the point of view of the Other.

Day 4, the second-longest segment (thirty minutes), is titled "The Wall," with the sardonic subtitle "Adventure Park." Here Ottinger cites Benjamin's "One-Way Street" in the ironic epigraph about blindness, as if the Wall were rendered invisible by its hypervisibility in the mass media. Benjamin writes,

> The blind will to rescue the prestige of one's personal life, rather than to free, through the sovereign denigration of its impotence and collaboration, one's own existence (at least) from the background of general blindness, asserts itself everywhere. That is why the air is so crowded with theories of life and world views, and that is why they all seem (at least here in Germany) so arrogant, since they refer ultimately to the self-justification of a completely insignificant private situation. It is precisely for such reasons that the air is so full of delusions, projections of a nevertheless upcoming and flourishing cultural future, since everyone is bound to the optical illusions of his own isolated point of view.[33]

As with other references to Benjamin, the original context of this passage in "One-Way Street" gives Ottinger's film its sharpest edge. Ottinger points to this context by referring spectators back to the written text, aphorism 8 in "Imperial Panorama: A Tour of German Inflation." The context, in both film and text, is thus explicitly a monetary policy that spins off enormous imperatives throughout society and culture. As Benjamin wrote in "Tour 3," "All close relationships are lit up by an almost intolerable, piercing clarity in which they are scarcely able to survive. For on the one hand, money stands ruinously at the center of every vital interest, but on the other, this is the very barrier before which almost all rela-

33. Compare the translation in Benjamin, "One-Way Street," 74.

tionships halt; so, more and more, in the natural as in the moral sphere, unreflecting trust, calm, and health are disappearing."[34] Benjamin's dire warning about the way that reactionary, nationalistic forces would/could exploit a worldwide economic crisis was written in 1928, at the time of the first global stock market crash and looming hyperinflation. His prophecy—like Cassandra's and Ottinger's in the film—is couched in a metaphor of visibility and invisibility. And so, "Filth and misery grow up . . . like walls, the work of invisible hands"[35]—as Ottinger will repeat in the intertitle for day 7. For the time being, the task of destroying the wall of impoverishment is linked to making the "invisible hands" visible in an alternative medium such as cinema. And there is urgency. For, according to the subtext, "there is no hope so long as each blackest, most terrible stroke of fate, daily and even hourly discussed by the press, set forth in all its illusory causes and effects, helps no one uncover the dark powers that hold his life in thrall."[36] In addition to repeating Benjamin's written mastertext as part of an "illustrated lecture,"[37] Ottinger reinforces it with filmic images and sounds.

In Ottinger's first image in the Wall section, a giant bulldozer methodically moves chunks of concrete, dismantling a structure not clearly identifiable; the workers evidently control the bulldozer but are dwarfed by their mechanical hyperprosthesis. Ottinger's camera then cuts to an elderly woman pushing a pram through a break in the Wall, finally recognizable as such. And, for the first time in the film, we hear the voice of an interviewer, probably Ottinger herself, asking the woman if it is her first time "over," because the ability to cross over the wall has been there for some time. Ottinger likely chose to integrate this footage as a counter to the exuberant images of border crossings that dominated the mass media when the Wall first fell. After the unionized workers complete the demolition, Ottinger shows some of the unofficial workforce and children: a little girl and a particularly energetic group of boys who ham for the camera, becoming the film's only "actors." And there are tourists with their own cameras—notably people from Japan. But Ottinger also momentarily shows the Wall as if it were still intact, before 1989, and then pans once again to show its ruination. As on day 2, when Ottinger finally provides the film's first extended look at the Wall—or what remains of it—in situ, viewers "hear" it before seeing it: the noises of chipping and ham-

34. Benjamin, "One-Way Street," 72.

35. Benjamin, "One-Way Street," 72.

36. Benjamin, "One-Way Street," 73.

37. This is J. Ronald Green's term for what I and others tend to call essay film (see Green, "The Illustrated Lecture," *Quarterly Review of Film and Video* 15, no. 2 [1994]: 1–23).

mering are heard before see the agents or the object are seen. Only gradually do the workers' shadows appear, then their bodies. A veritable wall of sound of dismantling is given before the visual images, which include those already projected so many times by the mass media.

What is the motivation behind the extremely long sequences of footage of the Wall—this great requisite—as it is deconstructed by both machinery and human hands? Ottinger's tracking and lingering on the Wall serve a metaphoric end. Again, this is what Bill Nichols calls "cinematic excess" and "a surplus of meaning."[38] The Wall is the iconic sign par excellence, first for the division of Germany and second for its reunification. Its surplus meaning forms a multiple social-historical-political layer of signification. It can be read, like Ottinger's reference to Benjamin's "One-Way Street," as a sign pointing out the paradoxical blindness and optical illusion of an event irrevocably hypersaturated by the mass media. This is Ottinger's way of making the viewer look at it again, this time seeing beyond the "air so full of delusions" and cutting through the material concreteness—a concreteness that only attempts to disguise an ideological abstraction that sustains it as a mere visibility. Borrowing from Henri Lefebvre's critique of "everyday life," Ottinger is trying to make viewers perceive the otherwise imperceptible abstract space that exists in and around quotidian-cum-extraordinary events: her vision of the reunification. According to Lefebvre,

> We already know several things about abstract space. As a product of violence and war, it is political; instituted by the state, it is institutional. On first inspection it appears homogeneous; and indeed it serves those forces which make it a tabula rasa of whatever stands in their way, of whatever threatens them—in short, of differences. These forces seem to grind down and crush everything before them, with space performing the function of a plane, a bulldozer or a tank. The notion of the instrumental homogeneity of space, however, is illusory—though empirical descriptions of space reinforce the illusion—because it uncritically takes the instrumental as a given.[39]

Replacing Lefebvre's "space" with "wall," it becomes apparent that the relentlessly homogeneous media images of the Wall's destruction carried out by human hands and bulldozers conceal the presence of something more enduring and much harder to destroy: the ideological barrier

38. Bill Nichols, *Representing Reality: Issues and Concepts in Documentary* (Bloomington: Indiana University Press, 1991).

39. Henri Lefebvre, *The Production of Space,* trans. Donald Nicholson-Smith (1974; Cambridge: MIT Press, 1991), 285.

between the two German states—an introjected wall more indestructible than concrete could ever be. This problematic was anticipated already in Helke Sanders's essay film *Redupers* (All-Round Reduced Personality, 1977).[40] But now that the removal of the Wall also removes East Germany as the Other of West Germany, what will fill that space and fulfill the function of Otherness?[41] Ottinger points to this question as she demands that we re-view the Wall and its fall, lingering as long as filmically possible on its dismantlement and testing the audience's patience not only with her own film but also with the echoes of all media hyperbole.

Not all is political (or monetary) in *Countdown.* For Ottinger, Otherness inevitably also always means sexual difference, even though in deference to the film's special topic, she considerably downplays that difference this time. Thus, close to the film's midpoint, day 5—"Vital Signs"—opens with footage from the "first public gay demonstration in [former East Berlin] on Alexanderplatz." It is followed, the intertitle announces, by a "drive down the death strip, graffiti artist on Wollankstraße, Oberbaumbrücke, Turkish restaurant at Schlesisches Tor." A large banner, soaked by the rain that will eventually dampen the spirits of the demonstration and disperse it, mentions "Christopher Street," another manifestation of cosmopolitan geopolitical consciousness, this time pointing to the United States. Alongside the shot-reverse shots of drag queens and incredulous passers-by, the camera shows the banner that reads *Wiederguttun* (making good, or recompensation) for the victims of fascism and Stalinism—a double-edged thrust against both the Nazi and the communist regimes, both of which were intolerant of the gay and lesbian Other. In this instance, at least, Ottinger allows that the Wall's removal might have brought about a liberation, if only the freedom to demonstrate openly against continuing public and private homophobic harassment. The next sequence doubtless implies some progress, as the camera cuts to what used to be the infamous death strip, where former citizens of the German Democratic Republic lost their lives in their desperate attempts to leave socialism.

The physical geography of a transport route or strip continues to tell Ottinger's story, evoking other memories. Now, though, the camera slowly tracks through Berlin from a moving automobile, temporarily pro-

40. On this film, see Judith Mayne, "Female Narration, Women's Cinema: Helke Sander's *The All-Round Reduced Personality/Redupers*" [1981–82], in *Issues in Feminist Film Criticism,* ed. Patricia Erens (Bloomington: Indiana University Press, 1990), 380–94; B. Ruby Rich, "She Says, He Says: The Power of the Narrator in Modernist Film Politics" [1983], in *Gender and German Cinema: Feminist Interventions,* vol. 1, *Gender and Representation in New German Cinema,* ed. Sandra Frieden, Richard W. McCormick, Vibeke R. Petersen, and Laurie Melissa Vogelsang (Providence, R.I.: Berg, 1993), 143–62.

41. Zygmunt Bauman, cited in Wark, *Virtual Geography,* 51.

viding the viewer with the point of view of guards who used to ride along that strip, poised to kill. Ottinger points to the remarkable durability of roads and streets—more lasting than government regimes, wars, or walls. Their names may change, buildings may come and go, but the paths endure, inscribed in minds when no longer in space, the real if ironic vital signs of a dying world. The film goes back and forth, as it did previously, from East to West, transgressing borders as the car moves from the death strip to a city street and back again, uncannily evoking how a normal street can be momentarily transformed into a conduit of death, and vice versa. With the end of this sequence (after a brief stay in a Turkish restaurant), the film's temporal progression takes a break as it reaches its exact middle, figured, significantly, by the empty space between day 5 and day 6.

Day 6, "'Farewell to the Past' Festival and the Children," expands the break into geography as it leaves metropolitan Berlin for small former East German towns, one of which was formerly patronized by GDR leaders and now hosts a private party. Here, working women who have closed shop to talk recall dignitaries (notably Egon Krenz) who used to revitalize themselves there. This second major "interview" resembles an unconventional focus group. Ottinger steps back and voyeuristically allows the waitresses and cooks to talk freely among themselves. As the intertitle suggests, this conversation constitutes for these common people their own "Farewell to the Past Festival," echoing Ottinger's memories in day 1. The women speak in very low, barely audible, monotone voices. The topic turns to the Stasi, but in a very quiet way, without much emotion. This moderation clearly contradicts the sometimes hysterical mass-media coverage of citizens—family, lovers, and friends—involved in spying on one another. Ottinger chooses here to play down a traumatic experience but not to cover it up or to legitimate it; rather, by trivializing it, she wants to force viewers, Germans or not, to reflect on their own complicity with power or their own guilt and frailties. This minor re-creation of the "banality of evil" shows laundry drying on the line and modest table settings (composed with the care of a classical still life); there is also, as monetary integration draws near, a quiet discussion of unemployment and other social problems. Other towns appear, and finally the film shows children, who play between houses, on the roofs of which storks come and go and preen themselves.

These banal symbols of regeneration and hope may be too overt to be taken seriously, yet nothing indicates that Ottinger intended them to evoke an ironic, because illusory, image of East Germany or a melancholic vision of a paradise lost as a result of monetary integration. In fact, the longest segment of the film (forty minutes) seems to delight in its surprisingly refreshing representation of rural life with sheep, chicken, geese, and other farm animals as well as men pitching hay into wooden carts. How, then, to read the oddly disturbing romanticization of premodern countryside that characterizes "Farewell to the Past" and that will recur on day 9, which asks a more trenchant question: "What's left?" That penultimate segment, initially set in Plaue, a fishing village, is again relatively quaint, focusing primarily on children, people fishing, and animals. In contrast to the Western streetcars and trams, the typical mode of transportation here, as on day 6, remains the horse and cart: a further example of "Ostalgie," an idyllic counterpoint to the mediatic cliché of East German industrial pollution. But are these two pastoral scenes—days 6 and 9—as intentionally innocent as they seem? Perhaps Ottinger was unaware that she was treading on dangerous ground with these lengthy, highly nostalgic takes, particularly in light of her earlier statements linking Jews, nomads, and all Others to an ambiguous modernity. In this sense, the village would become a site for locating a pure German identity.

Moving back to Berlin, day 7, "What Counts?" asks to choose between a "Multicultural Diversity or a New Ghetto." Here Ottinger cites Benjamin's remark that "poverty grows 'like a wall built by invisible hands.'" Closer to Benjamin's original text—and giving the film more edge—is the following translation and its context, which begins,

> "Poverty disgraces no man." Well and good. But *they* disgrace the poor man. They do it, and then console him with the little adage. It is one of those that may once have held good but have long since degenerated. The case is no different with the brutal "If a man does not work, neither shall he eat." When there was work that fed a man, there was also poverty that did not disgrace him, if it arose from deformity or other misfortune. But this deprivation, into which millions are born and hundreds of thousands are dragged by impoverishment, does indeed disgrace. Filth and misery grow up around them like walls, the work of invisible hands.[42]

Ottinger adds laconically and somewhat cryptically, "That's why it's good to see the hands count. With a gesture of counting that gets translated directly and thus stays alive." Whether hands of oppression or hands of protest, the manual metaphor points to poverty and, in Berlin's context, to its poor Others looking out from their walls at their own Others: the German Berliners. Ottinger's camera moves from one group to the other on board the Magnetbahn: from the market on Potsdamer Platz to the Tiergarten, to smiling picnickers and, in counterpoint, to homeless camps. The

42. Wark, *Virtual Geography,* 51.

choice of identifying the picture as a "multicultural diversity" or as "a new ghetto" is left to the viewer. Here again the tacit context of Benjamin's "One-Way Street" gives dire urgency to the threat of a one-way street of economic countdown and provides the documentary its proper pedagogical function of *docere*—to teach and warn. The concrete material Wall, never predicted by Benjamin but built by visible hands, has collapsed to reveal intact the old walls of poverty built invisibly by capitalism. Should they keep protecting the Others, or should they too be erased?

Another series of questions—to which one answer is given—is raised in the intertitle of day 8, "The Empty Shop Window of the East": "Why doesn't one wait until the ideological evacuation creates new contents? Why doesn't one take the time to react to realities now that one can no longer pursue politics with ideas? Why must every vacuum that could emerge undergo instant colonization by the old and familiar? Why does one never slow down and only accelerate? Because slowing down could bring with it its own acceleration, one which does not always already count on being done with the next step." Presumably, these rhetorical historical questions describe the problematic *Countdown* itself as it attempts through its pace to slow down the rush to reunification of currency and nation. Poverty still looms in the background. The camera pans across row after row of more or less empty shop windows in East Berlin (which may not have been better supplied before the fall of the Wall). Then, in day 9 in Plaue, an old East German sign offers a play on words that sums up the future change with an overdetermined meaning: *Konsum* had served as a standard term for "co-op" (cooperative store), but now, integrated in the economic context, it will become an injunction, the basic imperative of the impending new capitalistic order and its "terror"—"Consume!" Queues of people begin to form past the empty shops leading toward an old savings and loan building, the telos of countdown. Gypsies appear—no monetary reunification in sight for them. The camera focuses on an outdoor café, and a conversation is overheard, recorded in Ottinger's idiosyncratic interview/noninterview style. At one point a woman who has just stripped a chicken leg with her teeth looks into the camera lens and says, flatly but with slightly ironic smile, "This is our last bone."

Day 10, titled "Currency Lines," has a sardonic intertitle (as in a Brecht or Piscator play): "25 million marks are available, 16 million people are waiting in line for them." The new spatial coordinates are "Karl-Marx-Allee, Frankfurter-Allee (formerly Stalin-Allee), roller coaster, amusement park"—all bright Berlin spots. Ottinger again slowly tracks along lines of people; her camera again picks out the children for momentary relief of tension. Behind the lines one can read a snippet of new graffiti on the Komerzbank—"Geld macht nicht glücklich" (money doesn't make you happy)—but no one but the camera seems to notice it. In a sequence showing women walking dogs, a statue commemorates East German–Soviet collaboration: "Gemeinsam auf der Erde und im All" (together on earth and in space). These two monuments loop back to the film's monumental beginning, suggesting the question: Will international communism—as reality or as ideal—be as erased from history, as were the Jews? Then comes an amusement park, complete with a Ferris wheel and the requisite haunted house—a dual allegory for triumphant capitalism and communism reduced to the status of a "hauntology." Finally a group of children, this time in medium close-up, is shown making eye contact with the camera, foregrounding the device. They wait for a group of musicians who are getting ready to pack up their instruments after having played. The film's show, too, is nearly over. It ends abruptly, almost in media res, back in the boat with a view of the unified Berlin skyline. But a shrill siren strikes the last jolting note, just before the film's end: the siren signals the precise moment of monetary unification with the same anticipation of dread as did the sirens that signaled air raids during World War II.

By its nature, the meaning of *Countdown* (constructed both formally and through explicit and implicit commentary) is obviously polyvalent and is open rather than closed. Hence, it has received a wide variety of responses in the press. An early reviewer wrote that, with a few exceptions, "Ottinger's languorous technique" fails to communicate a definite meaning, "becoming disengaged rather than revelatory."[43] Few could disagree wholly with this remark, especially with regard to the weaker (or most confusing) film sequences, but not necessarily for the same reasons as the critical reviewer, who questions Ottinger's ideological commitment and hence manipulation of perspective. "Except for the few brief times, when she speaks from behind the camera," the reviewer complains as he tries to support his claims, "Ottinger refuses to acknowledge her role as not just a recorder of events but also an organizer and orchestrator of subjects and events. As in the trip on the canals or the later records of the East German villages, *Countdown* threatens to become little more than an elegiac, and soporific postcard."[44] And so the review ends. The problem here is less the critic's unstated premise (the old *Cahiers du cinéma* notion that foregrounding the filmic device is necessarily meaningful) or his overlooking the openly heavy editing of the film with a selective camera and more an issue of cinema as theory and practice: Ottinger's views, closer to those of the essay film, therefore simply and clearly differ from her reviewer's more traditional views. The film may be elegiac and soporific in some regards. It

43. Knight, review of *Countdown,* 55.
44. Knight, review of *Countdown,* 55.

interweaves in a very complex pattern its otherwise tightly constructed allegorical plot lines: concrete metaphorical linear chronology; oscillating highs and lows, moments of hope and apprehension; monetary and political subtexts; variations of subversion. All this may appear chaotic and fragmentary, even in reductive summaries, reflecting Ottinger's deconstruction of the reunification. But *Countdown* does not set out to record events with an illusory objectivity. That is precisely what the mass media do so well—and so poorly. In contrast, Ottinger's intent in this essay film was to warn by documenting. Specifically, she set out to warn—surreptitiously more than explicitly; cannily as well as uncannily; in short, im/perceptibly—that German reunification was not merely an event that spoke somehow all by itself or that its protagonists could necessarily speak all by themselves. Rather, she attempts to allow objects and structures to speak, as it were, and to allow Walter Benjamin to issue his dire warning from out of the crisis of Weimar. The hard truth is that if Ottinger's un/canny technique works properly, then that early reviewer, and those who share his opinion, might never fully know how much or little they have been changed by *Countdown.*

III. Reunification as Musical Comedy: Ophüls's *November Days*

> The musical has only recently received its share of serious critical attention. A tone of incredulous disdain still tends to prevail, even though the claims of other genres have long since been accepted. . . . [M]usicals are increasingly coming under investigation for their ideological projects, their relationship to social moments and their orchestration of structures of pleasure.
>
> —*The Cinema Book*

Reacting, like *Countdown,* to the homogenized mass-media wave of approval—indeed, celebration—of Germany's 1990 reunification, Marcel Ophüls's *November Days: Voices and Paths* (1990) adds a note of original fantasy to the second, definitely critical, stage of response to that historical watershed. Ophüls took the somewhat unusual tack, in the context of this historical conjuncture, of selecting as his medium a type of essay film that he dubs "musical comedy"[45]—a multilayered genre straddling the unstable boundaries between highbrow and lowbrow, image and sound. Much like Ottinger's *Countdown,* this film ends with money and the monetary unification. It deals in earnest with many weighty social and political

45. Ophüls, cited by Kevin Jackson in "Just Singin' Round the Wall," *Independent* (London), November 9, 1990.

issues, but all it says is kept at an (ironic) distance, as if Ophüls remained on the outside looking in.

Born in 1927 to a Jewish household in Frankfurt, Germany, Marcel Ophüls fled to France with his filmmaker father, Max (1902–57), when Hitler came to power, moving to Hollywood in 1940. Marcel grew up alongside Bertolt Brecht's daughter, Barbara, a childhood friend. In 1950, the war over, he returned to France, where he became active in radio and television before turning to film. Ophüls's return to Germany to shoot *November Days* could be compared to a prodigal son's brief return to a reunified ancestral land. But Ophüls's feelings toward the new Germany—or, indeed, toward the notion of a German nation—are more ambiguous. And in his film, the Germans themselves—or at least those he interviewed for *November Days*—view reunification as a mixed bag: for some it is good news, for others an alarming development. The opposed ends of this spectrum are represented in the film by Michael Kühnen, a Nazi who hopes neo-Nazis in eastern Germany will rally to his cause, and by Barbara Brecht-Schall, who admits in her California-inflected English that she "has never liked the Germans," maintaining despite Ophüls's caveat that they are "still the same" and should be mistrusted.[46]

November Days was not Ophüls's first attempt at cinematographic expression of his ideas and/or reactions to forms of social or political violence. Ophüls conceived a 1967 work, *Munich, ou, La paix pour cent ans* (Munich, or, The Hundred-Year Peace), as the first part of a vast historical trilogy. This work began with the events leading up to World War II but, like all Ophüls's subsequent films, interwove past and present in a unique audiovisual style, making a genre that he calls not "documentary" but "nonfiction." Ophüls described his next major film, *Le chagrin et la pitié* (The Sorrow and the Pity, 1970), as "the movie of my life, like Conan Doyle and *Sherlock Holmes*—I try to get rid of it but it won't go away" and as a "biased film—in the right direction, I'd like to think—as biased as a Western with good guys and bad guys."[47] Tackling head-on the ultrasensitive topic of France's complicity with and resistance against Nazism, *The Sorrow and the Pity* was denied broadcast on French television but had a deep impact in movie theaters elsewhere. As the reviewers noted, it scandalized not only because of its specific subject matter because it punc-

46. In the same interview, Brecht-Schall asserts that she will not clean the Nazi graffiti off her father's gravestone, which Ophüls then shows us. It reads: "Sau Jud raus!" (Jewish pig, get out!), which can be taken to refer more directly to, say, Ophüls than to any Brecht.

47. Cited in Annette Insdorf, *Indelible Shadows: Film and the Holocaust,* 2d ed. (Cambridge: Cambridge University Press, 1989), 245. On the film, see further James Roy MacBean, "*The Sorrow and the Pity:* France and Her Political Myths," in *New Challenges for Documentary,* ed. Alan Rosenthal (Berkeley: University of California Press, 1988), 471–79.

tured the Gaulist myth of *grandeur française* but also because of the perfection of a new personal "compilation style" with which Ophüls smoothly shuttles back and forth among hard facts, montage, and narrative intervention.[48] Not least disturbing was the less-noticed use, in a minor key but in an otherwise deadly serious context, of what could already be called musical comedy. Thus, music enters as ironic commentary in the final scene, when Maurice Chevalier, the prototypical Frenchman, sings with his patented nonchalance, "Let the whole world sigh or cry, I'll be up in a rainbow, sweeping the clouds away."[49]

Over the years, Ophüls refined his compilation style but not the musical component. His next major film after *The Sorrow and the Pity* was *The Memory of Justice* (1976). Four hours long, it articulated responsibility and guilt in an often deeply personal way (through interviews with Ophüls's German wife and with American college students) between the Nuremberg war trials and not only Nazi war crimes but also global violence: Dresden, Algeria, and Vietnam. With some irony but also with genuine emotion, the film turned the judgments at Nuremberg back on the accusers, though without falling into the revisionist trap of denying the significance of the Holocaust. But in response to his wife's wish that he make a different sort of film, more along the lines of "Lubitsch or *My Fair Lady,*" he did include popular songs ("New Sun in the Sky," "That's Entertainment," and "I Guess I'll have to Change My Plan") that contrast with the bleak landscape of Schleswig-Holstein, where he had gone in search of a former Nazi physician. Less ironic and overall grimmer were other of his movies, such as *A Sense of Loss* (1972), on Northern Ireland; and *Veillees d'armes* (Trouble I Have Seen, 1994), on the rape and destruction of Sarajevo. All these films are informed by forays into the interplay between audio and visual tracks that have the spotlight in *November Days.*[50]

November Days was conceived in 1990, when Ophüls was commissioned by BBC 2 to make a film marking the first anniversary of the coming down of the Wall. The resulting work is just over two hours long. On the serious side, it comprises a series of interviews, mainly of former GDR citizens from various walks of life. Ophüls first shows parts of the BBC's

48. *Le Monde* (Paris), August 18, 1981.

49. Richard M. Barsam asks a pointed question: "Does this song damn Chevalier and, through extension, the French, for avoiding reality? Or is it just another piece of wartime footage reminding us that history is a complex mosaic? Ophüls asks audiences to think for themselves about how others behaved, about how they might behave in the face of the great human challenge" (*Non-Fiction Film: A Critical History,* rev. and exp. ed. [Bloomington: Indiana University Press, 1992], 348).

50. Insdorf first called attention to this audiovisual "counterpoint" in *Indelible Shadows,* 245.

November 1989 television coverage of Germany and then, with a remarkable detective work manifest in his earlier films, tracks down a select group of people to interview them again. The basic form of the film is a documentary, the brand of nonfiction that defined his style in earlier works—that is, a montage of found footage and live interviews, interrupted frequently by Ophüls's comments and even hummed bits of songs. Disregarding the whimsical notes of the musical comedy, *November Days* twists the documentary norm in the direction of a seriously committed essay film.

A dominant strategy is to show typical before-and-after sequences. For some East Germans, unification has a happy ending; for others, the result has been economic disaster, with loss of jobs and ideological anxiety, to the point of dysfunction; and the former Stasi fear incarceration. Ophüls has long been reputed to use film to attack what he called in 1972 "the horribly bourgeois attitude of believing that one can separate what is so conveniently called 'politics' from other human activities—e.g., profession, family life, love. This popular attitude constitutes the worst conceivable evasion of life, and the responsibilities of life."[51] The average person is not the only focus of Ophüls's camera in *November Days:* he interviews former high government officials and police, including Egon Krenz (who replaced Erich Honecker as general secretary of the Communist Party), Günter Schabowski (the Politbüro member who announced that East Germans could travel to the West), Markus Wolf (a major Stasi figure), and Walter Momper (the mayor of Berlin). Ophüls traces the disintegration of the German Democratic Republic in several levels of civil society, suggesting the complexity of internal pressures that led to its destruction and subsequent unification with the West. Ophüls seems less interested in the external pressures from both West and East, although he does let through some veiled allusions to them. Several significant passages were omitted from the final (released) version of *November Days.* As Ophüls recollects in a *taz* article, "Was nicht zu sehen ist," they include an interview with Marceline Ivens, a concentration camp survivor and the widow of Joris Ivens.[52] During this conversation, both parties reflect on Kristallnacht and the camps, with a cut to the neo-Nazi Kühnen. Another sequence contains an exchange with former East German gold medal–winning swimmer whose daughter has permanent bone damage as a result of her mother's consumption of steroids during her time as an athlete. Other omitted scenes include a talk with Beate Uhse, Germany's self-

51. Ophüls in *L'Avant-scène du Cinéma* 127–28 (July–September 1972): 10.

52. "Was nicht zu sehen ist," *taz,* November 14, 1991, in *Marcel Ophüls: Wiederreden und andere Liebeserklärungen: Texte zu Kino und Politik,* ed. Ralph Eue and Constantin Wulff (Berlin: Vorwerk, 1997), 238–40.

styled porn queen, and some reflections by Heiner Müller about the hatred of foreigners in the East. There is no apparent ideological, social, or functional link among these people, and it is possible only to speculate about why these scenes were ultimately cut.

Alongside the representation of the political economy of the GDR are those from its culture industry on several sides of the 1989 velvet revolution. Ophüls has particularly long exchanges with writer Stephan Hermlin, playwright Heiner Müller, Barbara Brecht-Schall, symphony director Kurt Masur, and artist Bärbel Bohly, referred to as the mother of the revolution. Oddly, fellow filmmakers are not interviewed. Some key figures, such as Christa Wolf, refused to meet with Ophüls, although they come up in conversation. And there is the interview with Michael Kühnen: a polite, articulate, high-ranking neo-Nazi—or, to use Žižek's preferred term, just plain Nazi.[53]

Heiner Müller. (Video caption from *November Days*.)

In all of the interviews (many pitted against each other and all interrupted in some way by editing), Ophüls recreates his signature version of the montage type that Benjamin (uncritically) and Adorno (critically) might call dialectical image.[54] Ophüls splices in, often with disruptive ironic effect, clips from old feature films, documentary footage from various periods of history, and other devices that undercut the verisimilitude and empathy commonly exuded by live interviews. For instance, after Brecht-Schall's denial that she fraternized with Erich Honecker, the camera cuts first to Heiner Müller (chomping a cigar à la Bert), asserting that

53. See again Žižek, *Tarrying with the Negative,* 200–237.

54. See Buck-Morss, *Dialectics,* esp. 33, 67, 73, 209–15, 219–22.

Brecht-Schall's statement is simply untrue, then to documentary footage of Brecht-Schall talking amicably with Honecker at a Berliner Ensemble production. This interview-editing technique surely is not the least reason why some people (including Christa Wolf) refused to be interviewed.[55] Ophüls also likes to interject himself into his interviews (at one point, his recording team is shown in a mirror), demonstrating the falsity of the still common assumption that a documentary is objective and its mechanism invisible, at least when compared to feature films. Ophüls's privileged outsider-insider status enables him to take his simultaneously committed and ironically distant stance, which infuriated some of his interview subjects. Tension is particularly evident when conductor Kurt Masur interrupts Ophüls's attempt to pressure Masur into saying that in his endeavors to construct a socialism with a human face, he feels "betrayed" by the "banana people" who have rejected all socialist ideals for consumer capitalism. Masur abruptly terminates the interview, stating that "no one has a right to ask such questions" without having been there. Here a major blockage or aporia is reached, not only for Ophüls but also for his audience; in a sense, we become the silenced interviewee. Nonetheless, Ophüls's ambiguous status gives *November Days* a certain international and cosmopolitan critical perspective that is missing in films more obsessively self- and nation-centered. Interestingly, the Nazi Kühnen defines *Jew* as (among other things) a "cosmopolitan" without national roots and allegiance (somewhat like Ophüls). Ophüls himself wavers on this issue. To Bohly's request (the only one in the film) that Ophüls say what he thinks of unification, he replies that "the Germans have a right to self-determination just like other *Völker* [nations or peoples]." He adds that this process is "so positive that I can't understand people's anxiety, including yours." Whereupon Bohly responds anxiously but forcefully that she is worried about the "little people" crushed by the juggernaut of privatization, to which Ophüls offers no comment. His considered response, it seems, comes in the form of *November Days* as a whole and perhaps as a musical comedy most specifically.

Why, indeed, a musical comedy about German reunification? The need for a new form of some kind may have stemmed from Ophüls's effort to destabilize a "spectacularized" topic to which audiences were already becoming numb, to force them to review it critically, and, in Brechtian terms, to become alienated. As Ophüls told reporter Kevin Jackson, "peo-

55. Ophüls publicly admitted in the early 1970s that there is an element of "exploitation" in all filmmaking and of "con game" in his manner of interviewing in specific. See "A Discussion with Marcel Ophüls," *Filmmaker's Newsletter* 6 (December 1972); Calvin Pryluck, "Ultimately We Are All Outsiders: The Ethics of Documentary Filming," in *New Challenges,* ed. Rosenthal, 255–68.

ple will be thoroughly fed up and jaded with the subject. I knew that I wanted to have a highly personal, subjective approach."[56] As with some previous films, he chose to interject music, stressing the musical comedy concept. Reviewers duly responded in various ways. Some praised Ophüls for attacking "the traditional style of the documentary by injecting snippets of popular musical culture into the serious discussion to delightfully subversive effect."[57] Others denounced "a 20th-century European melody in which nothing much happened very slowly, because Ophüls's editing had all the discipline and clarity of a sponge."[58] Such superficial praise and snide remarks do scant justice to Ophüls's gambling on the self-designated musical comedy.

At least two dialectically related channels or tracks operate here in combination—music and comedy—moving the film out of its expected documentary mode. Musical comedy qua genre, whether filmed or not, typically threatens to exceed classification—hence perhaps the contradictory reactions by reviewers. From its inception, musical comedy has been a legitimate form of popular culture (not inappropriate for a people's revolution) but also has been informed by more or less explicit social commentary (sometimes linked to a psychosexual problematic), as has been claimed for the use of sound in cinema generally.[59] Ophüls's choice of genre may be ambivalently placed between highbrow (documentary) and lowbrow (musical comedy), but his editing is hardly "spongelike." One must also resist the all-too-common tendency to view music in specific and sound in general as cosmetic to the film proper. Ophüls's carefully edited interpolation of songs and other music, alongside old film clips and stills,[60] are themselves bits of documentary evidence or requisites that paradoxically prohibit *November Days* from being mistaken as documentary pure and simple. Nor does he resort to another possible technique of protest nonfiction filmmaking, the feigned feature segment (yet another

56. Ophüls, as cited in Jackson, "Just Singin'."

57. Hillel Tryster, "Friends, Romans—and Stasi," *Jerusalem Post,* July 22, 1991.

58. Sheridan Morely, "Too Polite by Half," *Times* (London), November 12, 1990.

59. See, for example, Rick Altman, *The American Film Musical* (Bloomington: Indiana University Press, 1987); several essays in Rick Altman, ed., *Sound Theory, Sound Practice,* (New York: Routledge, 1992); Caryl Flinn, *Strains of Utopia: Gender, Nostalgia, and Hollywood Film Music* (Princeton: Princeton University Press, 1992); Kaja Silverman, *The Acoustic Mirror: The Female Voice in Psychoanalysis and Cinema* (Bloomington: Indiana University Press, 1988).

60. Films alluded to by Ophüls in *November Day*'s minihistory of cinema include various documentaries about everyday life in Berlin, including *Menschen am Sonntag* (written by Billy Wilder, codirected by Robert Siodmak and Edgar Ulmer, with Fred Zinnemann, 1929); Joseph von Sternberg, *The Blue Angel* (1930); Ernst Lubitsch, *To Be or Not to Be* (1942); and Joseph Mankiewiecz, *Julius Caesar* (1953). Noteworthy is Ophüls's tacit allusion to significant filmmakers with émigré status—that is, to insider-outsiders.

legitimate film genre or medium), as adapted in *Far from Vietnam* or *Germany in Autumn*. Thus, Ophüls's musical comedy inhabits the shadowland between fiction and truth while remaining more on the side of nonfeature, essay cinema.[61]

Ophüls adds to his diegetic soundtrack (mostly interviews) a musical score that is not quite background or nondiegetic but, rather, operates between the lines of diegesis, just as he adds film clips and stills more or less disjunctively to the image track. Ophüls's occasional voice-over comments on neither these dialectical images nor this dialectical sound track. As was the case for the nexus of political un/consciousness between the lines of the interviews with Schall-Kühnen-Bohly-Masur, any significance must be coproduced by the audience, which is not presented with the significance by metacommentary within the film. These audiovisual insertions exceed the diegetic world of the film (which further includes Ophüls's incorporated BBC broadcasts). The overall sound track might be called "A," the musical "a"; the visual footage would then be "B," with the incorporated docufootage "b"—but only if it is understood that the priorities can reverse themselves semantically. Sometimes the minor key turns out to be major. To grasp their function, which is neither strictly diegetic nor nondiegetic yet is contaminated by both, it is important to note those moments when Ophüls hums or sings words to a song, sometimes encouraging his interviewees to sing along, before or after the same song is heard as professionally recorded. Ophüls's own "prodigal body," as it were, serves as the point of articulation between diegetic space and nondiegetic space, both of which contain elements that are fictional or artistic as well as nonfictional or factual.[62] In terms of his notion of musical comedy,

61. Ophüls normally avoids the designation "documentary" and earlier calls *Memory and Justice* nonfiction. He is not alone in making this specification. Thus, Vietnamese filmmaker Trinh T. Minh-ha has said, "I never think of my films as specifically documentary or fictional, except when I send them off to festivals" ("From a Hybrid Place" [interview with Judith Mayne, 1990], in Trinh, *Framer Framed* [New York: Routledge, 1992], 139). Bill Nichols duly notes that "documentary practices are strictly governed and institutionally bound and determined" (*Representing Reality*, 14–15).

62. Bill Nichols clarifies the relation in documentary between narrative voice-over and sound/image track: "Whereas the appearance of a narrator speaking in direct address almost invariably ruptures the diegesis of fictional narrative, it can *constitute* the 'diegesis' of documentary exposition. Hence, the 'diegesis' cannot be ruptured by the narrator's presence, although it sometimes can be by his absence, by the lack of a logical principle ordering the whole which the narrator usually makes manifest" (*Ideology and the Image: Social Representation in the Cinema and Other Media* [Bloomington: Indiana University Press, 1981], 184). Thus, throughout *November Days*, Ophüls can be felt to be present in his absence at certain moments, even while generally shunning overt voice-over. On the problematic presence of bodies in documentary films, including the body of the filmmaker/narrator, see Nichols, *Representing Reality*, 229–66.

then, the main point seems to be that Ophüls is attempting to direct his documentary much as he might direct a musical comedy. This is not to argue that Ophüls comes across as a cabaret artist manqué but rather that for *November Days,* German reunification has aspects that can be illuminated by—indeed as—musical comedy.

Nevertheless, the critic who referred to the editing of Ophüls's "20th-century European melody" as having the "discipline and clarity of a sponge" was not entirely off the mark, though for the wrong reasons. (And self-effacing deception was evident in Ottinger's remark that her film was "arbitrary.") If Ophüls's work is not easy to decipher, it is because it echoes Roland Barthes's thesis about the "obtuse" or "third meaning" in film. Barthes argues that signs are read in cinema first on an informational level, second on a symbolic level, and finally on a third level that eludes designation and that he calls "obtuse meaning."[63] It originates in a surplus structural and carnivalesque excess—not unlike comedy, music, and prodigal status. While Barthes applies his theory to visual imagery (he was analyzing stills from a silent film by Eisenstein), it can extend to sound track and a fortiori to self-conscious musical comedy. The cinematic excesses in *November Days*'s audio and the visual tracks thus elevate meaning to another, more properly dialectical—and properly musical-comical—level of articulation of the aesthetic and the political.

November Days opens with newsreel footage of Honecker at the East Berlin Airport on October 6, 1989, the fortieth anniversary of the creation of the GDR, awaiting the arrival of Mikhail Gorbachev, who the next day will decline to intervene in German affairs. Honecker shouts to Western journalists, "Die Totgesagten leben lange! [Those declared dead live long!]" At this historical moment pregnant with in/decision, Ophüls freezes his frame and his voice propels the narrative past this still point (Benjamin's "dialectics at a standstill").[64] The effect of Ophüls's freeze frame is dialectically similar to that of Ottinger's attenuated tracking shots—by pausing in the past, this technique gives the spectator time to reflect on the current situation and speculate on its future possibilities.

63. See Roland Barthes, "The Third Meaning," in *Image-Music-Text,* trans. Stephen Heath (New York: Hillandwane, 1977), esp. 322–30.

64. See Walter Benjamin, *Das Passagen-Werk,* ed. Rolf Tiedemann, 2 vols. (Frankfurt am Main: Suhrkamp, 1983), 1:570–611.

Image of Rostropovich. (Video caption from *November Days*.)

If a disembodied, controlling, authoritative voice-over is standard fare for many documentaries, Ophüls inserts himself into the interviews in a vastly more aggressive and obtrusive way than does Ottinger, countering such neutral pretensions. His next cut is to a series of still photographs of the American, British, French, and Soviet military immediately after World War II, cheerfully photographing one another as they carve up Berlin into its four sectors. The obtuse chiasmus is striking: in 1945, still photos captured at once a unity of purpose in the defeat of Nazism but also the division of Germany; in 1989–90, moving pictures capture the reunification of Germany as well as, by the im/perceptible logic of the chiasmus, a return toward fascism. The sound track is Marlene Dietrich singing in English the melancholic "September [November] Song": "It's a long, long while from May till December, and the days grow short when you reach September, when the autumn weather turns the leaves to flame, one has no time for the waiting game." Two visual cuts follow: first to stills of children playing by the Berlin Wall, their ball frozen in midair, then to an old man playing his cello against the palimpsest-graffitied Wall. This is a widely disseminated photograph of Mstislav Rostropovich (dubbed by *Time* Magazine "one of America's cold war trophies" after his return to his native Russia in 1992),[65] playing in front of a graffiti image of Mickey Mouse. Ophüls's camera zooms in on Rostropovich and his cello, while "September Song" plays in the background. Thus, the sound sutures the disparate visual narrative spaces as if still photographs were generating the

65. *Time,* December 28, 1992, 73.

musical score to the sound track. The cello player establishes the role that music will play throughout the film against the text or score of the Wall, and the image also anticipates later images of cellos in the footage of Masur's Leipzig Philharmonic playing Schiller's "Ode to Joy" from Beethoven's Ninth or Choral Symphony—the icon of transtemporal human solidarity. Dietrich's "September Song" thus has at once diegetic and nondiegetic significance and is as important as the visual track in struggling to represent the looming days of November. Against the graffitied Wall (an image proliferating in the Western mass media as the symbol for resistance to tyranny), one hears music signaling audio graffiti—graffiti that flows via sound waves breaking through history and the subconscious. It is again a reminder of Sanders's *Redupers,* in which 1970s Berlin is shown and heard before the collapse of the Wall, with a montage of radio broadcasts in English, French, German, and Russian generating an ideological sound space that at once severs and unites East and West. All music in *November Days* becomes a form of graffiti, the image of Rostropovich forging an audiovisual loop. In Barthes's terms, on the informational level, "September Song" tells how quickly time flies from May to December; on the symbolic level it reminds the listener both of the waiting game and of how quickly and peacefully, in the larger scheme of things, the Wall and the East fell; on the third, or obtuse, level, Dietrich singing in English recalls not only her self-imposed exile from Germany and Weimar Cinema but also Ophüls's father, forced to find a career in Hollywood. (And, looking ahead, in 1996–97 a heated debate raged in Berlin about whether to name a street after Marlene Dietrich, who was a "traitor" to her country. The street was named for her and is located in the heart of the once vibrant, then desolate, and today vibrant again Potsdamer Platz.) The next sound after Dietrich is English schoolchildren reciting the lines "Humpty Dumpty had a great fall . . . and all the king's horses and all the king's men couldn't put Humpty together again"—superimposed first on an illustration from *Alice in Wonderland* and then on footage of goose-stepping GDR soldiers changing the guard, momentarily suggesting that perhaps the Nazis have returned with their march. Ophüls chooses this moment to insert his own recitation from *Alice in Wonderland* about Humpty Dumpty—the epigraph of the first section of this chapter—as the image track shows old, cancer-riddled Honecker walking with his entourage away from the camera into the October woods of his botched wonderland.

Ophüls's obtuse audiovisual, intertextual, and existential loop thus includes his prodigal return to turn his film about German reunification into a "comedy" in the common sense that it appears to have a happy ending. A layered history of meanings can overdetermine the re/presentation of one tiny snippet of song. The location of these surplus meanings is not so much in the film, as either information or symbolism, but just below the level of conscious perception, which is to say musically. But the obtuse status of this musical comedy is not best described as "a very subjective film about Marcel Ophüls going back to Germany."[66] Each time Ophüls intervenes, especially linked with music, he also points his musical comedy away from himself to larger history. Thus, he first starts humming Gershwin's "It's Wonderful" (before the recording is played) during an interview with West Berliner Susi Fischer, who was captured by BBC cameras as she crawled over the Wall toward the East. Ophüls tracks her down and asks her to recall her feelings at the time. The word *wonderful* pops up, leading Ophüls to a discussion of flirting—standard fare of the musical comedy. Further associations with flirting bring up East German Werner Schäfer, who hints at the sexual freedom that the fall of the Wall promises. He admits to leaving his wife in the East (*drüben,* or "over there") and moving in with a West German woman for a few months, the women of the West representing an allure of the sexual erotic and exotic.[67] As in many Hollywood musical comedies, song and sex form a momentary bridge between national and class identities. But at this point Dietrich starts "Ich bin von Kopf bis Fuß auf Liebe eingestellt, denn das ist meine Welt und sonst gar nichts!" After lingering on Schäfer and contemporary Berlin, Ophüls recuts to *The Blue Angel* (1930), one of the first German sound films, starring Dietrich the singer of the future even as the old—in effect, nineteenth-century—order was fast fading away.[68] The repressed sexuality of Weimar Professor Unrat may echo and reinforce the perceived repression (sexual and other) of the former GDR.[69] With Dietrich still singing on a record, the camera moves to Armistice Day footage in 1945, then to current West Berlin discos. Ophüls then interviews former East German waiter Mario Kähl, who frequents these scenes. Not formerly shy, the waiter notes that with Western women, he has "inhibitions" (*Hemmungen*). It seems that West German women, symbolized as trophies, indicate the persistence of

66. See Jackson, "Just Singin'."

67. In *Germany 90 Nine Zero,* Godard's camera captures the Berlin cigarette advertisement "Test the West" with a sexy, leather-clad woman who entices the viewer to smoke (to buy and buy into) not merely a brand (West) but an entire economic system.

68. On the importance of this film both in film history and in Dietrich's career, see Wolfgang Jacobsen, Anton Kaes, and Hans Helmut Prinzler, eds., *Geschichte des deutschen Films* (Stuttgart: J. B. Metzler, 1993), 95–98.

69. Dietrich has long been a lesbian and gay icon, though this subtext is probably more a projection by some film viewers than Ophüls's own; generally speaking, sexuality is not one of his filmic concerns.

a great class divide that still separates East from West, (some) men from (some) women.[70] But Kähl's inhibitions do not prevent him from showing off a dance step for Ophüls's camera, although he is no Fred Astaire. This moment adds yet another layer of cruel/funny social satire to the musical comedy.

Bing Crosby's "Song of Freedom" evokes post–World War II Cold War democracy, which allows old friends Ophüls and Brecht-Schall to debate the significance of the lyrics on both sides of the Wall: freedom to "speak and hear," freedom from "want and fear," and freedom to "sail the seven seas." They pose momentarily as rival critics of this bit of popular musical culture. Ophüls later turns to a once famous German musical of the 1930s, *Weisse Rössl.* The male lead, "Der gute Sigismund," was originally supposed to be a Jew. As Ophüls (who sings some of the lyrics) informs the current actor in the role, Carl Jung, the Jewish referent has entirely dropped out of the 1990 performance in West Berlin. But Ophüls also would have us recall Krenz's plea that "not all the 40 years of the GDR were shit."[71] The obtuse meaning is musical-comically complex. If Jews have been erased from German history (and Nazism out of East German history with the argument that the Nazis were a mere by-product of capitalism), then, by filmic syllogism, will the years of communism also simply be eradicated? Where will they go? Will they resurface?

Ophüls's penultimate musical score is Masur's chorus of men and women in the former GDR singing "Alle Menschen werden Brüder." But even this quintessential highbrow, feel-good, and happy-ending paean to unification becomes suspect. For the accumulated associations in the film (notably the inconclusive conversations earlier with Brecht-Schall and Bohly about the German *Volk*) suggest that in Germany today this song is taken to refer less to a unified Europe—let alone unified world—than to German hegemony. (The irony pointed out by Ophüls seems to elude the official Goethe Institute film about unification, which uses the same Beethoven as its sound track.) Again Ophüls takes pains to position his musical comedy as social commentary spanning horrific past, ambivalent present, and uncertain future. With Beethoven, the symphony reached its maximum form of purely musical expression and so required the interpolation of sung words, Schiller's paean to revolution and hope for utopia. This was Wagner's analysis of the situation, choosing as he did the Ninth Symphony to instaurate Bayreuth—its "music drama of the future," its

70. The terrible reality of sexual abuse and violence, to which women in both the GDR and the Federal Republic have been subjected over the years, is the theme of Helke Misselwitz's controversial recent film, *Herzsprung.*

71. Egon Krenz in an interview with Ophüls, as filmed in *November Days.*

claim to unify Germany. This was arguably the modernist origin of the peculiarly powerful *Gesamtkunstwerk* known as cinema.[72] By middle or lowbrow analogy, Ophüls's film stakes out a new position for musical comedy in the analysis of cultural politics.

Asked why Ophüls uses the vehicle of unification to experiment with film genre, and vice versa, one possible answer might be that the fall of the Wall is analogous to the fall of walls between fiction and documentary realism. If *Hotel Terminus* disclosed something lethal hidden in darkness, then "1989" is too visible to the world. By clouding an ostensibly black-and-white issue, Ophüls points to the importance of what is not seen, said, and heard: the in/visible and in/audible text of history. But, to his un/canny credit, this principle does not exclude *November Days.*

Scene from *November Days*

In footage of Communist Party members singing "The International" for the last time in early November, an old proletarian apparently waves his party card in time to the music. The old man denies that he did it. Our first reaction is that this rank-and-file communist is lying, like Brecht-Schall about her relationship to Honecker. But Ophüls replays the clip without verbal comment, and we see that the man is waving not his card but a clenched fist. In the sea of cards raised by others, it only seems that he too is holding one. The difference may appear inconsequential (though one difference is significant: the fist does not necessarily denote party adhesion), yet it is not insignificant in terms of the complexity of the events

72. See Flinn, *Strains of Utopia*, esp. 13–17, 24–34, 65–68, 86–87.

at hand, the struggle to differentiate truth from falsehood, and the often extreme import of the most minuscule distinctions. This sequence cuts two ways. The old man may seem to have evaded the issue by a technicality, and since he still describes himself as a communist, communism itself may seem further discredited by an apparent sophistry. Conversely, the deeper point is that Ophüls has misread documentary film footage in his own film and that he allows us to see and hear this misleading fact. This is a standard problem in the psychology of perception, "the phantom percept," as developed for painting by E. H. Gombrich and for film by Teresa de Lauretis.[73] Briefly, the phantom percept permits a viewer to extrapolate from fragmentary sense data a unified whole that may or may not turn out to be accurate. As De Lauretis notes, the percept is also a basic "*social* contract by which external consistency is given up or traded against the internal coherence of the illusion."[74] In *November Days* the phantom percept as contract is ironic, foregrounding not only an audiovisual problematic but also the social, even as the ringing promise of communism in "The International" seems to echo away historically and filmically.

For his final audiovisual "song," Ophüls's picks "Money," from another—perhaps the most famous—musical comedy about Berlin, *Cabaret,* "Hollywood's first foray into decadent chic."[75] Bob Fosse's 1972 film was based on *Berlin Stories,* by the pacifist and homosexual Christopher Isherwood, yet another kind of exile from Weimar Germany.[76] *November Days: Voices and Paths* ends with a montage edited back and forth between Liza Minnelli's eroticized singing of "Money" in *Cabaret*'s Weimar and East Germans exchanging their now worthless currency for deutsche marks, linking viewers to Ottinger's *Countdown.* Earlier in his film, Ophüls failed to get interview subjects to sing along (notably, Brecht-Schall and the mayor of Berlin) and did not presume to pressure conductor Masur. But now former East German commoners cheerfully comply—almost. Ophüls apparently has reminded them of the lyrics to "Money," and some stop just short of breaking into song, intoning the keyword from the chorus: "Money! Money! Money!" This is not the first time in the history of cinema where reference to money puts a sinister final spin on a feel-good film.[77] Ophüls's dialectical sound-image is diachronic and syn-

73. See Teresa de Lauretis's elaboration of this argument in *Alice Doesn't: Feminism, Semiotics, Semiotics, Cinema* (Bloomington: Indiana University Press, 1984), 60–62.

74. De Lauretis, *Alice Doesn't,* 62.

75. Pam Cook, ed., *The Cinema Book* (1985; London: BFI, 1992), 112.

76. Christopher Isherwood, *The Berlin Stories* (1935; New York: New Directions, 1963).

77. Think of the grotesque, ostentatious depiction of money at the end of Frank Capra's *Its a Wonderful Life* (1946), as noted by Robert B. Ray, *A Certain Tendency of the Hollywood Cinema, 1930–1980* (Princeton: Princeton University Press, 1985), 179–215.

chronic: back to Weimar's point of transition to the Third Reich; fast-forward to the twenty-first century; and laterally to a psychosocial space of un/canny location in the serious musical comedy also called late capitalism. Ophüls's and Ottinger's cameras leave inconclusive final images of monetary unification in the summer of 1990. What and who will survive in the new Germany is left open to debate and to the media.

Epilogue. History in the Making: The Children of Golzow Project

Spare no Charm, Spare no Passion.

—Hanns Eisler

It seems somehow fitting that this book, opening with the study of a committed East German film collective—the H&S that collapsed together with the Berlin Wall[1]—would conclude with the story of the Junges, two relatively successful East German filmmakers who are alive and active today. This structure could be considered paradoxical, as it seems to assign to East German cinema the overarching function of brackets encompassing a subordinate West German production. In reality, of course, with the sheer volume and dynamism of its output, applauded by critics all over the world, West German cinema has been playing the dominant role since the end of the war, and the East German production looks like a parenthesis—and a short-lived one at that—in the history of German-language films. But paradoxically it is tempting, one could argue, to create an alternate reality where a politically correct poetic justice would reverse the relation of winners and losers. Such a virtual world, absurd by logic, could generate new answers to the old question of whether talent or money, art or power, creation or politics determines cinematographic value judgments. One could also claim, still in a paradoxical mood but with more respect for realism, that the harsh conditions of filmmaking in East Germany, stifled by material, ideological, and political constraints, were in fact more typical of film production in most Western countries, hampered by comparable financial problems and pressures to conform. The beginning and end chapters of this book could thus be claimed to serve as an initial and final reminder of the tough reality of film production everywhere,

1. After the reunification, Heynowski and Scheumann became unemployed and lost control and possession of most of their films and materials. Scheumann died in 1998.

whether state or free-market driven, with a suggestion of strategies that have been essayed to deal with the most offensive aspects of that reality and perhaps with a lesson for the future. On a more serious note, I admit expecting that this radical spatial polarization of the two East German experiences, diverging within the same system, will structurally repeat and therefore reinforce the contrast between the cinemas of the two separated parts of Germany and the final resolution of their opposition. Compared to the Junges' saga discussed here, the H&S story in the first chapter appears more typical of left-wing filmmaking, with its ideological aggressiveness and political commitment—overt or covert but always somewhat revolutionary. That story has an unhappy end, the total silencing of H&S by the public and political pressure of a reunited anticommunist Germany, epitomizing the silencing of most East German culture. In contrast, the Junges, who survived as filmmakers, had always been closer to Western documentary film practices. Indeed, as Noël Burch notes, "The documentary idea after all demands no more than that the affairs of our time shall be brought to the screen in any fashion which strikes the imagination."[2] The Junges' Children of Golzow series, examined in this chapter, stresses many of West German topics and attitudes: focus on romance and family problems, generational conflicts, progress (or failure) in society, urban growth. In fact, it seems occasionally to look very much, with a communist instead of capitalist slant, like the small West German town chronicled in Edgar Reitz's *Heimat.* No wonder, then, that the most recent Children of Golzow episodes have come out in the reunited Germany, integrated as it were in the flow of the victorious West German cinema. Of course, such a survival has its price: the renunciation of a previous identity. But in this sense, too, this chapter reflects or optimistically anticipates the eventual integration of former East Germany, still resented on both sides of the political divide. The story of the Junges thus exemplifies history and can be read in that light in a pseudochronological order.

"Everything flows, no one can bathe in the same river twice," intones the voice of a schoolteacher, echoing Heraclitus's famous dictum, at the beginning of Barbara and Winfried Junge's 1980 compilation film *Lebensläufe* (Paths of Life). Winfried Junge (b. 1935), was part of the 1958 class (the first class to graduate) of the East German School for Film Art (Deutsche Hochschule für Filmkunst) in Potsdam-Babelsberg. Junge followed the advice of his film-school mentor, Karl Gass, and in August 1961, a few days after the GDR sealed its borders, embarked on what

2. Noël Burch, *Theory of Film Practice* (Princeton: Princeton University Press, 1969), 156–57.

would become a lifelong project to document the life of the people of Golzow in Oderbruch, an East German village near the Polish border. The result has been sixteen films to date, collectively referred to as the Children of Golzow Project. The most famous of these is *Lebensläufe.* Another compilation film, the four-and-a-half-hour *Drehbuch: Die Zeiten* (Screenplay: The Times, 1992), was made from selected footage from the 1980s and early 1990s. In 1978, Junge's wife, Barbara, became fully involved in the editing, directing, and production of the subsequent Children of Golzow films. According to the Junges, their project marked the first attempt in the history of the documentary genre to produce such a long-term ongoing chronology. And, indeed, it preceded by three years the start of Michael Apted's better-known 7-Up series, which in 1964 began filming at seven-year intervals the lives of seven-year-old British children, following them until they reached age forty-two.

For his initial subjects, Junge chose children born in 1954–55 who entered school for the first time in the fall of 1961. The decision to record the lives of these children at school was influenced by the background for the initial funding of the project: in 1960, the GDR had introduced a new ten-year educational schema, and Junge's children were being tracked partly to determine the effectiveness of that new system. As the titles of the initial films indicate, they generally focused on major events connected to the children's school life: *Wenn ich erst zur Schule geh* (First Day of School, 1961), *Nach einem Jahr-Beobachtungen in einer ersten Klasse* (One Year Later—Observations on a First-Grade Class, 1962), *Elf Jahre alt* (Eleven Years Old, 1966), *Wenn man vierzehn ist* (When You Are Fourteen, 1969), *Die Prüfung* (The Examination, 1971), and *Ich sprach mit einem Mädchen* (I Spoke to a Girl, 1975). Following their graduation from school, the participants were then asked to keep the Junges abreast of significant moments in their lives, such as marriage, birth of children, career changes, and the like. As it turns out, though, the subjects did not always honor their contract, as happened in the case of Jürgen, who "forgot" to notify the Junges of his marriage and the birth of his child. One of the challenges that confronted the Junges in the late 1970s was that of selecting a small number of continued "stars" for their project because funding did not permit them to track all twenty-six of the initial children. In addition, some of the former students had to be dropped from the study as result of various circumstances, and in one case, filming had to be rethought because of the sudden death of one person. None of their lives is extraordinary. And because of the Wall, all of the subjects remained in East Germany until unification, greatly facilitating the task of tracking them. The result is a remarkable account of everyday life. As one reviewer put it, "In all these years, nothing really sensational has happened to these children. . . . Yet the film in its totality is truly sensational."[3] Furthermore, the film testifies to the quality of trust that has grown among the Junges, their filmmaking crew, and the subjects, whose often intimate discussions indicate a rare degree of understanding, compassion, and empathy.

Unlike most directors working for the GDR state-owned film company, DEFA, especially those producing documentaries, the Junges did not see their project come to an end as a result of German reunification in 1990. Richard von Weizsäcker, former president of the Federal Republic of Germany, stated in a letter to the Junges that "for decades you have documented a world, a time of revolutionary chance along with its consequences, that in the meanwhile has become alien even to the baffled protagonist. Today, the *Chronicle of the Children of Golzow* is a unique document."[4] And because of this uniqueness and the project's historical value as record and archive, the Junges' project has survived and continued to receive funding. Indeed, five more films were made during the 1990s, each one focusing on an individual person instead of on a collective event. For example, the Junges made *Das Leben des Jürgen von Golzow* (Jürgen of Golzow, His Life) in 1994, followed by *Die Geschichte vom Onkel Willy aus Golzow* (The Story of Uncle Willy of Golzow, 1995), and *Was geht euch mein Leben an Elke—Kind von Golzow* (My Life Is My Own Affair, Elke—A Child of Golzow, 1996). More recently, *Brigitte und Marcel* was shown at the 1999 Berlin Film Festival, and *Dieter* is nearing completion. A shift in emphasis clearly took place, from a communal history to life of liberated bourgeois individuals.

At this point, then, the Junges' work has been going on for nearly forty years and constitutes a unique examination of the second half of the twentieth century from the perspective of one small German town. No wonder that the resulting tapestry of testimonies that Junges' films weave together present an incredibly rich sociological record of the former GDR *wie es eigentlich gewesen ist* (as it truly was). The series also evokes the shifting social conditions brought about by the transition to life in a unified Germany. Each of these films merits a thorough investigation in its own right, but I will focus only on an overview of *Lebensläufe* and *Drehbuch* and, as a point of contrast, *Da habt ihr mein Leben: Marieluise, Kind von Golzow* (Here You Have My Life: Marieluise, Child of Golzow, 1997).

Lebensläufe is divided into biographies of four men (Jürgen, Bernd,

3. *Süddeutsche Zeitung* (Munich), April 15, 1995.

4. As cited by Barbara Junge in Ron Holloway and Dorothea Holloway, "Interview with Barbara and Winfried Junge," 44. (From the personal archives of Barbara and Winfried Junge.)

Dieter, and Winfried) and five women (Gudrun, Brigitte, Elke, Marieluise, and Ilona), framed by a prologue and an epilogue. One central question the film raises is to what extent portraying an individual life can reflect a historical process of which it is a part. While the films are surely historical because they chronicle the lives of real-life children and follow their transformation from youngsters into adults from an anthropological perspective, the Junges' films are also ethnographic in that they limit their observations to a very specific geographical location—Golzow—a quasi-premodern village where a farming cooperative introduces a factor of change. According to Winfried Junge, Golzow was chosen because it was "a village that had survived the war but had been heavily damaged during the battles on the Oder River. So now the youth there should be given a new chance to profit from the area's reconstruction: one of the first buildings to be erected in Golzow was the school. And since the children in this rural community were now given the opportunity to benefit from ten years of schooling, this was the place we wanted to film—a devastated village now getting back on its feet."[5] Their subjects are for the most part children of farmers and agricultural workers, a constraint that obviously reduces the scope and validity of the group as an ethnographic sample. But as Winfried Junge states in the prologue, "We did not aim for a sociological cross-section." By following the evolution of the chosen group, the camera simultaneously records the parallel development of Golzow from a pretechnological rural farming community to a modernized small town. Important innovations such as soil reform, the introduction of a new high-tech tractor, and the implementation of more advanced irrigation system are highlighted in *Lebensläufe.* Both prologue and epilogue offer long tracking shots of a country landscape, but the epilogue also shows new houses in the village, the first apartment building, new hothouses for plants; furthermore, trucks and cars have replaced the old steam engine so markedly present in the early years.

However—and this is particularly pertinent here—not only changes in society and the environment are documented: the Junges' project is also significant because it shows the developments in documentary filmmaking practices from the 1960s to the 1990s, moving from black-and-white to color (1978) and updating interview techniques and strategies, including a reassessment of the role of the interviewer. Finally, in a most informative bonus, the later films such as *Marieluise* encourage provocative comparisons between their new style, influenced by the West, and the style of earlier films, which reflects the filmmakers' training in an ideological tradition that differs radically from the Western European or American tradition.

5. As cited by Winfried Junge in Holloway and Holloway, "Interview," 42.

In the process of viewing the entire series, one becomes increasingly more conscious that the Junges had been first educated in a system dedicated to historical and dialectical materialism, with an explicit political commitment to East German communism and to an aesthetic practice derived not from high modernism but from socialist realism. Conversely, one notices more clearly that the postunification films are marked by the parallel transition and integration into Western capitalism affecting both the life of the people and the style of filmmaking.

More specifically, one realizes how much, in opposition to Western conventions about the documentaries at that time—that is, the respect of an idealistic objectivity—the early documentary style practiced by the Junges (and evidenced in *Lebensläufe*'s earlier quotes) is confrontational, overtly politicized, and in that sense both subjective and manipulative. If, during the 1960s and 1970s, the Anglo-American direct cinema and the French cinema verité outwardly strove toward as much formal neutrality as possible, concealing their own irreducibly subjective ideological support of the bourgeois society, the Junges in contrast rejected all spurious objectivity and tended toward assuming a more subjective stance that continuously reminds the viewer of the constructiveness of their filmic text. True, the cinematic apparatus is not visually foregrounded in the early films, but there are many references to the function of the film and to the presence of the filmmaker. In the first episode, for example, it is revealed that the cameraman chose to chronicle one particular little boy's experiences because that boy (Jürgen) was particularly photogenic. Furthermore, the opening scene, which features the first day of school, had to be reenacted and refilmed because the shots of the real action were deemed inadequate: only Jürgen's back was visible. This is not the only instance in the film where the filmmakers restaged a real episode and hence inevitably deformed it out of concern for the aesthetics or message of their film. Two other such reconstructed scenes are included in Gudrun's sequence, both of them scripted and acted out (instead of experienced) by the participants—in one case by Gudrun and her father, in the second by Gudrun and her mother. In a somewhat naively formulated statement, Dieter's segment proclaims, "We are acting out the scene exactly as it took place a few minutes ago," as if such an equivalence were possible.

This strategy of self-reflexivity that draws attention to the artificial reconstruction of reality—a strategy that became popular in the West in the mid-1980s and 1990s—was not totally uncommon in other East German documentary practices; H&S carried it out. It certainly raised some basic theoretical questions about the nature of filmmaking and its relation to reality, and the Junges were not alone in experimenting with it. Their more personal contribution was the new stress on the related perennial question about the extent to which a documentary film is indeed directed by the filmmaker. The Junges would argue that from a dialectical perspective, the inevitable subjective and partisan manner in which the editing camera intervenes in the presentation of reality does not necessarily entail the violation of that reality but rather reorganizes it for the sake of the truth as it is revealed by the camera. However, a capital and yet still controversial distinction must surely be made here between arranging and directing. The Junges' practice oscillates between the two, undermining in either case the supposedly unique documentary value of their record of real life—that is, a long-term filmed reality.

Another striking technical characteristic of *Lebensläufe* is the dominating and controlling voice-over of the narrator/director (Winfried Junge—Barbara is heard only once in the series, in *Marieluise,* when Marieluise and her two daughters pay an unexpected visit to the studio). Winfried Junge's questions are often quite provocative and/or aggressive, fulfilling the function of a partisan commentary. In one instance, he tries to start a political discussion with the adult Jürgen, who does not respond, preferring instead to watch television. This prompts Junge to state that Jürgen just sits around at home and does nothing. It is true that, in the spirit of Bakhtin's dialogism, Junge immediately retracts his comment and rhetorically asks exactly what is wrong with Jürgen wanting a private space after working all day. Here, Junge comes as close as he ever will within *Lebensläufe* to explaining the strategy underlying his political questions, which, he implies, are nothing more than rhetorical devices. "How could he understand that I am trying to provoke him?" he wonders in a tone that hesitates between compassion and condescension. In another scene in which he interviews Brigitte, who works in a poultry-processing factory, Junge makes a point of saying just how disagreeable he found her work—disemboweling chickens—and in general her working conditions: "Here we counted the minutes before we could go, and if we hadn't begun filming in color, this is not the moment we would have started. The smell was not recorded." Inside the plant, Junge asks Brigitte, who has a serious heart condition (from which she dies, as related in the 1999 film *Brigitte und Marcel*), the same question he asks of all his subjects: "Do you enjoy your work?" Brigitte, covered in blood, repeats incredulously "Enjoy it?" Then, after a long pause, which continues until she abruptly remembers that the camera is rolling, she adds halfheartedly "It's OK." Significantly, Junge again claims that his aggressive style was only a rhetorical strategy: "The last question was intended to provoke. I could have saved it." But he did not do it, neither then nor in the final editing process. And later, in 1975, when he visits Brigitte, who is sitting on a couch watching TV in an obvious mood of depression, Junge's voice hypocritically intones, "We stay a little longer. We wonder why she lets us film her like this. Perhaps because it's normal life, everyone can do it. Nevertheless, it is uncomfortable playing the role of observer—should we renounce the part simply because we can't help?"

This is a remarkable passage, even though the commentary, as in the examples given earlier, is disguised as a rhetorical question. Junge enters the debate about the nature of the relationship between the observer and the observed. Should (documentary) filmmakers become dialogically involved in the lives of their subjects? And to what extent ought filmmakers accept or reject an underlying ethical responsibility for the results of such an interference? Better or worse, does such an involvement with real filmed people affect the filmmakers' existence, creating problems that must be solved? This overall issue frames the much later *Marieluise*—filmed at a distance of many years—between the opening (rhetorical) question of whether the Junges' project is or was worth the effort and the closing (rhetorical) somewhat cynical interrogative musing, "What is the point of continuing? Who will pay for it?" In a similar pessimistic mood, viewers may also wonder why Junge includes so many bleak scenes in his earlier films. Was it by choice or by random selection? And how did he react to these bleak scenes? If indeed they simply recorded the bleak character of the raw material of his film, how is it possible to account for a seemingly total reversal in mood in the later film about the life of Marieluise, which reads almost like a Hollywood success story? Did the outside reality change? Or have the Junges? Or was their new optimism designed to appeal to the new regime and public, which no longer wanted to hear depressing voices? And finally, where must one look for the answers to these questions? Not in the voiced-over commentary that raised them in the first place. Which leaves the films themselves, but are they really as transparent and as informative as their simple true/false plots imply?

Filmed in 1995 and released in 1997, *Marieluise* opens with an overhead shot of a car traveling on a highway. It is 1991, and Marieluise and her family are on vacation in Denmark, finally able and happy to travel outside the borders of the former East bloc. She is now thirty-seven years old—the Junges have tracked her for a full thirty years. The film next jumps ahead five more years, to 1995. Marieluise is on the couch with her husband and two daughters; they are in the process of watching the video of early films about Marieluise's life. It is an extraordinary sequence that exemplifies a rare blending of raw documentary filming and highly contrived artistic manipulation. On the one hand, the scene—like all scenes of the series—is presented as taking place in the same time and space continuum as its recording by the camera, an exemplary instance of cinematographic objectivity, an on-the-spot document. On the other hand, the video pictures fulfill the now classical function of a film within a film—that is, they trigger a sequential reverberation between two mirror images on two levels of reality, each one screened by the artificial lens of the camera. Marieluise is thus twice filmed by the same filmmaker, and the second time she is shown seeing herself as that filmmaker saw her in the past but no longer as she sees herself in the new present, and as she perhaps never was. By the same token, of course, the Marieluise who watches the video becomes similarly problematic—a shadow of a character, a film image that recedes into an artful past with each new frame. In fact, the dizzy effect of that brief episode creates a doubt about the authenticity of the entire Golzow Project, merging facts and fiction to the point where both the cinematographic genre and the Junges' intentions become blurred notions. This issue will subsequently be examined in detail.

The Junges seem to have been aware of these ambiguities and perhaps were eager to play on them. The next sequences re-present some of Marieluise's life as it has been captured by the Junges while she experienced it but then framed and edited and hence distorted several years later. The film constantly cuts back and forth from 1995 to the various segments of the past while offering editorial or voice-over comments by Winfried Junge, Marieluise, and her husband, Steffen Seidel. One wonders which of these testimonies are reliable and which are mere bits of interpretation. However, there is also some order to this chaos. Underlying the paradoxical and somewhat unsettling shifts in time and perspective, three distinct chronological time flows are retrieved from the past: childhood; 1980–89; and 1989–95. The first part draws on footage from the earliest films and adds little to the Junges' project. The second part is more puzzling, though it does not reveal much by itself as it tears apart the systematic if arbitrary pattern of re created history. Without warning, a substantial gap is registered between 1984 and 1992. When questioned about this break, the Junges explained that during the last years before the fall of the Wall, while they still received funding to continue the filming of their project, the authorities did not allow the release of the final edited footage.[6] The reasons for this censorship will be discussed later. It suffices now to note that, judging by the video, Marieluise's life was neither more nor less remarkable than that of any of her compatriots. Its only exceptional feature was that she was the first of the Golzow children, and in 1996 still the only one, to leave the former East and take up residence in the West. The film ends when, at forty years old, she is starting a new life and setting up house on the outskirts of Cologne. A success story indeed, at least from the Western perspective. It would seem then that Marieluise is a positive symbol of a

6. Interview by author, Berlin, June 8, 1998.

seamless integration of former East Germans into the new greater Germany, leading to—one might infer—a happy adaptation of the East German cinema to the new postunification conditions of cinematographic industry.

But the Junges, likely not naive enough to promote an oversimplified optimism, use their narrative skills to undermine that apparently happy message. Marieluise is not the only true-life character endowed with iconic meaning in her story, and her story is not the only one. In fact, she is one of six children fathered by a stern, churchgoing Christian. Eventually, a radical shift in emphasis will set up that father, and by extension religion and all ideological values, as the dialogical opposition to the "happy end" myth. In contrast to Marieluise's father is her father-in-law: a former Communist Party secretary, he had been 100 percent committed to the East German communist cause. His son, Marieluise's husband, was a faithful officer of the communist army, in which he reached the rank of major. Because of his position, he did not allow himself to be filmed during the crucial years of the 1980s, appearing estranged from his wife and from the entire Golzow Project. Then, after the reunification, he gives up his beliefs without compunction, undergoes a smooth retraining in the West, and, keeping his rank, is chosen as one of the lucky few who are reassigned to the Bundeswehr. In his case the success story clearly rewards cynical pragmatism rather than idealism or simple political neutrality. Before discussing him further, it is important to make it clear that Marieluise is not above suspicion. Initially employed in an East German chemical lab, she later changes jobs but remains in the tainted chemical industry. As might be expected in view of the prevailing censorship at that time, the pre-1989 footage shows a relatively impartial view of her workplace; however, even then Winfried Junge evidences doubts about the ethics of the entire industry when he asks pressing, anxious questions about chemical warfare. At first evasive, Marieluise admits in 1995 that she was directly involved in manufacturing chemical weapons during the Cold War. She adds that she believed she was helping to save mankind. Only with the collapse of East Germany does the very pragmatic Marieluise, like her husband, change her outlook—and with it, her looks: shortly after unification, she visits a chic West Berlin establishment to get a new face that will make her appear more Western and thereby increase her job opportunities. It is a very painful scene in many ways, showing the pure power of superficial signs—the sign of the Western woman and the extremes to which she must go to erase her identity and values to fit in and get a job in a society dominated by sign value. Watching the artifice of makeup, viewers must ask what makeover the Junges have had to undergo to allow their extraordinary project to continue. One may argue that

Marieluise had no choice but to adapt to the new reality, that there is nothing ethically wrong with her pragmatism. The narrator certainly voices no criticism. And Marieluise remains friendly with the Junges during and after their filming of her private and vulnerable makeover scene. Like the other subjects, she keeps her trust in them. It is an open question whether that special relationship results from familiarity with the camera since the age of seven or attests to a Hollywood-style breakdown between private and public life.

A more important question is whether the Junges' outward neutrality about Marieluise's pragmatism verges on complicity, manifesting their own acceptance of a pragmatic perspective, or whether they trust that, with various oblique stratagems, they will manage to convey a negative moral judgment about her, her husband, and many of her peers? To what extent can one trust the Junges' explicit statements before and after the unification? The answers are not easy, perhaps purposefully difficult to find. Yet in some cases viewers are invited and even compelled by the logic of the film to cut through the narrator's controlling voice to reach, or at least approach, a meaning that transcends the objective goal of a documentary recording.

One can start with Junge's initial statement that "August 1961 as a starting point is arbitrary." This contention obviously must be taken with a grain of salt: the year of the closing of borders between the two Germanys could not have been totally arbitrary. Setting aside all its other possible meanings, including the atmosphere of political threat it inserts in the film, one must acknowledge that it provided the filmmaker/anthropologist with an almost sterile and scientifically controlled laboratory-like field of study. The Golzow Project could not have succeeded without such an enclosure, such a separation from the world. Conversely, one must not oversimplify and view the actors of the drama as totally alien inhabitants of an artificial milieu. Like other German filmmakers of the times, whether in the East or in the West, the Junges were aware of global changes not only in politics but also in overall modern culture and in particular of the intrusive impact of the most powerful anticinema medium, television. External global news interfaced with Golzow through TV. It is thanks to TV, for example, that the Vietnam War could be used for many years as the main argument of anticapitalist propaganda. When, as an adult, Dieter explains that solidarity with Vietnam had been taken for granted since he was a boy, Junge's voice interjects, "Vietnam: the television screen brought it to him, the well-known shots from 1966." The camera then crosscuts between TV footage of U.S. army planes and their bombing victims and shots of Dieter's troubled face. It is logical then that TV sets figure prominently throughout the series, even to the point of distorting by their image (as do other film tricks) the filmed reality. As Marieluise recalls, when Junge filmed her at age twelve playing Eisler's "Spare No Charm, Spare No Passion" on the piano, he had a TV set brought in for the recording session.

This ubiquitous television presence may carry a symbolic message as well. As discussed earlier, practically all German filmmakers regarded television as the medium par excellence of illusory real documents—that is, pseudodocumentaries that deform reality and demand to be read between the lines to be understood and made to release any concealed truth. As serendipity would have it, the relentless reminder of television might have been thus intended by the Junges, with a duplicitous slyness, to prompt their audience to read between the lines of these documentary films. A political interpretation of the Golzow series, as well as other less provocative meanings, would surely require such a reading.

True, as noted before, the Junges generally avoid taking sharp political positions, at least in the form of voiced statements in the early series films. But reading between the lines yields some surprises. Outwardly, the Golzow films hew closely to the official communist line protected by censorship: the inhabitants seem to like their jobs, their labor is honored and rewarded, all occupations are equally respected, and so on. Underneath that image, however, the Junges show the not-so-faint traces of a different picture: lack of adequate medical treatment, problems in housing, unwanted pregnancies, problematic freedom of choice of careers, dead-end marriages, boring lives, poor education—all potentially explosive issues bubbling just beneath the surface of the Junges' documentary. None of these topics are strongly highlighted or developed, but they can be perceived in the cracks of the text, in the meanders of family discussions. There is no global condemnation of the communist regime—it is, rather, praised—but it does not come through unscathed. At least some doubts are sown, and some are nurtured. Others are scattered at random, as if the Junges had no preexisting definite agenda (as they probably did not). But as in most essay films, spectators must draw their own conclusions. I believe that the Junges truly had no well-structured political views, steeped in a definite ideology, but were interested in and had compassion for the life of simple people bypassed by the powers. The Junges judged communism and then democracy in part by their promises and in part by what they did for less favored groups and individuals; in short, the filmmakers were disillusioned with the two regimes, thereby learning to appreciate a certain ideological integrity without becoming social rebels or political revolutionaries. In the West the Junges would have been called humanists but not always liberals. Paradoxically, their story, with its two streaks of success, somewhat evokes the same type of pragmatism that they observed, with mixed feelings, as the key attitude among their most successful subjects.

Reading between the lines also enables the viewer of the series to identify a couple of taboo topics that the Junges do not discuss openly but at which they hint, even through denial. One is predestination. In the first episode of *Lebensläufe,* the grown-up Jürgen works as a housepainter; he is then shown as a child, having fun painting. The voice-over quickly cautions the viewer not to romanticize this image because it cannot foreshadow Jürgen's career choice. Yet over and over again, the Junges chose to illustrate precisely this sort of romanticism. Brigitte is surrounded with hatching eggs when we first encounter her, and she later takes up a career in poultry production; Gudrun, whose father chairs Golzow's agricultural co-op, is elected to the district assembly and works as a district councilor. Of course the notion that one could be born into a social role was anathema in East Germany, and these sequences could (or should?) be understood as an implicit criticism of state ideology, which would explain the taboo treatment of their explicit meaning.

Another sensitive topic verging on taboo is the military. Even though the Junges praise conscription as a way of transforming undisciplined young men into rational and productive workers, as preached by the political line, the filmmakers introduce an exchange that evokes a more questionable historical function of soldiers:

> *J:* "And if you look back, your forefathers were all soldiers, too . . .
> *B:* "It must have been incredibly more difficult to be a soldier then."

The "then" is not clarified. The viewer is left to fill in the blanks, to go back perhaps to Nazi times and the shame attached to Hitler's army's behavior in the Soviet Union. Could the East German army be much better? Nothing definite is stated—only innuendoes can bypass the taboo. By a different stratagem but with the same discretion and disguise of the target, the viewer is permitted if not invited to judge the entire GDR army by the negative example of Major Steffen Seidel, whose rank sets him up as a model and whose slick pragmatism turns into religious hypocrisy as required by the new Bundeswehr. Through him, the Junges suggest but do not affirm the interchangeability of all military, authoritative, totalitarian hierarchies that recruit passive personalities to maintain power.

There is one more problematic item related to the war: the Holocaust. In sharp contrast to what was being done in West German cinema at the time, there is barely any mention of the Nazis or the Holocaust in the core of the Golzow series. This rather surprising silence may have been self-imposed out of guilt or forced by fear of censorship. It is improbable, however, that it could reflect an actual ignorance of the Holocaust tragedy. In the 1992 compilation film *Drehbuch,* made after reunification with footage from the 1980s that had never before been shown, the Junges included a sequence of the Golzow children's class trip to Buchenwald, explaining that the previous regime had insisted that these scenes be cut. There is also a brief allusion in *Marieluise* to the guilty silence of the military during the *Hitlerzeit* (but only as a pretext for a criticism of the GDR). Why is no more said or shown? Occasions were not lacking for quoting some adults, and it is hard to believe that as the Golzow children grew up, they remained oblivious of the killing of millions of Jews. No doubt the taboo worked well to protect older communists from reminders of a relatively recent guilt by association. But why keep silent after the reunification, two generations later? Were the Junges timid, overcautious, or just indifferent to anything that could distract from their films as films? Were they totally uninterested in values?

Not quite. At least one character becomes, during a historically drawn out process, a positive icon for integrity, nonconformity, and eventually political subversion: Marieluise's father. Starting with his initial 1961 appearance, a slow but dramatic change takes place in the way in which he is seen by the Junges. In thirty-five years he evolves from a conservative religious zealot, forcing his six children to attend church as a challenge to the communist policy, into one of the last defenders of the socialist system in 1995. His voice is revealed as the genuine voice of principled subversion, and his obstinacy, censored in earlier footage as backward Christian fanaticism, later becomes a serious and levelheaded critique of a totalitarian system. This shift likely reflects the Junges' growing disillusionment with the system during the 1980s, when it became clear that communism was not working and needed a major revision and restructuring—a dream gone sour. And perhaps the constant contact with the children of Golzow, who became rather dull citizens, made the Junges aware of the system's contradictions and dead ends. That growing critical sense must have been one of the reasons why the Junges's films were not released in the 1980s—a form of punishment for their inability or reluctance to conceal the regime's most obvious weaknesses. Marieluise's father received a parallel punishment. He was accused of spreading the "Polish virus"—that is, the ideas of Solidarity—then was caught with pamphlets, and finally was demoted with his wife to a lowly position as a milker, taking care of cows on the same farm he had directed in the good/bad old days. During a conversation about Marieluise's father's now open dissent, Winfried Junge admits that it was less an interview than a boxing match where he, representing the state, was on the losing end. However, ironically at the film's end, the irrepressible father is the most critical of reunification, stating that things are worse off than before and that the CDU is not to be trusted. He is the only protagonist truly committed to the forsaken socialist project.

With this note, however ambiguous (for who is the real Marieluise's father? What was real East Germany?), the Golzow cycle acquires a more balanced finish: there were some bad and some good people during these four decades, and one should not praise or condemn then hastily. In fact, since the story is still going on, any retrospective judgment about them and about the East German part of reunited Germany risks being shown to be as mistaken as the early predictions about communist victory in the GDR. History is more shrouded in mystery for the Junges at this stage of their work than at its beginning. The tapestry of people and events, enriched with ever new threads, grows to be more confusing rather than simpler, and the shades of its colors run into each other without a clearly visible pattern. For the spectator—and, no doubt, for the filmmakers—it is as puzzling as a historian's history or at least as history grasped by the Junges' camera. Indeed, reversing the usual formula, one might argue that all that what was only a record of history, the documentary film, has become part of the only history that is known—the history that it claimed to represent. Winfried Junge's postmodernist dictum, "History only exists in film," may be rephrased as "History only exists as film." And vice versa.

In other terms, throughout the chronicle of Golzow, the audience witnesses the progressive transformation of the documentary into history, but a history that in turn has been made into an art as screen images substituted for memory. "Things," says Marieluise, "look better on film." Perhaps. But they certainly have a different look than raw reality has for those who experience it. And therein lies the greatest paradox of the Golzow films. Turning their back on fiction, to be sure, but also on the pseudodocumentaries that mutated into essay or art films, the Junges could have expected—and probably did—that their series, filmed in step with the daily events of an uneventful existence of a group of people during their entire lives, would escape the tempting traps of restaging post hoc the deeds of their subjects and thus would create a personal history. I believe I have shown that these expectations, if indeed the Junges entertained them, were not fulfilled, despite the exceptionally suitable conditions experienced. Yet this failure as a documentary was more than compensated by the correlated success of the series as an episodic nonfiction film—perhaps the most ambitious if not the most aesthetic in inspiration.

"Everything flows; you can never bathe in the same river twice," repeats the voice-over at the end of *Lebensläufe.* Bits of reality have become virtual, and the most promising documentary has become a fiction unlike any other. But that perpetual change should not be deplored. People and events may indeed deteriorate, ultimately betrayed by their surviving images on the screen. Future generations will hardly watch mid-twentieth-century newsreels to learn about their past. Interfacing with history, even the best documented essay films are hardly reliable as sources of a truth. If, however, Winfried Junge is right when he claims in *Drehbuch* that "filmmaking is the topic" of filmmaking, then all cinematographic archives, including the Children of Golzow as well as Farocki's essays or Wim Wenders's poetic reportages, may hope to escape their fixed limits as solipsistic pieces of art and flow back into the stream of history as moving elements of the history of art. Everything may be changing before our eyes, including cinema, but there is satisfaction in watching that particular history, like water in a river, being continually refilmed and renewed, even as we look at it. And if the first centenary of filmic production was marked by the success and domination of the fiction film, perhaps, as the recent successes of documentary films such as Wenders's *Buena Vista Social Club* attest, the next century will bring about an ascendancy of nonfiction image production.

Index

Social History, Popular Culture, and Politics in Germany
Geoff Eley, Series Editor

(continued from pg. ii)

Contested City: Municipal Politics and the Rise of Nazism in Altona, 1917–1937, Anthony McElligott

Catholicism, Political Culture, and the Countryside: A Social History of the Nazi Party in South Germany, Oded Heilbronner

A User's Guide to German Cultural Studies, Scott Denham, Irene Kacandes, and Jonathan Petropoulos, editors

A Greener Vision of Home: Cultural Politics and Environmental Reform in the German Heimatschutz *Movement, 1904–1918*, William H. Rollins

West Germany under Construction: Politics, Society, and Culture in Germany in the Adenauer Era, Robert G. Moeller, editor

How German Is She? Postwar West German Reconstruction and the Consuming Woman, Erica Carter

Feminine Frequencies: Gender, German Radio, and the Public Sphere, 1923–1945, Kate Lacey

Exclusive Revolutionaries: Liberal Politics, Social Experience, and National Identity in the Austrian Empire, 1848–1914, Pieter M. Judson

Jews, Germans, Memory: Reconstruction of Jewish Life in Germany, Y. Michal Bodemann, editor

Paradoxes of Peace: German Peace Movements since 1945, Alice Holmes Cooper

Society, Culture, and the State in Germany, 1870–1930, Geoff Eley, editor

Technological Democracy: Bureaucracy and Citizenry in the German Energy Debate, Carol J. Hager

The Origins of the Authoritarian Welfare State in Prussia: Conservatives, Bureaucracy, and the Social Question, 1815–70, Hermann Beck

The People Speak! Anti-Semitism and Emancipation in Nineteenth-Century Bavaria, James F. Harris

From Bundesrepublik *to* Deutschland: *German Politics after Unification,* Michael G. Huelshoff, Andrei S. Markovits, and Simon Reich, editors

The Stigma of Names: Antisemitism in German Daily Life, 1812–1933, Dietz Bering

Reshaping the German Right: Radical Nationalism and Political Change after Bismarck, Geoff Eley